Parent Articles
About ADHD

Clare B. Jones, Ph.D., Senior Editor
H. Russell Searight, Ph.D., Co-editor
Magda A. Urban, Ph.D., Co-editor

**Communication
Skill Builders®**®
a division of
The Psychological Corporation

555 Academic Court
San Antonio, Texas 78204-2498
1-800-228-0752

Reproducing Pages From This Book

As described below, some of the pages in this book may be reproduced for instructional use (not for resale). To protect your book, make a photocopy of each reproducible page. Then use that copy as a master for photocopying.

About the Editors

Clare B. Jones, Ph.D., Senior Editor

Clare B. Jones received her Ph.D. from the University of Akron in Ohio, her M.Ed. from Cleveland State University, and her B.S. from Drake University. She is a diagnostic specialist for children and young adults with learning disabilities and attention disorders. The former education director of Phoenix Children's Hospital, she has been a classroom teacher for 20 years. She was recognized in Ohio as Master Teacher of the Year. Dr. Jones is an adjunct professor at Northern Arizona University and a nationally recognized presenter. She is the author of *Sourcebook for Children With Attention Deficit Disorder: A Management Guide for Early Childhood Professionals and Parents* (1991), *Attention Deficit Disorder: Strategies for School-Age Students* (1994), *A Sourcebook on Attention Deficit Disorder For Early Childhood Professionals and Parents, Revised* (1998), and *The Young and the Active* (video) for elementary teachers. She is also a contributor to several textbooks and journals. Dr. Jones operates a private practice, Developmental Learning Associates, in Phoenix.

H. Russell Searight, Ph.D., Co-editor

Russell Searight received his Ph.D. in clinical psychology from St. Louis University, his M.S. from St. Louis University, and his B.A. from Butler University in Indianapolis. Dr. Searight is the director of behavioral sciences at the Residency Program of Family Medicine of St. Louis. He is an adjunct professor of community and family medicine at St. Louis University, and was formerly an associate professor of psychology at Southern Illinois University. Dr. Searight is the author of numerous articles, and his books include *Family of Origin: Therapy and Diversity* and *Behavioral Medicine: A Primary Care Approach*. He runs a practice with an emphasis on the psychological problems of children and adolescents. His primary area of current interest is teaching behavioral science to residents in family medicine.

Magda A. Urban, Ph.D., Co-editor

Magda A. Urban is a clinical learning specialist in private practice in Tucson, Arizona, and has been a general and special educator for over 20 years. She is a professionally recognized educator in special education teaching and educational diagnosis. She received her Ph.D. in special education from the University of Arizona. On campus she coordinated Project ADEPT: Attention Deficit Disorder Education for Teachers, which developed and implemented a model for teacher education. Her publication interests pertain to parent education and teachers' knowledge and attitudes about ADHD. As a complement to her published works, she also has conducted many workshops, conference presentations, and radio and television broadcast presentations for professionals, parents, and the general public.

Contents

Section 6: Adolescence

Section 7: Associated Disorders

Section 8: The Adult With Attention Deficit/Hyperactivity Disorder

Introduction

Parent Articles About ADHD includes over 60 reproducible articles written specifically for parents of children who have or who are at risk for attention disorders. The diagnosis of Attention Deficit/Hyperactivity Disorder requires a team process, and the professionals who wrote the articles for this handbook are all experienced members of that team process. As well as being experts on Attention Deficit/Hyperactivity Disorder, they also have expertise in the fields of medicine, psychology, education, speech-language pathology, nursing, social work, occupational therapy, recreational therapy, and the law. The articles provide current, hands-on, easy-to-read information. Parents will find immediately usable suggestions on a variety of typical experiences. The articles cover a variety of topics that are relevant to families, friends, professionals, and caregivers who work or live with individuals who have attention deficits.

Professionals who serve families with attention disorders will find the articles to be a valuable resource throughout the course of diagnosis, treatment, and intervention. The articles are useful in conjunction with ongoing interventions and patient/student/family counseling. Attention deficit is a lifelong disorder and these articles can provide support at different times in the life span, from early childhood through adolescence to adulthood.

How to Use This Book Most Effectively

The articles in this book are organized by topics. A clinician might duplicate specific articles as a supplement to a meeting or therapy session or give a copy of an article to a parent at the end of a session to provide a reminder of what they discussed. The articles could serve as a focal point for an upcoming workshop or lecture. Educational facilities will find the articles helpful in staff training and as a resource for staff members conducting parent conferences. Multidisciplinary clinics may duplicate copies of specific articles (for example, article 2.1 on Medical Evaluation) and make these available to clients in the lobby or in informational packets to support families after they leave the clinic.

Parent Articles About ADHD provide a practical, clinically sound resource for support to the many teams, schools, and clinics aiding families in their challenges with ADHD.

A very special thank you...

The editors sincerely wish to thank all of the contributing authors for their wonderful effort and their perceptive insight. Many experts and leaders in the field of attention deficit contributed to this book, and we are honored that each author chose to submit an article for this handbook. We are indebted to the team of authors who made this book a reality.

Section 1

Attention Deficit/Hyperactivity Disorder: General Information

The Facts About Attention Deficit/ Hyperactivity Disorder

Sam Goldstein, Ph.D.

Attention Deficit/Hyperactivity Disorder (ADHD) is characterized by a constellation of problems with inattention, hyperactivity, and impulsivity. These problems are developmentally inappropriate and cause difficulty in daily life. ADHD is a biopsychosocial disorder. That is, there appear to be strong genetic, biological, experiential, and social factors that contribute to the extent of problems experienced. ADHD affects 3% to 5% of the population. Early identification and proper treatment dramatically reduce the family, educational, behavioral, and psychological problems experienced by individuals with ADHD. Accurate diagnosis and treatment can help individuals with ADHD manage or even avoid the many life problems usually associated with ADHD, including school failure and dropout, depression, behavioral disorders, vocational and relationship problems, and substance abuse

At one time, clinicians thought that symptoms of ADHD diminish by the adolescent years. However, subsequent research has found that the majority of individuals with ADHD mature into adulthood with a very similar pattern of problems. Adults with ADHD experience problems at work, in the community, and in their families. These adults also exhibit a greater degree of emotional problems, including depression and anxiety.

Researchers first described the characteristics of the impulsive, inattentive, and hyperactive problems of children with ADHD in 1902. Since that time, writers have referred to the disorder by different names, including Minimal Brain Dysfunction, Hyperkinetic Reaction of Childhood, and Attention Deficit Disorder. The American Psychiatric Association's *Diagnostic and Statistical Manual of Mental Disorders* (fourth edition)—the standard diagnostic handbook—currently describes this set of problems as Attention Deficit/Hyperactivity Disorder.

The Disorder

ADHD interferes with an individual's ability to sustain attention (particularly with repetitive tasks), manage emotions and activity level effectively, respond consistently to consequences, and, perhaps most importantly, inhibit. Inhibition refers to the ability to prevent the expression of dominant urges to act on impulse, so as to permit time for self-regulation. Individuals with ADHD might know what to do, but they are inconsistent in doing what they know because of their inability to stop and think efficiently before responding, regardless of the setting or task.

Characteristics of ADHD arise in early childhood for most individuals. The chronic behaviors last at least 6 months, with onset often occurring before 7 years of age. Researchers have identified four subtypes of ADHD.

1. **ADHD—inattentive type.** The individual demonstrates at least six of the following characteristics:

    a. Fails to give close attention to details or makes careless mistakes.

    b. Has difficulty sustaining attention.

    c. Does not appear to listen.

    d. Struggles to follow through on instructions.

    e. Has difficulty with organization.

    f. Avoids or dislikes tasks requiring sustained mental effort.

    g. Often loses things necessary for tasks.

    h. Is easily distracted.

    i. Is forgetful in daily activities.

2. **ADHD—hyperactive/impulsive type.** The individual has six of the following characteristics:

    a. Fidgets with hands or feet or squirms in seat.

    b. Has difficulty remaining seated.

    c. Runs about or climbs excessively (in adults might be limited to subjective feelings of restlessness).

    d. Has difficulty engaging in activities quietly.

    e. Acts as if driven by a motor.

    f. Talks excessively.

    g. Blurts out answers before questions have been completed.

    h. Has difficulty waiting in turn-taking situations.

    i. Interrupts or intrudes upon others.

3. **ADHD—combined type.** The individual meets the criteria for both inattentive and hyperactive/impulsive ADHD.

4. **ADHD—not otherwise specified.** The individual demonstrates some characteristics but an insufficient number of symptoms to reach a full diagnosis. These symptoms, however, disrupt everyday life.

School-age individuals with ADHD are at greater risk for grade retention, school dropout, academic underachievement, and social and emotional problems. The symptoms of ADHD seem to be catalytic, making children vulnerable to failure in two of the most important arenas for developmental mastery—school and peer relationships.

With increasing medical, educational, mental health, and community knowledge about the symptoms of and problems caused by ADHD, professionals are identifying, diagnosing, and treating an increasing number of cases. Nonetheless, it is likely that a significant number of individuals with ADHD remain undiagnosed or are misdiagnosed. Their problems intensify and create significant hurdles to meeting life's demands.

ADHD often has been portrayed inaccurately as a learning disability. Instead, ADHD is a performance disorder. Children with ADHD are able to learn, but they have difficulty performing in school because of the impact of ADHD symptoms on efficient school performance. However, approximately 20% to 30% of children with ADHD also have a learning disability, which further complicates identification and treatment. Children with ADHD also have an increased risk of developing problems related to Oppositional Defiant Disorder, delinquency, Conduct Disorder, depression, and anxiety. Researchers suggest, however, that it is not ADHD alone but rather ADHD in combination with the development of Conduct Disorder that predicts the most dire adolescent outcomes, particularly those related to criminal behavior and substance abuse.

Adults with ADHD also experience increased problems related to antisocial behavior, vocational and educational underachievement, depression, anxiety, and substance abuse. Unfortunately, many adults with ADHD were not diagnosed properly as children. These individuals grew up struggling with a disability that often went undiagnosed, misdiagnosed, or untreated.

The majority of adults with ADHD have symptoms very similar to the problems children encounter. They often struggle to sustain attention and are restless, easily distracted, impulsive, and impatient. They have problems with stress intolerance, which leads to greater expression of emotion. Within the workplace, they often fail to achieve vocational positions or status commensurate with their intellectual ability.

Cause

Commonly suspected causes of ADHD include toxins, developmental impairments, diet, injury, ineffective parenting, and heredity. Researchers have suggested that these potential causes affect brain functioning and, as such, they consider ADHD a disorder of brain function. A

number of studies have demonstrated significant differences in the structure and brain function of individuals with ADHD, particularly in areas of the right hemisphere of the brain, the prefrontal cortex, the basal ganglia, the corpus callosum, and the cerebellum. These structural and metabolic studies, combined with family, genetic, and drug response studies, demonstrate very clearly that ADHD is a neurobiological disorder. Though the severity of problems experienced by individuals with ADHD seems to vary based upon life experience, genetics appears to be the primary underlying factor in determining whether an individual will have symptoms of ADHD.

Diagnosis

The diagnosis of ADHD is a multifaceted process. Many biological and psychological problems can contribute to symptoms similar to those exhibited by individuals with ADHD. For example, inattention is one of the nine hallmark symptoms of depression; and impulsivity, another ADHD trait, is also a characteristic of delinquency.

To establish the diagnosis of ADHD, professionals must conduct a comprehensive evaluation to eliminate other possible causes and determine the presence or absence of co-occurring conditions. The most important aspect of the diagnostic process is obtaining a careful life history. An evaluation for ADHD often includes assessment of intellectual, academic, social, and emotional functioning. Medical examination is also important to rule out infrequent but possible causes of ADHD-like symptoms (e.g., adverse reaction to medications, thyroid problems). The diagnostic process also must include input from teachers and other adults who interact routinely with the individual. There are several new computerized tests that have become popular in the assessment of ADHD. However, researchers haven't proved yet that these computerized programs make for an accurate diagnosis.

When assessing an adult for ADHD, it is extremely important to obtain a careful history of childhood, academic, behavioral, and vocational problems. Because of increased recognition that ADHD can be present throughout a person's life, there are more standardized questionnaires and related diagnostic tools for assessing adult ADHD.

Sam Goldstein, Ph.D., is a nationally certified school psychologist specializing in child development, school psychology, and neuropsychology. He currently is the director of the Neurology, Learning, and Behavior Center, Salt Lake City.

Treatment of Attention Deficit/ Hyperactivity Disorder

Sam Goldstein, Ph.D.

Treating Attention Deficit/Hyperactivity Disorder (ADHD) in children requires a coordinated effort between the parents and medical, mental health, and educational professionals. This combined set of treatments offered by a variety of individuals is called multimodal intervention. A multimodal treatment program for ADHD should include:

- Parent training about ADHD and effective behavior management strategies.

- An appropriate educational program.

- Individual and family counseling, when needed, to minimize the escalation of family problems.

- Medication when required.

Behavior management is an important intervention for children with ADHD. Positive reinforcement combined with punishment in a model referred to as "response cost" is particularly effective for children with ADHD.

Classroom success for children with ADHD often requires a range of interventions. Most children with ADHD can stay in the regular classroom with minor adjustments in the classroom setting, the addition of support personnel, and/or special education programs provided outside of the classroom. However, children most severely affected with ADHD often experience a number of recurring problems and require specialized classrooms.

Psychostimulants are the medications most frequently used for managing ADHD symptoms. At least 70% to 80% of children and adults with ADHD respond positively to psychostimulants. These medications enhance performance, and most children with ADHD who take these medications show dramatic improvement, with reductions in impulsive and hyperactive behaviors and increases in attention span.

Adults with ADHD respond to psychostimulant and other medications at a rate similar to children. These adults also benefit from learning to structure their environment, developing organizational skills, receiving vocational counseling, and, if needed, short-term psychotherapy to cope with life experiences and current personal problems. For some individuals with a combination of ADHD and other problems (particularly depression), extended psychotherapy can be helpful in teaching behavior change and coping strategies.

ADHD treatments are effective in reducing the immediate, symptomatic problems experienced by individuals with ADHD. However, long-term research for children with ADHD indicates that symptom relief alone has little effect on long-term success. Professionals agree that the factors predicting positive life outcome for *all* children are also extremely important for children experiencing problems caused by disorders such as ADHD. Increasingly, clinicians are recognizing the importance of "balancing the scales" for individuals with ADHD. Thus, professionals prescribe treatments to relieve symptoms while also helping the individual to build life success. The motto, "Make tasks interesting and payoffs valuable," is critically important for individuals with ADHD.

Prognosis

Compared with their peers, children with ADHD are at greater risk for school failure, emotional difficulties, and significant social problems. However, these children can beat the odds with early identification and treatment. The topic of ADHD likely will continue to be the most widely researched and debated area in mental health and child development. New ground is broken daily. The 5-year multisite, multimodal ADHD treatment study underway at this time by the National Institute of Mental Health will provide an even better set of answers concerning the diagnosis, treatment, and outcome of individuals with ADHD. In addition, ongoing studies of molecular genetics might identify the genes related to this disorder. With the increasing awareness and understanding in the community about the significant impact of ADHD symptoms on individuals and their families, the future appears bright.

Sam Goldstein, Ph.D., is a nationally certified school psychologist specializing in child development, school psychology, and neuropsychology. He currently is the director of the Neurology, Learning, and Behavior Center, Salt Lake City.

Attention Deficit Disorders Without Hyperactivity

Thomas E. Brown, Ph.D.

"If only he would pay attention to his schoolwork in the same way he concentrates on his sports and video games." "She knows the lyrics to all the top 40 songs, but she doesn't remember what she has learned in her homework from one day to the next." Many parents are frustrated and worried about their sons and daughters who can concentrate very well on activities in which they have a special interest but chronically seem unable to sustain attention and effort for their schoolwork or other assigned tasks.

Children and teenagers who chronically are very inconsistent in their ability to sustain attention and effort for work tasks might have Attention Deficit Disorder (ADD). Typically, parents and teachers readily notice students whose problems with inattention are accompanied by hyperactive behavior. Such students tend to be disruptive in classrooms and relentlessly demanding at home. Hyperactive children and adolescents are difficult to overlook.

However, it is easy for parents and teachers to overlook inattentive children and adolescents who are not hyperactive. Often they are "spacey" and preoccupied with their own thoughts, but generally they are not disruptive. Their primary difficulties in school usually involve failure to complete homework, forgetting to prepare for tests, and not getting their assignments in on time. Teachers and parents often assume that these children are just unmotivated, lazy, or immature.

Sometimes these students get their work done well, but far more often they drift off into daydreaming or simply forget what they were supposed to be doing. They chronically lose track of their books and materials for homework; or they laboriously complete an assignment and then leave it in the backpack, forgetting to turn it in to the teacher for credit. These inattentive children who are not hyperactive can suffer from ADD impairments just as much as those who are "hyper."

Boys or girls can be inattentive or inconsistent in their studies for many reasons. Family stresses, emotional problems, learning disorders, inadequate teaching, and other factors can cause any child to have difficulty in sustaining attention and effort for schoolwork. Qualified professionals must assess carefully to determine whether a child's attentional difficulties result from ADD or some other factors. Evaluation for ADD should include careful assessment for learning disorders, mood disorders, anxiety disorders, etc., because individuals with ADD often have one or more other disorders as well.

APA Guidelines

The American Psychiatric Association (1994) has developed guidelines for identifying children and adolescents whose chronic inattention problems might be due to an attention deficit disorder. These guidelines are as follows:

1. Often fails to give close attention to details or makes careless mistakes in schoolwork, work, or other activities.

2. Often has difficulty sustaining attention in tasks or play activities.

3. Often does not seem to listen when spoken to directly.

4. Often does not follow through on instructions and fails to finish schoolwork or chores.

5. Often has difficulty organizing tasks or activities.

6. Often avoids or is reluctant to engage in tasks that require sustained mental effort (such as schoolwork or homework).

7. Often loses things necessary for tasks or activities (e.g., toys, school assignments, pencils, books)

8. Often is distracted easily by extraneous stimuli.

9. Is often forgetful in daily activities.

If a child or adolescent has six or more of these nine symptoms and is significantly and chronically impaired by them, there is a significant chance that the student has an attention deficit disorder. Although the current official diagnostic label for ADD without hyperactivity is "Attention Deficit/Hyperactivity Disorder, predominantly inattentive type," it is not necessary for the child to have any hyperactive or impulsive symptoms to qualify for this diagnosis.

ADD without hyperactivity, as with ADD with hyperactivity, often appears to be a willpower problem. Actually, it is a neurochemical disorder that tends to run in families and often is inherited.

If untreated, ADD, even without hyperactivity, can contribute not only to chronic and serious school problems but also to substance abuse, low self-esteem, and chronic family stress.

When careful evaluation indicates a diagnosis of Attention Deficit Disorder, the first step is for parents to become well-informed about what ADD is and what it is not. Often the family pediatrician or school psychologist will be helpful. Other good sources of accurate information are listed in the References and Resources section of this article. In addition, parents can contact the support group, Children and Adults With Attention Deficit Disorder (CHADD) at (301) 306-7070 or online at http://www.chadd.org.

After getting adequate, objective information about ADD, parents whose child has been diagnosed as having ADD should consult with their school staff, their pediatrician, a psychologist, or other experienced professionals to consider what accommodations, treatments, or other interventions might be appropriate and desirable for their son or daughter.

The most effective treatment for most individuals who have Attention Deficit Disorder, with or without hyperactivity, is carefully fine-tuned medication. Numerous scientific studies have shown that 70% to 80% of persons diagnosed with ADD experience significant improvement of their ADD symptoms when treated with appropriate doses of stimulant medications. Other interventions such as tutoring and behavior reinforcement systems are most effective when combined with medication treatment.

References and Resources

American Psychiatric Association. (1994). *Diagnostic and statistical manual of mental disorders* (4th ed.). Washington, DC: Author.

Barkley, R. A. (1995). *Taking charge of ADHD.* New York: Guilford Press.

Brown, T. E. (1995). *Attention deficit disorder, predominantly inattentive type.* Fact sheet #9. Plantation, FL: CHADD.

Brown, T. E. (1995). Differential diagnosis of ADD vs. ADHD in adults. In K. G. Nadeau (Ed.), *Comprehensive guide to Attention Deficit Disorder in adults* (pp. 237–259). New York: Brunner/Mazel.

Brown, T. E. (Ed.) (in press). *Attention deficit disorders and comorbidities in children, adolescents, and adults.* Washington, DC: American Psychiatric Association.

Dendy, C. A. (1995). *Teenagers with ADD: A parents' guide.* Bethesda, MD: Woodbine House.

Hallowell, E. (1996). *When you worry about your child.* New York: Simon & Schuster.

Koplewicz, H. (1996). *It's nobody's fault.* New York: Random House.

Dr. Brown is a member of the faculty at the Department of Psychiatry, Yale University School of Medicine. He is the author of the Brown Attention Deficit Disorder Test.

Girls With Attention Deficit/ Hyperactivity Disorder

Sari Solden, M.S., LMFT

Girls with Attention Deficit/Hyperactivity Disorder (ADHD) often are not identified at an early age. However, even when they are identified and treated successfully for the primary symptoms of ADHD, these girls often face other significant difficulties as they become young women and begin to confront the effects of their attentional challenges on their ability to fulfill gender role expectations. Parents increase the chance for long-term success when they help their daughters develop an internal voice that both explains and values their differences so that by the time these girls leave home, they feel confident and capable of leading satisfying, successful lives as women with ADHD.

Early Identification

For girls, especially those who are primarily inattentive, ADHD is as much a set of cognitive and attentional differences as it is a description of behavior. As a result, girls with ADHD often are difficult to identify at an early age. In addition, the struggles of these girls often go unnoticed because of their tendency to "people please" and to internalize instead of act out their difficulties, and because protective factors in their environment, such as parental support and structure, can mask the extent of the problem.

Discussions that recognize ADHD in girls as a significant and severe condition that needs to be treated emphasize the importance of early identification in alleviating the distress of the ADHD symptoms themselves as well as preventing the development of secondary negative consequences. One study, for example, discusses "the risk to the attention-disordered girl who is passive, doesn't disrupt other children, is not a problem to anyone and so remains undiscovered" (Berry, Shaywitz, & Shaywitz, 1985, p. 562). The authors warn, "this makes her vulnerable to academic underachievement and social and emotional disturbances."

Beyond Early Identification

It is important to recognize, however, that early identification and even successful management of the primary problems with attention through standard treatment methods (organizational strategies, behavioral management approaches, and medication) might not be enough to ensure long-term successful outcomes for these girls as they become women with ADHD. The secondary effects of living with ADHD often develop in spite of early treatment for the primary symptoms and need to be the focus of a separate, parallel set of interventions.

In my work with women with ADHD, I have observed that, when girls reach early adulthood and lose the structure and support that home might have provided, they very often encounter a whole host of new challenges. When young women begin to see ADHD's effect on their ability to fulfill gender role expectations, the deeply held views about their differences they have developed are often the determining factor in whether they will continue to employ successful strategies or, instead, retreat behind a wall of shame. Above and beyond treatment for primary ADHD, then, we must take a longer view when we think about helping these girls. We must be just as vigilant about the subtle *messages* they are receiving about their ADHD as we are about the *methods* aimed at their primary symptoms.

Providing an Internal Explanatory and Valuing Voice

An important goal for parents is to help these girls, from early on, begin internalizing an explanatory and valuing voice that they can carry with them as they confront their ADHD as women. Parents can become internal partners with their daughter by talking with her in an objective, explanatory way about her experiences and thinking through strategies together until she is able to think through situations for herself. As a result, she will develop a strong internal voice on which she can rely as she encounters new challenges throughout her life. While it's important to provide structure, support, and strategies after identification of ADHD, it also is critical for parents to help their daughter gradually learn how to approach and analyze increasingly complex and important situations.

With this ability to act in her own best interest comes an increasing feeling of control and confidence and a growing sense that she is someone who has options and can affect her own life in a positive way. Then, when attention-related difficulties arise throughout the girl's life, she will be more likely to ask herself, "How can I make things work?" rather than saying, "I'm a jerk, I'm hopeless, I'm stupid, I'm a slob." Once this positive and confident self-talk becomes natural and routine, she will be able to communicate much more effectively with others about her differences and needs. Instead of defending, apologizing, or withdrawing, she will focus on getting what she needs to make her life work.

Gender Role Models

All parents need to provide healthy role models to their daughters and teach them to resist the pressure to conform to gender role expectations that have damaging effects on girls as they become adolescents and young women (Pipher, 1995). Girls with ADHD have less opportunity to be exposed naturally to successful models with whom they can identify, so parents of these girls must be even more deliberate in providing examples of successful women who break the traditional mold. Mothers who have ADHD themselves must remember that their daughters will internalize not only what these mothers say directly to their daughters but also will absorb what their mothers say and feel about their own difficulties and differences.

It is especially important for a mother with ADHD to model "asking for help" in filling in her own gaps. If a mother has difficulty in specific areas relating to her daughter, she can show her willingness to involve others in the process. For example, she could ask her sister or husband to take over certain activities with her daughter, such as shopping for school supplies or organizing her notebooks. At the same time, though, the mother with ADHD needs to be clear about the abilities and strengths she does possess and provide. This attitude models interdependence, conveys an appreciation of variations, and demonstrates an ability to move beyond traditional gender role expectations.

Fathers also play a very important role in the lives of their daughters with ADHD by telling and showing what they value in women. In this way, their daughters can integrate the idea that perfect organization and following the cultural norm are not the essential elements of what makes a woman valued. If his wife has ADHD, a father can discuss with his daughter what special qualities he appreciates in Mom, such as integrity, individuality, creativity, warmth, and sensitivity. This will go a long way in helping the girl with ADHD resist the shame and the fear that often arise when she becomes a young woman who doesn't match the idealized cultural image of what is important in a woman. Father also can contribute to the healthy development of these girls by modeling task division on the basis of strengths, not gender. As a result of this modeling, the girl, by the time she becomes a young woman, will feel capable of developing an intimate and equal relationship in which she feels valued by her partner, instead of assuming or accepting a one-down position.

Talking to Her so She Will Talk to You

It is vital to remember that, even if her difficulties are not apparent, the girl with ADHD might be compensating by overworking and internalizing her feelings rather than acting out behaviorally. This eventually can lead to feelings of isolation, anxiety, and depression. An atmosphere of safety will encourage your daughter to confide her struggles to you. We want to prevent a climate that establishes a lifelong pattern of "hiding" in which a girl might say to herself, "Well, I'm doing all right even though I'm working very hard just to keep up, so I won't say anything to anyone. I wouldn't want to wipe away the good opinion they have of me." Hiding herself this way deprives the young woman of the benefit she could derive from partnership with, modeling of, and teaching by a caring adult.

Five Reminder Questions Parents Can Ask Themselves

Begin by listening to yourself as you talk to your daughter with ADHD about her differences and challenges. Think about what you might be conveying indirectly to her or what other subtle messages she might be absorbing. Ask yourself:

1. "Will what we're saying to her not only help her succeed or get better grades now, but will it improve her ability to make choices for herself later as she faces more complex challenges?"

2. "Are the messages we're conveying, or the models we're providing, going to help her feel safe to ask for help when she needs support as an adult?"

3. "How might the way we talk about our own differences or treat our partner's difficulties be contributing to her view of herself as an individual of worth and value, even with her set of challenges?"

4. "Are our words giving her false reassurance or minimizing her struggles?" Statements such as, "Don't be silly, nothing's wrong with you," have the effect of pushing her to cope silently on her own. Validate and take her problems very seriously, but always keep them separate from a characterization of *her* as the problem.

5. "Are our words or messages subtly conveying the message that treatment means we want her to get over who she is?" It is important for your daughter to understand that the purpose of treatment is to help her be able to express *more* of who she is and to make it easier for her to do this. Guard against subtly conveying that she is valued or acceptable only when she's not displaying ADHD symptoms.

Summary

Young girls with ADHD need parents to be partners in their challenges from an early age. We need to teach them to understand how their brains work so they learn early how to manage their difficulties, in order to access their strengths. We must teach them interdependency and give them appropriate role models to internalize other than traditional images of women. We must be good role models ourselves, showing we aren't afraid to get help with our difficulties, and that we value differences in other people. If girls are diagnosed early with ADHD, receive interventions designed to help them with their significant difficulties, *and* simultaneously and vigorously receive interventions that focus on their developing self-concept, they will grow into young women who see themselves as valuable and unique individuals, capable and competent to live successful lives with their particular set of abilities and complex challenges.

References and Resources

Berry, C. A., Shaywitz, S. E., & Shaywitz, B. A. (1985). Girls with attention deficit disorder: A silent minority: A report on behavioral and cognitive characteristics. *Pediatrics, 76(5),* 801-809.

Pipher, M. (1995). *Reviving Ophelia.* New York: Ballantine Books.

Sari Solden, M.S., LMFT, is a psychotherapist in Ann Arbor, Michigan, working with women and men who have ADHD. She is the author of Women With Attention Deficit Disorder. *(Underwood Books, 1995).*

Controversial Treatments for Children With Attention Deficit/Hyperactivity Disorder

Sam Goldstein, Ph.D.

In the past decade there has been a tremendous upsurge of scientific and public interest in Attention Deficit/ Hyperactivity Disorder (ADHD), reflected not only in the number of scientific articles but also in the explosion of books for parents and teachers. Research has made great progress in understanding and managing this common childhood disorder. Children with ADHD who would have gone unrecognized and untreated only a few short years ago are being helped now, often with dramatic and positive results.

It is critical for parents to seek the best in evaluation, as well as the best in treatment. Evaluations that consist of a single checklist or 10-minute discussions run the risk of misdiagnosing the disorder or misunderstanding the problems that often accompany ADHD. Symptoms of inattention, restlessness, impulsivity, and social and academic difficulties can reflect a variety of childhood disorders. It is essential to understand the problems thoroughly before attempting to intervene, especially because many children with ADHD have other learning and behavior problems. A good treatment plan follows logically from a thorough evaluation.

There are still many questions in need of answers about cause, treatment, and outcome of ADHD. Although there are a number of effective treatments, they might not be equally effective for all children with ADHD. Parents sometimes become desperate in their efforts to seek effective help for their children. In their desperation, and confused by misinformation in the marketplace, some parents turn to treatments that claim to be useful but have not been demonstrated to be truly effective in reliable scientific research. We refer to such treatments as controversial; that is, they are marketed beyond their proven worth.

Unfortunately, most parents, no matter how intelligent or well-educated, do not have the training or expertise necessary to evaluate the effectiveness of various treatments that have not as yet met scientific standards for effectiveness. Some of these treatments merit continued research, others do not.

Evaluation of New Treatments

Proving the effectiveness of a treatment can be difficult and lengthy. The process starts with an idea based on information that is already known. The second step is to develop a way to test the effectiveness of the proposed treatment. The scientists must define the treatment and the way they will implement it very carefully. The researchers also must specify how they will measure the effectiveness of the treatment. They must be careful that any results they see aren't due to the "placebo effect." A placebo is a pill or a treatment that doesn't have any effect on the condition, but the person taking it doesn't know that. People respond to all sorts of ineffective treatments as long as they believe that the treatment has the power to help them. Placebo effects can be more dramatic than most people realize.

The researcher also must take care that all who participate, researchers and research subjects alike, are not aware of who is receiving the active treatment and who is receiving the placebo. Otherwise the expectations of either group could influence the findings. Researchers also must use appropriate measurement techniques and statistical tests so that the entire scientific community can evaluate the findings. Finally, the scientists must allow other qualified individuals to evaluate their work before publication so that other researchers can examine the findings, perhaps even trying to duplicate the results to see if they are reliable.

Alternative Treatments: Another Path

There is also a second path that some practitioners follow, sometimes in an effort to shortcut the longer, more accepted process. This path, unfortunately, has many problems. Here, some practitioners propose treatments that are outside the mainstream of existing knowledge or just along its border. Individuals sometimes prescribe these treatments long before there is any research supporting their effectiveness—often after brief, poorly designed trials involving only a small number of subjects. Measurement techniques and means of evaluation are scanty at best, and single-case studies often serve as "proof" of the treatment's effectiveness.

Individuals publicize these controversial treatments in books or journals that do not require independent review of the material by recognized experts in the field. Often, in fact, advocates of particular treatments publish the work themselves. This method of self-publication should raise a warning for consumer parents. Additionally, although parent support groups have an essential role in the treatment of childhood disorders, those advocating one and only one treatment for a disorder can tend to substitute enthusiasm for careful scientific research.

These alternative treatments and interventions commonly claim effectiveness for a broad range of problems. When asked for proof to support these claims, however, proponents are unable to produce more than scanty documentation. Additionally, proponents sometimes claim to have access to knowledge and information not shared by the medical community at large. When their treatments are criticized, they respond by explaining that this criticism reflects a conspiracy against them in the scientific community.

Controversial Treatments for ADHD

We do not recommend the methods described here as proven treatments. Parents do need to be informed about such approaches, because they might be offered as proven and accepted treatments for ADHD, which they are not.

Dietary Intervention

The Feingold Diet, one of the best-known dietary interventions, proposes that some children are sensitive to a variety of foods and food colorings, including preservatives. It is claimed that such children can develop symptoms of ADHD as a toxic reaction to these substances. Advocates of these dietary interventions claim that additive-free diets will improve most, if not all, of the learning and attention problems children experience. They describe case studies in which children could be removed from drug therapy if their diet interventions (no sugar, etc.) were maintained. When the children did not follow the diet, their learning and behavior subsequently deteriorated.

Although dietary interventions are popular, few studies have reported success, and for those few, statistical problems abound. Well-controlled studies also are lacking for those who propose a relationship between allergies and behavior or learning problems. Although proponents of these dietary approaches might acknowledge that careful scientific studies are necessary, such studies have not yet been conducted.

A large number of studies have examined the relationship between sugar and ADHD. However, most of them are difficult to interpret. A few well-designed studies have found some effects of sugar on behavior, but these effects are very small, and only a small percentage of children with ADHD appear vulnerable.

After careful analysis of the existing evidence, numerous researchers have concluded that there is limited, if any, support for a link between diet and children's learning and behavior. Of course, children with ADHD, like all children, require a healthy, well-balanced diet. At this time, however, research has not shown that dietary interventions offer significant help for children with learning and attention problems.

Megavitamins and Mineral Supplements

The use of high doses of vitamins and minerals, including currently marketed antioxidants such as vitamins A and E, pycnogenol, and ginkgo biloba, is based on the precepts of orthomolecular psychiatry. According to this theory, some people have a genetic abnormality that results in increased requirements for vitamins and minerals. The antioxidants remove "free radicals" from the blood stream that, according to this theory, cause problems in learning, attention, and behavior as well as accelerate aging.

In the early 1970s, some practitioners claimed that high doses of vitamins could decrease hyperactivity and learning disabilities. Proponents of this theory also claim that learning and behavior difficulties can result from deficiencies in minerals such as potassium and sodium as well as trace elements such as zinc and copper.

Although there is an instinctive appeal in this approach—after all, vitamins are synonymous with health—there is little scientific evidence showing that these additives make much difference in the lives of children with ADHD. Although these substances are natural, which lends an aura of safety, excessive use of these substances can in fact cause health problems.

Anti–Motion Sickness Medicine

Practitioners who recommend anti–motion sickness medicine believe that there is a relationship between ADHD and problems with coordination and balance stemming from a dysfunction in the inner ear system. Proponents of this theory treat ADHD with a mixture of medications, including anti–motion sickness medicine and several vitaminlike substances. Advocates of this approach have claimed a success rate in excess of 90% with this mixture. Unfortunately, these results are unpublished and have not been verified.

This theory is not consistent with what is known currently about ADHD. There is no research that supports a link between the inner ear system and a child's attention processes. Anatomically and physiologically, there is no reason to believe that the inner ear system is involved in attention and impulse control in other than marginal ways. In the single controlled study of this theory, researchers evaluated the use of anti–motion sickness medication to treat developmental reading disorders. The results failed to support the theory. This approach to treating ADHD is inconsistent with current knowledge, and research findings do not support it.

Candida Yeast

Candida albicans is a type of yeast that lives in the human body. Normally, the body's strong immune system and friendly bacteria keep yeast growth in check. When the immune system is weakened or when antibiotics kill the friendly bacteria, *Candida* can overgrow. This can lead to the vaginal yeast infection known as candidiasis and, less commonly, to infections of the skin, nails, and mouth.

Those who support this model believe that toxins produced by yeast overgrowth weaken the immune system, making the body susceptible to many illnesses, including ADHD and other psychiatric disorders. The purpose of the treatment is to discourage the growth of *Candida* in the body. This two-pronged approach includes anti-fungal medication and a low-sugar diet. Other aspects of the treatment include the use of vitamin and mineral supplements and an elimination diet to rule out food allergies.

Although *Candida* can cause infections of the vagina, mouth, and skin, there is little evidence to support the idea that it also causes the host of other illnesses listed by advocates of this approach. Instead, proponents offer anecdotal data and testimonials as proof that the approach is effective. The theory is not supported by evidence and most likely is not a helpful treatment for ADHD.

EEG Biofeedback

Proponents of this approach believe that children with ADHD can be trained to increase the type of brainwave activity associated with sustained attention and decrease the type of activity associated with daydreaming and distraction. They claim the result is improvement in attention and reductions in hyperactivity and impulsivity.

The technique of EEG biofeedback involves measuring levels of electrical activity in various regions of the brain. This information goes into a computer, which transforms it into a signal such as a light, tone, or video game. Using this signal as feedback, the child learns to increase certain kinds of brainwave activity and decrease other kinds (increase beta, decrease theta). Training involves 40 to 80 treatment sessions, with each session lasting 40 minutes or more. Sessions occur two or three times a week, which means treatment can last from 3 to 10 months or longer.

Although this treatment has become quite popular and is marketed throughout the country, there continues to be limited published, peer-reviewed research to support its use. Although there is an increasing interest in research in this area, the extensive claims initially made by proponents of this treatment (e.g., dramatic improvements in intelligence scores, dramatic reductions in ADHD symptoms) seem almost too good to believe. Many of the early studies were seriously flawed by the small numbers of children, many of whom had ambiguous diagnoses. Furthermore, published studies thus far have not included appropriate control groups to rule out the effects of maturation or placebo.

Biofeedback technology is not new. Although some believe it holds great promise in the treatment of ADHD, at this time parents must consider it at best a supplementary treatment used to support other treatments. Qualified researchers consider it unproven and advise parents to proceed with caution. It is an expensive approach whose effectiveness, until better studies have been completed, has not been demonstrated consistently.

Sam Goldstein, Ph.D., is a nationally certified school psychologist specializing in child development, school psychology, and neuropsychology. He currently is the director of the Neurology, Learning, and Behavior Center, Salt Lake City. This article is based on the work of Dr. Goldstein and Dr. Barbara Ingersoll.

Psychoeducational Therapy

H. Russell Searight, Ph.D.

Psychoeducational treatment is a term used to describe an integrated approach to managing difficulties with concentration, attention, and distractibility in children and adolescents with Attention Deficit/Hyperactivity Disorder (ADHD). Children and adolescents respond best to multiple approaches, including medication, skill building, and changes in the environment.

Basic Assumptions About Attention Deficit/Hyperactivity Disorder

ADHD Is a Biologically Based Disorder

Parents should recognize that ADHD involves the central nervous system (in particular, specific regions of the brain). Because of this biological imbalance, children with ADHD will have specific weaknesses in self-control, attention and concentration, and the ability to respond to directions.

Parents Do not Cause ADHD

ADHD is not caused by parental inconsistency, divorce, or a past history of emotional trauma. Although there certainly are skills you can acquire to manage the symptoms of ADHD more effectively, these children have a biologically based weakness that has been present since birth. About 70% of these children will continue to have symptoms in adolescence, and about half will continue to have some form of ADHD in adulthood.

There Are Varying Degrees of ADHD

There are two primary subtypes of the disorder—the hyperactive type and the inattentive type. Whereas hyperactive children are usually detected more easily, the inattentive type (more common in girls) often is not detected by teachers or adults because the child is not overly disruptive. Children with the inattentive type sometimes "space out" and have difficulty focusing but usually are not impulsive or disruptive. It is also important to recognize that some children have very pronounced forms of the disorder and others have relatively mild forms. In the milder forms, adults might not notice the inattention and distractibility until the child is older or has entered adolescence. At this later stage, the demands for greater independence in schoolwork can make ADHD symptoms more evident.

Medications Are Helpful

Medications, particularly stimulants, improve attention and concentration and sometimes help decrease aggression and improve social interaction. The majority of children do benefit from regular ongoing medication, and medication needs to be a part of their treatment. Although skills are certainly important, most studies suggest that medication is necessary to improve concentration so that children can benefit from specific skill training.

Attention and Concentration Vary

Because of children's vulnerability in the areas of attention and concentration, their weaknesses will be more or less evident depending on the situation. Tasks that are repetitive and tedious (such as trying to memorize the multiplication tables) will make inattention and poor concentration much more obvious. Tasks that are novel and unique (playing video games) often will make the ADHD child appear "normal."

Help Your Child Develop Skills to Compensate for Weaknesses

Children with ADHD struggle with inattention and distractibility. Unfortunately, many parents use logical consequences as a form of punishment for children with ADHD. For example, if a child doesn't complete assignments, the child will have to experience the consequences of a poor grade and the teacher's displeasure. Or, if the child does not have the room picked up and organized by a particular time, he or she will not be allowed to go to a movie with a friend.

Barkley (1990) notes very correctly that this approach only courts disaster for children with ADHD. Unless there is enough structure and assistance from the parents, such children will rarely, if ever, receive the reward. In attempting to organize school work without parental help, lists, schedules, or other time-management tools, the child with ADHD rapidly will become caught in a vicious cycle of frustration and academic failure. Nagging the child about this lack of responsibility to follow through is equally unhelpful. Again, it is important to remember that these children have a biologically based weakness.

You can help your child build skills to deal with these problems. You also might need to modify the type of discipline you use. You will want to find out what strengths your child has, then begin encouraging these areas. An academic therapist or diagnostic specialist can help identify special strengths.

Specific Skills for Structuring the Environment

Changes in the environment can help children with ADHD. This section describes several specific strategies for helping your child.

Help Your Child Organize

Children with ADHD often struggle with personal organizational skills. You can encourage such skills by helping your child establish a routine for the major tasks he or she must accomplish. For example, the child should have a routine in which he or she tidies the room, ideally every evening before going to bed. Additionally, the child should have school clothes and other material (back pack, homework) packed and set up the night before to avoid a mad, hectic scramble during the morning. Other strategies such as color-coded laundry baskets (dirty socks in the pink basket, gym clothes in the blue basket) will help the child with ADHD stay organized.

Use Visual Prompts or Cues to Remind the Child to Stay on Task

Visual reminders posted around the house can help your child remember and carry out specific activities. For example, a typical morning routine before school might include taking a shower, brushing teeth and hair, getting dressed, and eating breakfast. You could work with your child to create a series of drawings in a comic-strip format and place it in a central area of the house (e.g., kitchen). These drawings can help your child remember the routine, and if he or she seems to be off task, you can prompt the child to go look at the pictures to get back on track with the next step.

Break Down Tasks

Be very specific in defining the amount of work to be done when you are assigning your child specific homework or chores to complete ("I want this half of your floor picked up"). You also need to specify the time by which the child is to complete the task ("It needs to be done by 10:30. I'll set the timer"). Setting a timer for the specific length of time helps keep the child on task. In addition, it might be helpful to write down a schedule of the child's activities for weekends and after school.

Be Sure to See the Positive

It is important to praise children for desirable behavior. It is easy to focus on behavioral weaknesses with children who have ADHD, and many parents fail to reinforce children when they do perform tasks correctly. For example, a parent forgets to praise the child who has a coat on and is ready to leave the house at a specified time. The parent might be thinking that the child should know that he or she is supposed to be ready on time and should not have to be praised for it.

To ensure positive exchanges instead of these negative, nagging ones, it is helpful to set aside special time—perhaps 15 minutes a day—during which the child chooses an activity to do with the parent, such as playing catch, reading a story, or building a model airplane (Barkley, 1990). Because so much parent-child interaction often centers around task completion (homework or household chores), there sometimes is little positive interaction between the parent and the child with ADHD, and parents can become locked into a negative or critical pattern with the child. Allocating special time guarantees that you will have the opportunity to share enjoyable and positive exchanges with your child.

Repetition and Making Lists Will Help Memory

Make sure that your child understands rules and instructions. Encourage the child to restate the rules you have just described. This helps the child remember what you've said and gives you the chance to correct any misunderstanding. To help your child stay on task, write out instructions and have the child read them aloud. Using lists and written instructions helps the child with ADHD stay focused, and it is a skill that will be even more helpful as the child gets older. As your child enters the teen years, encourage him or her to begin making lists independently. Schedule books and planners also help teens develop these skills.

Parental Consistency Is Important

Consistency usually requires ongoing, constant communication. If you think you are being too lax on your child's misbehavior, or think you might be overresponding by being too harsh, check out the intended consequence with your spouse. It is also important to remember that if one parent assigns a consequence or task to the child, that parent (rather than the other parent) should be the one to determine if the child has completed the task or served the consequence.

For married couples, parenting children with ADHD requires a solid marital relationship with effective communication skills. If communication is a problem, consider seeking marriage counseling to be sure that you have this basic foundation. A strong marital relationship greatly increases the likelihood of successfully parenting the child with ADHD. It is important to schedule activities for yourselves so that you have adequate time and energy to devote to your marriage. A strong marriage will filter down to good parenting.

References and Resources

Barkley, R. A. (1990). *Attention Deficit/Hyperactivity Disorder: A handbook for diagnosis and treatment.* New York: Guilford.

———————————————————

H. Russell Searight, Ph.D., is the director of behavioral sciences for the Residency Program of Family Medicine of St. Louis. He is the author of several textbooks and an adjunct associate professor in the department of psychology and Community and Family Medicine at St. Louis University.

Section 2

Medical Aspects

Medical Evaluation of the Child With Attention Deficit/Hyperactivity Disorder

James E. Nahlik, M.D.

Why Go to the Doctor?

Parents often bring their children to the doctor's office when they or the teachers have noticed attention problems or overactivity. Sometimes the teacher or parent has said, "Get this child on medication!" The doctor must conduct a medical examination of the child before making the decision to begin using medications. You should stay with the child for at least the beginning of the exam. It also will help if you bring report cards or progress reports and examples of schoolwork for the doctor to review. If you have them, bring reports from school testing and letters from the teacher describing the child's behavior and academic work.

ADHD can be a difficult condition to diagnose. There is no simple blood test or x-ray that says a child has the disorder. The doctor compares the child's symptoms to a list of criteria described in the *Diagnostic and Statistical Manual of Mental Disorders* (American Psychiatric Association, 1994). Because there might be other factors causing disruptive behavior and inattention, the physician must evaluate your child's general health thoroughly as a part of the process of diagnosing ADHD. In addition, only a physician can prescribe medication for ADHD.

The Medical History

The pediatrician or family physician will measure the child for current height, weight, and blood pressure. The doctor will obtain a medical history from you and the child and will observe the child's behavior during this interview and the examination. Be sure to mention any difficulties with the youngster's early development and any hospitalizations. Report recent use of medications or nutritional supplements. If there is a family history of attention problems and hyperactivity in close relatives such as siblings, aunts or uncles, or either parent, please inform the physician. You also should let the doctor know if the child has been exposed to lead in the home because this can lead to behaviors resembling ADHD.

A Good Look

The doctor's physical examination of the child focuses on any of the problems that might be causing your child to be distractible. For example, the doctor will evaluate your child's vision and hearing carefully and make recommendations for treatment, if necessary. There might be signs of allergic irritation in the child's nose, throat, or lungs. The doctor will check your child's neck and possibly muscle reflexes to detect thyroid disorders, which also can cause hyperactivity. The doctor also will look for any signs of frequent physical injuries or conditions that could be causing the child pain. This is an opportunity to review with the doctor any other symptoms the child is having that concern you.

Further Studies

Depending on what he or she finds during the history and physical examination, the doctor might recommend blood tests for thyroid problems, allergies, or lead poisoning. Occasionally, the primary care doctor will want a brain wave test (EEG) or an x-ray of the brain (MRI or CT scan). Sometimes the physician will recommend an evaluation by a specialist such as a neurologist or a psychologist. The psychologist might use specialized testing to evaluate the child's verbal skills, problem-solving abilities, and visual-motor skills. The psychologist also might administer academic tests of reading, spelling, and arithmetic. These tests can detect learning problems that occur instead of or in addition to ADHD. Your child might not need these specialized tests and consultations.

Additionally, the doctor frequently will send the parents home with a questionnaire about the child's behavior. These checklists ask the parent or the teacher to rate how often the child shows different behaviors. Complete these behavioral checklists at a quiet time when you can answer the questions thoroughly and honestly. After you return the forms, the doctor scores the information and considers it before diagnosing the child with ADHD.

Skills as Treatment

If your child meets the criteria for the diagnosis of Attention Deficit/Hyperactivity Disorder, your physician might recommend behavioral treatments such as specialized teaching methods or a change in environment. Some schools have teachers who have received specialized training with children who have ADHD. Frequently they will recommend positive reinforcement and list-making skills. Some children improve by participation in such activities as scouting, sports, or martial arts, which can teach self-discipline and reward individual talents.

Pills as Treatment

Your doctor might prescribe medication to treat your child's ADHD symptoms. Methylphenidate (Ritalin) is the most common stimulant medication. These medications wake up the brain to use the attention centers. The medications often begin to help the child right from the start. Most of the time, children take the medication two or three times a day. There are strict laws to control who can give these medications.

You and your child should consider stimulants such as Ritalin as a tool to help the child pay attention, just as eyeglasses help people with poor eyesight to see better. Your child might use the medicine for several years, but he or she also must continue to work on improving behavioral skills. Ask your physician any questions you have about the medications, and report any side effects of the medicine (nervous movements, sleep problems, stomachaches). Your child might need to avoid these medications if anyone in the house would abuse them.

Some children under 10 can't swallow tablets. You can ask your physician to request that the pharmacist make Ritalin in a liquid suspension form. Other medications come in a sprinkle form (Dexedrine spansule) or chewable tablets (Cylert).

The Big Picture

The physician's evaluation is important in securing the diagnosis of ADHD. The doctor will go through several steps to look for other causes of difficulties with attention and hyperactivity. If the doctor does diagnose ADHD, there are treatments that will allow your child to succeed in school. You will need to work with your child's teachers to help your child succeed academically. As a parent, you can be a great advocate for the child and make sure that your child reaches his or her full potential. The physician is also an important part of this team, and communication between you and your child's doctor and teachers will help provide the best possible treatment package.

References and Resources

American Psychiatric Association. (1994). *Diagnostic and statistical manual of mental disorders* (4th ed.). Washington, DC: Author.

James E. Nahlik, M.D., is a clinical associate professor at St. Louis University School of Medicine and a faculty family physician at Deaconess Family Practice in St. Louis.

The Family Physician's Perspective on Attention Deficit/Hyperactivity Disorder: Collaborating With Parents and Teachers

Lloyd A. Darlow, M.D.

The family physician or pediatrician is usually the first professional to evaluate and treat the child with Attention Deficit/Hyperactivity Disorder (ADHD). Although educators' and parents' roles in assisting children with ADHD have been described thoroughly, many parents and teachers might not appreciate the physician's perspective. The physician is a vital and important member of the ADHD treatment team. This article can help parents, teachers, and others working with children who have ADHD better understand the physician's vantage point.

The management of children's health issues in primary care is quite complex. When dealing with adults, the physician engages in a one-on-one encounter with the patient. In pediatric settings, however, physicians always must remember that they are dealing with not one patient but two or more, namely the child's parent(s). In addition, issues that affect the child at school often bring more "patients" into the mix. Suddenly, the physician is involved with parents, teachers, school nurses, etc., all of whom have their own unique view of the child's difficulties. In order to provide the best possible service to all parties, especially the child, it is important for the physician to learn effective strategies for dealing with both parents and school personnel.

The Physician-Parent Relationship

From the first moment the parents walk into the doctor's office with a child for an "ADHD visit," the physician is presented with a unique opportunity. In very few areas of medicine does the physician have the chance to become such an important part of the child/patient's life, both immediately and for the future. But while the physician sees opportunity and promise, the child's parents might see trouble and despair. Often they feel overwhelmed with the child's difficulties at school, and they have no idea where to turn for help.

In addition, the parents might be encountering significant difficulties with their child at home. Common concerns include completing homework or other school assignments, compliance with household chores, "peace" at the dinner table, and getting to bed in a timely fashion. It is not unusual for that first physician-parent visit to include tears, frustration, desperation, and pleas for help. To make matters more complicated, the child with ADHD often will be quite well-behaved in the office setting. Children with ADHD frequently behave differently in various situations.

Therefore, the physician should attempt to accomplish several things in the first interview with the parents. This is a prime opportunity to establish rapport and gain the parents' confidence. It is also valuable to ascertain the parents' perception of their child's disorder. Close observation of the parent-child relationship in the office can be quite revealing in this regard (Barkley, 1990). There is a certain amount of information about the child's performance and behavior, both at school and at home, that is critical to obtain during this visit. The use of parental checklists or diagnostic rating scales is an effective method of describing certain behaviors that help to classify the child's disorder (Kelly & Aylward, 1992). The presence of other comorbid disorders such as Oppositional Defiant Disorder, learning disabilities, childhood depression, and Conduct Disorder can make the diagnosis of ADHD more difficult (Searight, Nahlik, & Campbell, 1995). These questionnaires are helpful as a diagnostic aid and, when given out at the initial visit, give the parents an immediate sense that "something is being done" to help their child. A number of behavioral scales are available, perhaps the best known of which is the Conners Parent Rating Scale. The physician should select a rating scale with which he or she feels comfortable and use it consistently.

Interactions With Teachers

In many cases, the person who has the most contact with the child (in terms of hours spent) during the course of a regular day is the teacher. Therefore, excluding the teaching professional from "the loop" (i.e., the diagnostic and therapeutic plan for that child) is neither practical nor helpful. Teachers are a source of invaluable information about the child's cognitive and behavioral performance. Their input aids in making the proper diagnosis of the child's condition(s) and also helps the physician determine whether or not any prescribed medication is accomplishing the therapeutic goal.

Teacher rating scales, similar to the parental rating scales, are available (for example, there is a Conners Teacher Rating Scale comparable to the Conners Parent Rating Scale). However, it might be helpful to have parents and teachers complete the same scale. It is important to recognize that teachers and parents might provide different yet often complementary ratings of the child's behavior. Certainly there are behaviors that are apparent only in the school environment, and parents might be unaware of these patterns. Similarly, teachers should not be surprised to hear a parent say, "My child never does that at home," and the physician must be careful about "choosing sides" should this prove to be the case. The teachers need to know that their input is desired and valued, and the physician should go to great lengths to communicate this.

An "Integrated" Office Protocol for ADHD

Attention Deficit/Hyperactivity Disorder is not a condition that can be diagnosed and treated in one 10-minute office visit. Therefore, physicians and parents should plan ahead so that the process from presentation to diagnosis, treatment, and follow-up is smooth and efficient.

At the first visit, the physician takes a thorough history from the parent, reviews any communication sent by the school, and performs a basic physical examination of the child. The physician gives a behavioral rating scale to the parents, along with copies for the child's teachers to complete, and stamped envelopes with the doctor's name and address. If there are two parents in the household, they should fill out their questionnaires separately and in private, no comparing of answers. Parents and teachers should return the completed forms directly to the physician.

After receiving all of the rating scales, the physician should analyze them promptly and, in combination with the history and physical findings, make a preliminary diagnosis of the child's condition(s). The physician should meet with the parents (with or without the child present) for a second appointment to review the entire process and discuss the diagnosis. The doctor should send a letter under separate cover to the child's teachers, summarizing what has taken place to date. The physician's office obviously must inform the school of any decision to start the child on medication, because the majority of medicines used to treat ADHD require the child to take at least one dose at school. The physician and parents also must inform the teacher if they choose to defer beginning medication. The physician should perform any further educational and/or psychological testing deemed necessary at this time.

The family must come in for monthly follow-up visits until the condition stabilizes to the point where these visits can be spaced out to every 3 months. Every child on medication for ADHD and/or other disorders should see the physician no less than every third month. It is important to track changes in the child's height and weight. Certain psychostimulants initially might slow the child's physical development, although this will normalize in the long term. Other medications, such as pemoline (Cylert), require periodic blood testing. A regular schedule for office follow-up prevents anyone's slipping through the cracks.

In preparation for the child's follow-up visit, parents will need to obtain a progress report from the teachers along with a review of the child's tests and homework assignments for the preceding period. Communication from the teachers is vital because mere paperwork does not tell the entire story of the child's progress, particularly in the social realm. Only by reviewing the work done at school can the physician determine whether the medication is producing the desired effect and whether the dose or type needs to be changed. Phone conversation with the teachers also might be appropriate before or after these regular visits.

Summary

When the question of ADHD arises, the physician often is the first, vital link between the parents, the child, and the school. There initially might be miscommunication and different opinions among these parties. The physician will need to understand these distinct points of view but also weigh information and make decisions about diagnosis and treatment. A consistent, coordinated treatment plan will help everyone keep in mind the most important thing— the health and welfare of the child.

References and Resources

Barkley, R. A. (1990). *Attention Deficit/Hyperactivity Disorder: A handbook for diagnosis and treatment.* New York: Guilford.

Kelly, D. P., & Aylward, G. P. (1992). Attention deficits in school-aged children and adolescents. *Pediatric Clinics of North America, 39,* 487-512.

Searight, H. R., Nahlik, J. E., & Campbell, D. C. (1995). Attention Deficit/Hyperactivity Disorder: Assessment, diagnosis, and management. *Journal of Family Practice, 40,* 270-279.

Lloyd A. Darlow, M.D., is a family physician in private practice with the Grandel Medical Group and a member of the faculty at Deaconess Family Practice in St. Louis.

Methylphenidate

A. Lesley McLaren, M.D., M.P.H

What Is Methylphenidate?

Methylphenidate, marketed under the trade name Ritalin, is a stimulant like caffeine. About 60 years ago, doctors noticed that stimulant medications seemed to help some children with behavior problems. Methylphenidate has been on the market since the 1960s and is the most common medication for treating Attention Deficit/Hyperactivity Disorder (ADHD).

How Does Methylphenidate Help Children With ADHD?

Methylphenidate seems to improve the workings of the particular parts of the brain that deal with the ability to pay attention and control impulsive behavior. Methylphenidate use usually results in success in the classroom. Children are less restless, are able to pay more attention to the teacher, and may perform better on classroom assignments, quizzes and weekly tests. Children also are more likely to think before they speak or act and, therefore, get along better with other people. However, acting-out behaviors such as stealing, fighting, and refusing to do household chores respond better to treatment with other medications that are aimed at changing the underlying aggression that is affecting the child's behavior.

Will Methylphenidate Help My Child?

Approximately 70% of children with ADHD show improvement in their behavior and do better in school when treated with methylphenidate. Used by itself, methylphenidate seems to work better for most children than other medications for ADHD, but sometimes, your doctor may need to add a second medication or use a different drug (such as clonidine) to help with other behaviors that affect your child.

Your doctor also may recommend that you and your child see a therapist to discuss behavior and family problems. Sometimes the most helpful treatment is a combination of medication and clear expectations for children's behavior with consistent consequences for breaking rules. Some children with other medical problems may not be able to take methylphenidate for ADHD, but there are other medications that may be helpful.

Does Methylphenidate Have Any Side Effects?

Very few children will experience side effects serious enough for them to stop taking methylphenidate. Sometimes a child will complain that a muscle will go into spasm repeatedly. This is called a tic. Your child may experience some loss of appetite, stomachache, headache, or difficulty sleeping, but these side effects are usually mild. Some children will become more irritable when the dose of medication wears off.

Your child may grow more slowly while taking it but will catch up after stopping the medication. Your doctor will want to keep an eye on your child's height, weight, and blood pressure. Methylphenidate doesn't cause nightmares, but it shouldn't be taken late in the day because the drug might make it difficult for your child to fall asleep.

How Do Children Take Methylphenidate?

Methylphenidate is made in immediate- and sustained-release forms. Immediate-release methylphenidate allows the whole dose of medication to go to work as soon as your child takes it. The sustained release form allows your child to receive the dose over a period of hours. Larger doses do not always give better results than smaller doses.

If your child has a hard time swallowing pills, you can crush the immediate-release form of methylphenidate and give it to your child in jelly or applesauce. The schedule that seems to work best for most children is a dose in the morning, before school, with a second dose at noon. A typical dosage of methylphenidate is 10 milligrams twice a day for a child in the middle elementary grades. Your doctor will choose the right dose of medication for your child. Older children may benefit from an extra dose of medication, given around 3:00 p.m., to help them concentrate on their homework.

Your doctor will ask you and your child's teacher to report on your child's progress, then adjust the medication to achieve the best results. Sometimes your physician will prescribe the sustained-release form or a combination of the immediate- and sustained-release forms so that it will not be necessary to arrange for the child's teacher or the school nurse to give a noon dose. If your child needs medication during the day, you must make arrangements with the teacher and ask your pharmacist to give you two bottles with labeled instructions, one of which you send to your child's school.

It is illegal for your doctor to write for refills or to phone in prescriptions for methylphenidate to your pharmacy. Physicians can prescribe only one month's supply at a time, and you must fill the prescription within 30 days of the date it is written. You must not share your child's prescription with anyone else. This is against the law.

If your child's behavior at home during the long school holidays is not a problem, your doctor may suggest trying a vacation from the medication.

Will Methylphenidate Have Long-Term Effects?

Methylphenidate helps children with ADHD in the short term, and scientists are trying to determine whether it helps these children in the long term. Sometimes children continue to benefit from methylphenidate into their teens and adulthood. There are no known long-term side effects.

Do I Need to Worry That My Child Will Become Addicted to Methylphenidate?

There is little evidence that physical addiction to or abuse of methylphenidate occurs when it is used for ADHD strictly according to your doctor's advice.

A. Lesley McLaren, M.D., M.P.H., is a faculty physician with the Family Medicine of St. Louis residency program. She is also an associate professor of community and family medicine and director of the preventive medicine/public health residency program at St. Louis University School of Medicine.

Other Stimulant Medication for Treating Attention Deficit/Hyperactivity Disorder

Michael T. Railey, M.D., and H. Russell Searight, Ph.D.

Stimulants are the most commonly used class of medication for Attention Deficit/Hyperactivity Disorder (ADHD). The most common stimulant, methylphenidate (marketed under the name Ritalin), results in improvement in approximately 70% of children. There are several other stimulant medications used to treat ADHD. These medications might be helpful in children and adolescents who do not respond to methylphenidate. The three most common alternative stimulant medications are dextroamphetamine (Dexedrine), pemoline (Cylert), and an amphetamine mixture currently marketed under the name Adderall. These medications all seem to improve attention and concentration. However, these medications work best in conjunction with behavioral modification in the child's family and school.

Dextroamphetamine (Dexedrine)

Dextroamphetamine was one of the first stimulants used to treat ADHD children. Most research indicates that it is about as effective as methylphenidate in addressing core symptoms of ADHD such as overactivity, impulsivity, and inattention. Dextroamphetamine is somewhat longer acting and slightly less expensive than methylphenidate. Dextroamphetamine comes in dosages of 2.5 mg, 5 mg, and 10 mg. Children usually take this drug in doses of 5–10 mg two or three times a day. Dexedrine also comes in a capsule form that is longer acting.

Common side effects of dextroamphetamine include difficulties falling asleep, decline in appetite, irritability, and mood swings. Less common side effects include stomachaches, headaches, and increased nervous habits such as fingernail biting. Children taking Dexedrine were somewhat more likely to have sleep difficulty and poor appetite than those taking methylphenidate. However, sleep and appetite usually improve after taking dextroamphetamine for several weeks. Because it is a slightly longer-acting medication, children and adolescents taking dextroamphetamine should be careful not to take the second or third dose too close to bedtime because it could interfere with sleep.

One caution in using dextroamphetamine is that people have abused it. Adolescents, particularly teenagers at risk for developing substance abuse problems, should take this medication with close supervision.

Pemoline (Cylert)

Pemoline, marketed under the trade name Cylert, is longer-acting than methylphenidate or dextroamphetamine. Pemoline comes in 18.75 mg and 75 mg capsules, and people usually take 18.75 mg, 37.5 mg or 112.5 mg once per day. Pemoline appears to be about as effective as other stimulants in improving attention and concentration, as well as reducing distractibility (Pelham, Swanson, Furman, & Schwindt, 1995). Pemoline's short-term effects can last up to 7 hours, but individual children respond differently to the drug. However, some researchers believe that it can take 3 to 4 weeks for the child to receive full benefit from pemoline (Elia, Rapoport, & Kirby, 1993).

One advantage of pemoline's longer mode of action is that individuals can take it just once a day. This might be an advantage in schools where staffing patterns do not allow medication distribution. Some children forget to take their noon dose of shorter-acting medication such as methylphenidate or feel self-conscious about going to the nurse's office. In addition, the effects of a noon dose of short-acting medication such as methylphenidate often will wear off by midafternoon. Children with longer school days or who have significant amounts of homework might require continued assistance with attention and concentration later in the day. Pemoline seems to be more effective for these children.

Possible side effects of pemoline include tics (repeated nervous movements) as well as jumpiness and restlessness. Pemoline does not appear to have "rebound" effects, in which children become irritable or restless after the medication wears off. This often is found in the shorter-acting stimulant medications such as methylphenidate. If your doctor prescribes pemoline for your child, it is important that the doctor run tests of the child's liver functioning several times a year. Pemoline has caused liver damage in a small number of children.

Amphetamine Mixtures (Adderall)

Adderall is a new ADHD medication that contains two slightly different forms of amphetamine. The drug comes in 10 mg and 20 mg tablets. Individuals take Adderall once or twice per day. Its effects are generally long-acting, and a single dose may be enough for the schoolday. More commonly, however, children take it twice—in the morning and at noon.

Children as young as 3 years have taken Adderall in lower doses (Prescription Drug Review, 1997). Children usually start at 5 mg twice a day (the tablets are scored to break in half). Adderall, like other stimulants, appears to improve attention and concentration. Side effects include loss of appetite, headaches, weight loss, and difficulty sleeping, particularly if taken late in the day. Because it is slower acting, there might be a more gradual onset of beneficial effects and less of a "crash" when the medicine wears off. At present, there is little research available on Adderall, but researchers are likely to study it more thoroughly in the near future.

Summary

Methylphenidate (Ritalin) is the most commonly used stimulant medication for ADHD. However, up to 30% of children and adolescents with ADHD don't seem to respond to Ritalin. Many of these children respond to another stimulant medication. If your physician prescribes these for your child, ask about the types of improvement you can expect and the possible side effects associated with these less commonly employed stimulants.

References and Resources

Elia, J., Rapoport, J. L., & Kirby, J. (1993). Pharmacological treatment of Attention Deficit/Hyperactivity Disorder. In J. L. Matson (Ed.), *Handbook of hyperactivity in children* (pp. 220-223). Boston: Allyn and Bacon.

Pelham, W. E., Swanson, J. M., Furman, M. B., & Schwindt, H. (1995). Pemoline effects on children with ADHD: A time-response by dose-response analysis on classroom measures. *Journal of the American Academy of Child & Adolescent Psychiatry, 34*, 1504-1513.

Prescription Drug Review. (1997). Adderall: The newest available option in ADHD. *Advance for Nurse Practitioners*, 73-74.

Michael Railey, M.D., is an assistant professor of community and family medicine and director of the family medicine clerkship at the St. Louis University School of Medicine. Dr. Railey is also a faculty physician in the residency program of Family Medicine of St. Louis.

H. Russell Searight, Ph.D., is the director of behavioral sciences for the Residency Program of Family Medicine of St. Louis. He is the author of several textbooks and an adjunct associate professor in the department of psychology and Community and Family Medicine at St. Louis University.

Antidepressant Pharmacotherapy

Ila V. Mehra, Pharm.D.

Often it is frustrating to parents when doctors switch their child with Attention Deficit/Hyperactivity Disorder (ADHD) from medication to medication. Why do doctors prescribe certain medicines more than others? Why doesn't methylphenidate (Ritalin) work for every child? Why are antidepressants used? Are there any risks or side effects with antidepressant medications?

Use of Medications

Remember, medication is only a part of the total therapy, not a "cure-all"! Children with ADHD also need behavior therapy, individual therapy, and/or family counseling. Medicines should never be the only treatment a child receives, unless other therapy is unavailable or too expensive.

Once your child starts on medication, he or she needs close monitoring and follow-up. Your child should not continue taking medication unless you see clear-cut benefits. If you or the teachers see no effect after several weeks, inform your doctor so your child can be reevaluated. Usually, drug therapy starts at a very low dose and increases slowly. Remember, do not change or increase the dose yourself, even if you or the child's teacher feels the child needs more. You need to speak first with your doctor.

Usually, the first medications tried are stimulant medications such as methylphenidate (Ritalin) because they are the most effective treatment for ADHD. Try not to be impatient or get frustrated. Stimulants can take several weeks before the child experiences maximum effectiveness, although you might notice some effect after 1 day of therapy. Although most children improve with stimulant therapy, it doesn't always work for everybody. The good news is that about 20% to 25% of children who respond poorly to one agent will have a good response to another. Typically, the physician would try different stimulant medications first.

The possible side effects of stimulants include decreased appetite, sleeping difficulties, stomachache, headache, palpitations, increased heart rate, increased blood pressure, and symptom rebound if the child stops taking the medication. However, the majority of children taking stimulants do not have any side effects.

After a child has tried and had no success with (or can't tolerate) the different stimulant medications, the doctor might try other drugs.

Antidepressant Medications for ADHD
Tricyclic Antidepressants (TCAs)

Although the U.S. Food and Drug Administration (FDA) has not approved TCAs officially for use in ADHD, researchers have found TCAs to be effective alternatives to stimulants. The most studied TCAs are desipramine (Norpramin), nortriptyline (Pamelor), imipramine (Tofranil), and amitriptyline (Elavil), although others have been used. These drugs might be a good alternative for children who also have tic disorders. Studies have shown that, although TCAs improved behavior as measured by clinicians, parents, and teachers, they seem to have little effect on academic performance. Stimulants work better. Some clinicians have used Ritalin and a TCA together; however, researchers have studied this combination in only a small number of children.

TCAs are not quite as effective as stimulants for ADHD (on both behavioral and performance measures) but work well in children who don't respond to or can't tolerate the side effects of stimulants or who have attention problems associated with anxiety, mood disturbances, or depression. The American Academy of Pediatrics Committee on Children With Disabilities and Committee on Drugs (1996) agrees that the TCAs are second-line drug therapy for the treatment of ADHD. Often, children for whom one or more stimulants have failed show the best response to TCAs.

There are a couple of key differences between TCAs and stimulants, other than the fact that they don't work quite as well. TCAs also don't work as fast as stimulants, taking about 2 weeks to show any effect. Be patient and don't give up! Also, children take these medications once daily at bedtime, which is more convenient than most of the stimulants. Unlike stimulants, which children can stop taking during weekends, TCAs require daily dosing, even on weekends. When children stop taking TCAs, they must taper off slowly and not stop abruptly.

Advantages of the TCAs include the convenience of once-daily doses at bedtime, no insomnia side effects, and no symptom rebound.

However, TCAs do have side effects, and some of them can be serious, including dry mouth, constipation, blurred vision, weight loss, tiredness, irritability, headaches, and mild cardiovascular changes such as dizziness on standing and increased heart rate. Although rare, serious cardiovascular changes can occur, such as arrhythmias (irregular heart rhythm) and problems with the electrical conduction in the heart. Physicians can detect the serious cardiovascular changes by using an electrocardiogram (ECG or EKG). Major EKG changes are more common when the blood levels of the drug are high.

Much of the concern about heart problems from TCAs stems from three sudden deaths reported in children with ADHD taking desipramine (Norpramin). However, none of these children had elevated levels of the drug in their bloodstream. Two of the children had a family history of early heart-related deaths, and one child already had a history of an irregular heart beat. Researchers have not determined whether these deaths were definitely the result of treatment with desipramine or perhaps due to another cause. These medications continue to be used for children with ADHD who cannot take stimulants and are rarely associated with serious adverse effects. TCAs appear to be at least moderately effective in treating core ADHD symptoms (Spencer, et al., 1996).

Because of the potential for serious cardiac side effects, your child's doctor should do a complete medical exam and history. The medical history you provide should include any history of irregular heart beat (arrhythmia), heart disease, dizziness on standing, hearing loss, or family history of heart disease or sudden cardiac death. Usually, before a child begins taking TCA, doctors check the child's blood pressure and heart rate. Most clinicians obtain an EKG before starting the medication, again while the dose is being increased, once the medication reaches steady levels in the bloodstream, and perhaps after each dose increase. There is some disagreement among experts whether or not an EKG is absolutely necessary, because researchers don't know if the EKG will identify all children who might have problems. If your child's doctor decides not to check an EKG, it usually is okay, because these types of problems are not common. However, you might want to discuss the issue with your doctor so that you have a better understanding.

It is common practice to check the level of the TCA in the bloodstream to avoid toxicities and to help determine what dose is needed. The frequency of such testing depends on the dose used and any other symptoms.

Children who have a history of acquired or congenital heart disease or murmurs, family history of cardiomyopathy, or diastolic hypertension absolutely should not take TCAs.

Buproprion (Wellbutrin)

Buproprion, also an antidepressant, works very differently from TCAs. It is not as well studied as the TCAs but seems to be as effective as stimulants on most measures.

Side effects of buproprion include dry mouth and insomnia. Uncommon side effects include anxiety, anger, irritability, stomach upset, headache, and seizures (although the risk is very low with recommended doses).

Buproprion remains an alternative to stimulants for the treatment of ADHD. It probably does not work as well as the TCAs, but it is an option.

MAO Inhibitors (e.g., Nardil)

MAO inhibitors are also antidepressants with yet a different mechanism of action. They are about as effective as dextroamphetamine.

The biggest problem with MAO inhibitors is the side effects and interactions with other medications and foods. The side effects and disadvantages include severe dietary restrictions, weight gain, drowsiness, and insomnia. If a person taking an MAO inhibitor eats foods containing tyramine (e.g., some cheeses and many other foods), hypertensive crisis (uncontrolled high blood pressure) is possible. Commonly used decongestants and stimulants also interact with MAO inhibitors to produce the same blood pressure elevation.

Fluoxetine (Prozac)

Prozac is another antidepressant medication that researchers have studied for the treatment of ADHD, both alone and in combination with methylphenidate. Very little information is available. Prozac seems to work better on behavior symptoms than performance symptoms.

The side effects include nausea, diarrhea, loss of appetite, insomnia, and nervousness. It shouldn't cause any serious problems with the heart.

Summary

The ideal ADHD medication would work immediately, provide benefit throughout the day, have few or no side effects, have no potential for abuse, work well for most patients, and be relatively inexpensive. Unfortunately, this ideal agent is yet to be discovered. In the meantime, stimulants are the first choice, with TCAs next in line after the child has tried several of the stimulants.

References and Resources

American Academy of Pediatrics. (1996). Report of the Committee on Children With Disabilities and Committee on Drugs. *Pediatrics, 98,* 301-304.

Spender, T., Biederman, J., Wilens, T., Harding, M., O'Donnell, D., & Griffin, S. (1996). Pharmacotherapy of attention-deficit hyperactivity disorder across the life cycle. *Journal of the American Academy of Child and Adolescent Psychiatry, 35,* 409-432.

Other Sources of Information:

American Academy of Child and Adolescent Psychiatry

3615 Wisconsin Avenue NW
Washington, DC 20016
(202) 966-7300
Website: www.aacap.org

American Academy of Pediatrics

141 North West Point Blvd.
Elk Grove Village, IL 60007-1098
(847) 228-5005
(847) 228-5097 (Fax)
Website: www.aap.org

Ila V. Mehra, Pharm.D., is an assistant professor at the University of Minnesota College of Pharmacy.

Section 3

Family Issues

Using Positive Communication With Your Child

Laura Falduto, Ph.D.

As a busy parent, you probably find that you have to shout across a room, up a flight of stairs, or into the backyard when you need to talk with your children. If you have a child with Attention Deficit/Hyperactivity Disorder (ADHD), he or she won't always hear you and doesn't always respond with behavior that is consistent with your expectations. Children with ADHD won't be able to stop what they're doing and listen, and they also will have trouble translating what you said into what they should do.

In most families, ineffective communication patterns become repeating patterns. If you are like most parents, you repeat what you said with more volume and frustration when your child doesn't comply. This cycle of repetition, anger, and noncompliance creates aggravation and tension. You probably end up feeling ignored and exhausted. Your child probably feels confused, worthless, and unloved. Over time you might feel chronically resentful and disapproving. The good news is that there are a number of things you can do to begin turning things around. It won't be easy right away, but it will be worth your efforts in the long run!

Cueing In

The most important step is to teach your child to "cue in" to you when you are saying something important. You must use visual and, if necessary, gentle kinesthetic (touching) cues, especially if your child is busy when you need his or her attention. When dealing with a small child, (toddler to second grade), begin by approaching the child while saying the child's name. When you reach the child, kneel down to make eye contact. You might need to ask specifically for eye contact by saying "Look at me" or "Find my eyes." Say the child's name, but with less volume. Finally, touch the child gently on the shoulder or arm. Using kinesthetic cues disrupts your child's **sensory perceptual** (touching and seeing) gratification and helps the child to focus on you.

Some children also need you to provide clear instructions about how to stop the activity in which they are engaged. Stopping and listening can be tough for all curious, actively engaged youngsters, but it is extraordinarily difficult for many children who have ADHD and function as though they don't have a "pause" button. As your child begins to develop some basic skills of tuning in to your communications, you will notice more follow-through and improved eye contact and attention. Give specific praise and approval.

Teaching With Questions

Rather than repeating the same things over and over, teach by asking questions. For example, when asking for attention, use questions such as, "Did you hear me call your name?" "Right now are you remembering what we are working on?" "Uh oh! What are you not giving me that I need right now?" Humor often works well to transform tension into laughter. With younger children, you could ask something silly, such as, "Are there bananas in your ears?" With older children, you need to be a bit more creative. Intense emotion does improve attention, but the outcomes are so much better when it's positive.

The best way to help your child internalize skills is to ask questions. Answering a question forces your child to engage in the cognitive (thinking) process of making the necessary links for success. For example, when helping your child to link thought and action, it is important to ask what the child thinks will happen. Be sure to include all the *what, when,* and *why* questions necessary to teach your point. If your child has not completed a requested activity, ask, "What are you supposed to be doing?" Believe it or not, this is often sufficient! By asking the question, you have helped your child develop an internal awareness of what is needed and required. The question connects the missing link by turning what is otherwise external "noise" into an internal awareness.

The next step is to teach your child how to link past experience with present tasks and imagine the future consequences. You might ask, "What must you do first?" or "What is most important now?" After you have clarified what is needed, start to help your child link the information with goal-directed actions. Spell out the connections between his or her lack of compliance and the likely natural consequences by asking questions such as, "When were you supposed to..." or "What were you going to be able to do if you...?"

Coaching children with questions really communicates that you are teaching them how to be successful and that you support them in reaching their goals rather than being mean or nagging them about the same things all the time.

If you can avoid the "You-screwed-up-again; I-told-you-so" tones of voice, the outcome will be especially successful. In addition, you quickly will see and feel, firsthand, how asking internalizing questions improves the quality of interactions with your child.

When you absolutely blow your cork, it is best to emphasize the specific reality of what led to your anger. Therefore, it is better to say things like, "I've got a million things to do, and right now I need your attention!" or "It's hard for me to stay calm when you don't look at me and listen to what I have to say! I feel ignored! It's disrespectful!"

In summary, the best news is that parenting a child with ADHD is the same as parenting any other child, with a few special exceptions. With a solid communications approach that places sufficient emphasis on the quality of your relationship with your child and recognizes the importance of keeping interventions kind, firm, and occasionally humorous, you can succeed. Be reassured that, just as your kids are learning new skills, so are you as a parent.

Laura Falduto, Ph.D., completed her postdoctoral fellowship in child and adolescent psychology at the Menninger Clinic in Topeka, Kansas. She is a clinical psychologist at the Institute for Developmental Behavioral Neurology in Scottsdale, Arizona.

Parent Articles About ADHD / ISBN 0761667512 / 1-800-228-0752 / This page is reproducible.

Coping Successfully With Attention Deficit/Hyperactivity Disorder in the Family

Linda J. Jones, Ph.D.

It is estimated that separation or divorce is three times more likely to occur in families that include a child with Attention Deficit/Hyperactivity Disorder (ADHD). Mothers of children with ADHD are more likely to suffer depression and feelings of self-blame. Additionally, friends and extended family members might not be emotionally supportive because of a lack of understanding about this disorder (Alexander-Roberts, 1994).

Factors for Success Within the Immediate Family

Many articles document the struggles of a single-parent family in today's society. However, being the only adult in the household allows that parent to make decisions regarding discipline, mealtimes, activities, bedtimes, homework, etc., without compromise or argument from a spouse. Parents of children with ADHD who have different opinions about child-rearing practices often envy single parents. When couples disagree about child-rearing practices, there is increased stress and disharmony in the home, not to mention lack of consistency with their child.

When one parent decides to use "time alone in your bedroom" as punishment and the other parent has difficulty getting the child to go to sleep in that bedroom, the child receives mixed messages that invite parental disagreement. One way to solve this problem is to discuss the discipline ahead of time and work out the details so that both parents feel comfortable when the need to discipline arises. Consistency is such a big factor in the success of any discipline or behavior management plan that you can ill afford not to support each other.

Many couples disagree on everything from "when to take the bottle away" to "whether or not the TV is on during dinner" to "why don't you go back to work so you're not dealing with this every minute of every day." Sometimes it is necessary to seek the advice and help of an objective third party, because each parent is sure the other person is wrong and needs to be set straight. With assistance and guidance from a professional who has knowledge about the challenges of raising a child with ADHD, parents can learn a tremendous amount about how to listen and communicate more effectively with each other. Professional counselors can provide couples with information and techniques specific to the parenting needs of the child with ADHD. Some counselors give "homework assignments" to

parents to improve their relationship as a couple and also to refine their parenting skills. Parent homework assignments might include planning a weekly date where neither partner can talk about the child; giving sincere, daily compliments and supportive statements to each other; and identifying the ways in which each partner can relax and relieve the daily stresses associated with the multiple roles as parent, spouse, employee, and so many others.

Parents often credit their work with professional counselors for saving their families from destruction. Though not everyone needs this particular kind of support, the job of parenting a child with ADHD calls for additional understanding and support from outside sources. These sources can include the extended family, friends, a support group, clergy, or a professional counselor. The point is that no matter how educated you are or how grounded you seem to be in your personal and professional life, parenting a child with ADHD brings a different level of stress to families. Parents cannot ignore it. They must recognize it and be able to reach out for support without feeling guilty or diminished in any way.

Factors for Success With Extended Family Members

Remind yourself over and over again that most of the negative and nonsupportive comments you hear from family and friends come from a lack of understanding about why the child is "behaving like that." Until you learned about ADHD and its effects in your family, you also might have wondered, at one time long ago, how parents could "let their child get away with that!" Now it has become your responsibility to educate your extended family members about ADHD. Be aware that family stress increases when parents serve as educators in addition to their other roles.

Some authors recommend that you send reading materials to members of your family to acquaint them with the diagnosis and current thinking about ADHD. This is a great suggestion if you know that your sister, brother, aunt, uncle, mom, or dad truly will read the information. When selecting reading material for extended family members, choose a very short, informative piece that explains ADHD in terms the general public can understand easily. You live with this child 24 hours a day, so it benefits you greatly to read alot about ADHD. Others probably don't need quite that much information. Family members who spend time with your child require more information than those who spend limited time with her or him, but relatives who rarely interact with your child don't need to read exhaustively to gain sufficient understanding to be able to be supportive and to enjoy their niece, nephew, or grandchild. Isn't that what we are looking for anyway, a typical relationship with grandparents for all of us?

A letter to relatives written from the child's perspective that includes descriptions of behaviors that the child exhibits (not all behaviors associated with ADHD are exhibited by all children) often has a softer touch than a brochure or article describing the full range of behaviors, medications, prognoses, etc. If your child is old enough, have him or her help you write the letter, taking care to specify what he or she likes about "visiting Grandma and Grandpa." A letter from a young (7-year-old) child might go something like this:

> Dear Nana & Papa,
>
> I can't wait to come see you and that beautiful Christmas tree you always put up in the living room. I love sliding down the stairs on my tummy and watching how the lights look from that angle. Don't worry, I know how to stop without hurting myself. And remember those special ball ornaments that spin? I can't keep myself from touching them, so Mom said you probably will put them up high this year so I can only look at them with my eyes. Will you put on some ornaments that I can touch?
>
> You'll be surprised how much better I'm getting at reading. I've been taking this special medicine that helps me concentrate better, so I'll bring a few of my favorite books if you will let me climb up in your lap, Papa, and read them to you. Nana, I love helping Mom at home in the kitchen—can I help you when you have a lot of work to do in there? I'm good at putting away dishes and stirring stuff.
>
> Mom and Daddy told me about your new puppy. Can I take it for a walk to the park (you know, the one with the swings and monkey bars) holding onto the leash? The puppy and I could run around a lot and use up some "extra" energy.
>
> I'll see you in 2 weeks. I love you.
>
> Kisses and hugs,
>
> Me

What grandparent wouldn't love to receive a sweet letter along with a drawing from a grandchild? Then, when you visit, describe what kinds of things they might see your child do, and explain your responses to specific behaviors. Be sure to fill them in on your behavior management plan. One plan that parents find helpful is *1-2-3: Magic!* by Thomas Phelan, Ph.D. It is portable and easy to teach to others. (See the References and Resources section at the end of this article for full publication information.)

Don't expect your parents to change their reactions to you or your child with ADHD immediately. If they questioned your child-rearing practices with your other children, it should be no surprise that, again, they are questioning your permissiveness or strictness. If you can explain to your parents the symptoms of ADHD as they see them happening, they will be better able to understand and support parental decisions. The more frequently grandparents are able to spend time with your child, the easier it will be for them to understand, accept, and deal with the misbehaviors. Be sure to praise the ways in which they interact effectively with your child, and don't be afraid to model ways in which you would like them to handle something differently.

Family vacations that include grandparents can have benefits for all family members. Mom and Dad are able to have some time alone (you brought the baby-sitters with you), grandparents get to see someplace they might not travel to on their own, and the child has so many more people to do things with that the adults don't seem to tire of the child's endless activity.

Holiday gatherings can be difficult with a child who has ADHD. A simple solution to the problem is to have family get-togethers at your house. The child with ADHD will be comfortable in that environment, knows the boundaries and expectations, and probably will be less active in the familiar surroundings than in someone else's home. Remember that a new environment is more likely to create additional problem behaviors. If you do travel to a relative's home, be sure to plan ahead and take appropriate toys, games, books, computer software, or magazines, anything that will make your child feel more comfortable, regardless of the age. When parents travel with infants and toddlers, they make sure they have the right "stuff." It's the same mentality now! Parents who take the time to plan ahead will find that the child is more comfortable and parental inconvenience decreases. Parents and children alike want to be able to enjoy family visits with the least possible amount of stress.

Summary

Research has documented the stress on families, both immediate and extended, of raising a child with ADHD. As parents, we are constantly learning more and better ways to raise our children effectively. We didn't learn how to accept and deal with ADHD overnight, and our understanding and strategies for behavior management have evolved over the time our child has been with us. We need to help our parents, grandparents, and other family members learn some of what we know, and give them the time to internalize it and practice it. Meanwhile, we are educating the world one family at a time. Support from professionals and educated extended family helps to nourish the couple who is parenting the child with ADHD so the family unit can remain intact, especially against the odds.

References and Resources

Alexander-Roberts, C. (1994). *The ADHD parenting handbook: Practical advice for parents from parents.* Dallas, TX: Taylor Publishing Co.

Phelan, T W. (1998). *1-2-3: Magic: Training your children to do what you want!* Glen Ellyn, IL: Child Management, Inc.

Linda Jones, Ph.D., is the parent of an 8-year-old boy with Down Syndrome and ADHD. She is an inclusion specialist/advocate and educational consultant.

Family Therapy

Susan L. Hubbard, M.S.W., LCSW

When a child has Attention Deficit/Hyperactivity Disorder (ADHD), the symptoms can affect other family members. Conversely, family dynamics and stresses can affect the behavior of the child with ADHD. Family therapy might be helpful in such situations.

Why Would a Therapist Want to See the Entire Family?

Family therapy involves the whole family in resolving a particular problem. For example, 10-year-old Jimmy was diagnosed recently with ADHD. His mother and father divorced a short time ago, and Jimmy lives with his mother and his two younger siblings. Jimmy has been having a lot of problems concentrating in school, and his grades have been falling. Jimmy's mother feels unable to help Jimmy, particularly since he was diagnosed with ADHD.

In this situation, a family therapist would ask to meet with the whole family, including the divorced parents, Jimmy, the siblings, and anyone else who lives with the family. The therapist would talk to all the family members about how the problem affects each one of them. The therapist might learn that Jimmy's father feels that if he were around more, Jimmy would be okay. His siblings might say that because Jimmy is in trouble and their mother is dealing with him constantly, they get little attention and feel neglected. The mother might feel that the problem results from something she did during her pregnancy. Finally, Jimmy might believe that his problems at school were responsible for his parent's divorce.

The therapist's job is to help sort out these feelings and the relationships that exist in the family. Once people can see how their behavior has a ripple effect on other people, they often can make small changes that affect the whole family. Jimmy's mother and father could help him and his siblings understand that the divorce was the parents' choice and not the result of anything the kids did. Jimmy's mother could talk to her doctor about the causes of ADHD to be reassured that she didn't do something to cause it. Both mom and dad might examine the quality of time they spend with all their children. Everyone can learn about ADHD and how they can help Jimmy by the ways they interact with him. In fact, the therapist might even help the family look at the "problem" in a new light, as a challenge rather than a stressful demand. The therapist might describe Jimmy's unique way of learning as creative spontaneity. He might need a "map" to help him learn that is different from those of other kids, and the therapist and family can develop that map together. A family is somewhat like an engine: When one piece of the engine is having trouble, the engine won't work properly.

The Origins of Family Therapy

There was a time when the thought of therapy brought visions of lying on a couch while a gray-bearded man said, "Tell me about your childhood." Actually, family therapy grew out of the realization that there were people who weren't being helped in traditional individual psychotherapy. In the 1950s, therapists began to look at systems theory and apply it to their work with individuals. They began considering the person's environment—including the family—as a necessary part of a person's health and well being.

Some people might wonder why the entire family needs counseling if only one person has the problem. The answer is twofold. First, one person's problem affects all members of the family. Second, the most logical source of help is in the strengths of the people who are the closest to the person needing help.

Another important difference between traditional counseling and family therapy is the role of the therapist. A family therapist sees that he or she is part of the entire system. A family therapist also tends be more active and involved in working with the family than a traditional individual therapist. The family therapist functions as a coach, but it is the family team who works together to find a solution.

How Long Will It Take?

In general, family therapy is fairly brief because the therapist and family decide on the goals of the therapy, and the family can assess the results readily. The therapist might meet a few times with the family in a short period of time or spread the visits out over a few months to allow time for the family to practice their new skills. Most family therapists emphasize that the family always can come back for a checkup or to address another problem that develops, just the way one would go back to the family doctor.

How Do I Find a Family Therapist?

Insurance that provides mental health benefits frequently covers the services of a family therapist. The first step is to call your insurance company and ask for a list of mental health providers. If you don't know which providers specialize in family therapy, you can call and ask them. Not all counselors are family therapists. Sometimes family therapists are psychologists, social workers, or psychiatrists. Ask therapists where they received their training in family therapy. The therapist you choose should be licensed and might have an extra professional affiliation, such as the American Association of Marriage and Family Therapists. Don't hesitate to ask each therapist about his or her credentials and philosophy. Once you have made your choice, meet with the therapist to decide if there is a good fit with your family. Some people who are perfectly qualified don't always fit with the family. If this is your feeling from the start, it's okay to try another counselor. However, if you've been working well with one therapist and then feel differently all of a sudden, don't give up until you've talked about it first with the therapist.

Summary

Family therapy helps the whole family work together to solve problems and support each other. Family therapists consider the patient's environment to be very important to the patient's ability to improve. Family therapists tend to be more interactive than individual therapists. In general, family therapy is brief. Family therapy with children who have ADHD might focus on communication between parents, improving sibling interactions, or helping the family develop a more structured and predictable daily routine.

References and Resources

German, A., & Kniskern, D. (Eds.). (1981). *Handbook of family therapy*. New York: Brunner/Mazel.

Gerson, M. (1996). *The embedded self*. Hillsdale, NJ: The Analytic Press.

Susan Hubbard, M.S.W., LCSW, is a behavioral science faculty member with the Family Medicine of St. Louis residency program. She received her master's degree from Washington University in St. Louis and specializes in medical psychotherapy.

Behavior Modification at Home: Parenting the Child With Attention Deficit/Hyperactivity Disorder

H. Russell Searight, Ph.D.

Effective parenting of children with Attention Deficit/Hyperactivity Disorder (ADHD) can be challenging. Although medication will help many children with ADHD to focus and concentrate better, structuring the home environment and using rewards and punishment consistently will help keep the child on track. The key word for any behavioral program is *consistency!* Parents must follow through and use these principles even when they are tired or when (in the short run) rewards and punishments do not seem to be working. Many parents might have used these principles effectively in the past, but implementing a behavioral system with a child who has ADHD sometimes requires some fine tuning of these skills.

Basic Principles of Behavioral Modification

The most important principle of behavior modification is that behavior is influenced by its immediate consequences. A reward (reinforcement) will increase the likelihood of that behavior occurring again. An unpleasant stimulus or event (punishment) decreases the likelihood of the behavior reoccurring.

Parents and teachers are modifying children's behavior all the time. They often are unaware of the extent to which they actually are rewarding behavior they don't want the child to continue. For example, a child who calls out in class might receive immediate attention from the teacher (reinforcement), which then results in the child's interrupting more frequently. Researchers have found that praising children for desired behavior (e.g., working quietly on their own in class or playing cooperatively with other children) will cause that behavior to occur more frequently. Rewarding desired actions is one of the most potent tools for changing problem behavior.

Punishing undesired behavior is effective but probably does not work as well as a reward. Punishment might not be effective because it often does not include any information about the desired behavior. Many of us have seen situations in public where a child has picked up a toy or candy bar in a store, and the parent responds with a harsh "No!" or a sudden spanking. The child then looks confused, not knowing the reason for the punishment. Because the child doesn't make the connection between the action and the punishment, and also because the parent doesn't describe the desired behavior, the problem behavior occurs again.

Physical punishment (spanking) often can lead to other problem behaviors, such as fighting.

Most young children will require *concrete* reinforcement, such as a sticker or a piece of candy. As children get older, *secondary reinforcement* (such as points or stars on a chart) that they accumulate and exchange for a privilege (staying up an hour later) or a reward (new shirt) will be effective.

Behavior Modification: Principles in Practice

Employing Consequences

Several of the principles of behavior modification are useful with children at home. First, it is important to describe the desired behavior to the child. You also should describe the consequence for undesirable behavior as well as the reward the child will receive for appropriate conduct. Give children—particularly children with ADHD—at least one and probably two verbal reminders when they are acting out. It also might be helpful to include some type of nonverbal hand signal to communicate the warning. (For example, when the child is talking out during dinner, hold a finger to your lips as you make direct eye contact with the child.) When you give the second prompt, remind the child of the consequence ("If you continue to talk out during dinner, you will have to leave the table and will not receive dessert this evening"). Most importantly, you need to follow through with both rewards and consequences.

When parents begin to think about which behaviors they would like to target in their children, they often will respond initially, "There are so many, I can't think of where to begin." Realistically, you can target only two or three specific behaviors at a time. When you first institute a behavioral program, pick two or three behaviors of particular concern or those you think you can affect most quickly.

It is important to remember that undesirable behavior most likely will increase when you consistently implement a behavior program. Parents often will say, "We tried a behavioral program for a week, but it didn't work. In fact, Johnny got worse." If, for example, the target behavior is staying with a parent in a store or following through on parental requests ("It is 3:30 now and time to pick up your toys"), the child's disobedience actually might increase for the first 2 weeks of the behavioral system. Why does this happen? Generally, parents have been inconsistent in the past and children have learned that if they just persist and even "turn up the volume," parents will give in and not follow through on the consequence. Increased problem behavior when parents first implement a behavioral system actually is a good sign that the system *is* working.

In developing a behavioral system, it is very important to have a good understanding of the "baseline" frequency of the problem behavior. For example, a child who requires eight prompts to get out of bed every morning is unlikely to begin getting up without any prompt just because you've instituted a reward system. Be realistic and reduce the number of prompts to four for a week or two, so that the child can receive a reward. If you use a "perfect" standard at the beginning, the child won't ever receive a reward, and the system will never actually operate (Searight, 1999).

Use of Punishments

Time out is probably one of the most helpful ways to reduce problem behavior, particularly in young children. In time out, the adult gives the child a warning, then removes the child from social interaction with others and any other pleasant activities (watching TV, listening to the radio) immediately after the problem behavior occurs. It is important that the time-out area be a place in the house where you can monitor the child but where there is little stimulation (e.g. no TV or conversation) actually taking place. Go on with your usual activities during the time-out period; don't sit in the room with the child unless it is absolutely necessary. Some young children will refuse to stay seated during a time out or will get up frequently and ask if their time out is over. If young children do not remain seated and you have given one or two warnings, you might need to restrain the child during time out. In this situation, you can hold the child in a "baskethold." For this form of restraint to be effective and the child not to be harmed, you should be seated on the floor cross legged, holding the child on your lap. You may put your arms around the child's arms and legs to prevent him or her from lashing out, kicking, or hitting (Searight, 1999). Hold the child until he or she regains physical control. During restraint, it is important that you not engage in conversation with the child. When the child regains control, allow the child to sit through the time out independently.

With older children, time out is often ineffective. Children older than 9 or 10 usually will benefit from some kind of *response cost* system. With inappropriate behavior, the child loses some of his or her accumulated points or stars. Loss of privileges such as TV or access to the computer for a specified period of time is also effective.

Behavior Modification and Children With ADHD

Because attention span is brief and short-term memory skills are a problem, children with ADHD often require a few modifications in a standard behavioral program. The child with ADHD needs immediate feedback about the behavior. Any delay between the child's actions and the parents' response makes it less likely that the child will make the connection. It is particularly important, when the 5-year-old with ADHD picks up toys, that the child receive a treat right away rather than an hour later.

For older children who are on a reward system, break down large increments of time into smaller periods. For example, your goal might be for the child to earn a star on a chart for going all day without fighting with a sibling. However, a whole day might be too long for many children with ADHD. Divide the day into morning, afternoon, and evening, and award a star for each part of the day that the child didn't fight.

Finally, as noted earlier, *consistency* is extremely important. For children with short-term memory problems to learn that there are consequences for their actions, rewards and punishments must follow *every time* the target behavior occurs.

References and Resources

Searight, H. R. (1999). *Behavioral medicine: A primary care approach.* Philadelphia: Taylor and Francis.

H. Russell Searight, Ph.D., is the director of behavioral sciences for the Residency Program of Family Medicine of St. Louis. He is the author of several textbooks and an adjunct associate professor in the department of psychology and Community and Family Medicine at St. Louis University.

Handling Everyday Routines

Linda M. Levine, Ed.D.

L isa has just put the cake into the oven. She sends 7 year-old Jeremy off to play, telling him that their measuring and mixing will be rewarded in 20 minutes when the cake is done. Before 10 minutes have passed, Jeremy has returned three times to ask, "Is it done yet? Huh? Is it done yet?" Lisa is patient with Jeremy the first time he comes back to the kitchen and tells him to listen for the timer bell to ring. When Jeremy comes back a few minutes later asking the same questions, Lisa is annoyed. When Jeremy reappears 2 minutes later and repeats his questions, Lisa loses her temper—again.

Lisa has a right to feel frustrated by Jeremy's impatience and compulsive behavior. By 7 years of age, Jeremy is old enough to judge the passage of short periods of time and to wait at least 20 minutes for the timer to ring. Although Lisa knows Jeremy has Attention Deficit/Hyperactivity Disorder (ADHD), she cannot keep from losing her temper when Jeremy acts inappropriately. After many years, she has come to understand that Jeremy's ADHD challenges require different behavior management strategies from those she used when her older children were Jeremy's age. Jeremy is impulsive and seldom thinks before he acts. He has difficulty paying attention, which makes it hard for him to be patient, especially when he is excited about a project.

Lisa has a list of things Jeremy has trouble with every day: He has a hard time concentrating on his homework, remembering to pick up his toys, waiting for events to happen, and staying at the table through the whole meal. He is always moving and can't seem to keep still for very long. These problems cause many stressful confrontations and make it hard for family members to live in a relaxed atmosphere. Lisa wishes there were a magic wand to change Jeremy's behavior automatically. Jeremy's behavior *can* be changed, but only if those who live with him are willing to change their behavior. They must learn a few new strategies that (a) establish written house rules for everyone to follow, (b) anticipate situations that might produce confrontations and plan for them, and (c) support and encourage Jeremy in his attempts to develop self-control.

House Rules

Although some degree of conflict is inevitable in every household, people have a basic right to live together peaceably and without the threat of harm. That is why families set up spoken or unspoken rules that *every person* in the family is expected to follow. Making up rules helps children understand what to do and what the consequences will be for breaking the rules. Although each family is unique and decides on whether to be structured or casual about making rules, it is important for the family of a child with ADHD to have very **specific, ongoing, nonnegotiable, written-down** rules that address the **basic expectations** for family members' behavior.

Keep the number of rules to a minimum and, when possible, state them **positively,** avoiding words like *no* and *don't.*

Here are some examples of specific rules:

- After playing, put your toys away in the toy box.
- Keep your hands to yourself when riding in the car.
- When you are angry, use your words, not your hands.

The following rules are too general and would not be helpful or effective:

- Clean up your room every day.
- Act nicely in the car.
- Treat others with respect.

One or two rules should address specific ongoing problems. For example, you might have rules about doing daily chores or about arguing if those are areas of difficulty for your child. The rules should state clearly the **exact behavior** you expect from the child (for example, "Ask permission to use something that is not yours"). When a family member breaks a rule, there should be a **specific consequence** such as a time out (separation from others) or loss of privileges. When your child breaks a rule, state the rule and the consequence: "The rule is, 'We talk instead of hit.' When you hit, you choose a time out."

It is important to be **consistent** in enforcing the house rules. That means that every time the inappropriate behavior happens, the consequences follow. Many children are argumentative and will try to negotiate when they break a rule. If this happens, you must become a "broken record." That means you state the expected behavior, and no matter how much the child argues, you repeat the rule in a calm voice. Adults should not argue but repeat the "broken record" twice before enforcing the consequence.

Anticipate Problem Situations

Many young children with attention problems have difficulty following daily routines. Often it is a struggle to get them up, dressed, and fed each morning. For many of these children, routine events such as waiting in the doctor's office, riding in the car, attending group gatherings, or going shopping result in behaviors that are not acceptable to the adults who take them to these places. It might be impossible as well as impractical for a frustrated parent to focus on changing more than one or two problem areas at a time. The parent of a toddler removes breakable items from low tables until the child can understand that some things are not to be touched. Similarly, family members of the young child with ADHD must anticipate when and where the child cannot exert self-control, and avoid setting the child up for failure. For example, Jeremy, who does not understand the passage of time and cannot contain his excitement, can hold the timer until it rings. When he asks his question, "Is it done yet?" Lisa can say, "Did your timer ring yet?" An hourglass timer with running sand is also a good idea, because the child with ADHD can see the passage of time.

Here are some ways to intervene before a difficult situation arises.

- If telling a child about an upcoming exciting event produces high anticipation, hyperactivity, and compulsive questioning, don't tell the child about the event until right before it happens, even if the event is a major change in routine such as a family vacation.

- Before the child gets out of the car to attend an event or go shopping, review the expectations for behavior in that place, whether there will be a reward for following the rules, and what will happen if the child breaks the rules. If there are three rules, for example, hold up three fingers to give a visual cue, state each rule, and have the child repeat them to you.

- Bring toys or books to occupy the child's attention if you expect that there will be a waiting period. Play is the normal behavior of children, and being expected to sit quietly for long periods of time is difficult for all young children. Plan for frequent walks around the facility or a special break when a hyperactive child can move around.

- Pick your battles. In other words, try to relax and let go of being upset about annoying behaviors that are less important, and concentrate on changing the behaviors that are of major importance.

Offer Support and Encouragement

One goal of changing behavior is to get the child to take responsibility for understanding what to do, and then to do it! To accomplish this, the child needs encouragement for doing the right thing, as well as discouragement for doing things that are inappropriate. Consider the example of Lisa's short temper in response to Jeremy's constant questions. Lisa needs to remind Jeremy about their house rule that he may not ask a question more than twice and that watching the timer will give him the answer, then praise him for remembering the rule. "Catching the child being good" is as important as reminding the child when behavior is inappropriate.

Many families use a token method such as a star chart to reward children for remembering responsibilities. However, this method is not a very effective incentive for young children and those who have difficulty waiting and understanding postponed rewards. A response-cost system works well for children with ADHD. This technique allows children to see or hold all the rewards at the beginning and uses "fines" to remove the rewards if the child cannot behave properly. For example, a child starts the day with an envelope full of privileges (TV viewing, play at a friend's house, bike riding) and loses a slip of paper each time he or she behaves inappropriately. Younger children need more concrete rewards (such as candy or small prizes) that are removed from a reward container when behavior is inappropriate. It is important to use shorter time frames (perhaps one day at a time) or even break the day down into segments when using the response-cost system. It is encouraging if there are always some rewards remaining at the end of a day, even if the child had a hard time behaving appropriately.

Summary

Children with ADHD can gain self-control when adults understand the developmental challenges of this disorder and structure the environment by providing fair rules and consequences. Child behaviors that are not appropriate will change only when adults are willing to change their own behavior toward the child. Helping the child succeed each day does not take a magic wand. It takes a dedicated adult willing to provide the structure needed to help a child establish self-control and self-responsibility.

Linda Levine, Ed.D., is an educational consultant and therapist in Tucson, Arizona. Her specialties include early childhood, advocacy, inclusion, and attention disorders. She is the author of several articles featured in Communication Skill Builders handbooks.

Managing a Difficult Child

Clare B. Jones, Ph.D.

When you see your child struggling with behavior problems, you must put on your "professional hat," ask yourself why you think your child is being difficult, and rule out certain physical factors. First, make sure there are no health problems involved. Did your child rub his nose or pull his ears, indicating that he might have an allergy or an ear infection? Is she eating well? Is he picking at his food? Are routines normal at home? Are there certain changes in the family? If such problems exist, you need to work with your physician on the physical concerns first.

Redirect the Child's Attention

Once you rule out physical concerns, try to note what your child likes, what he or she enjoys doing, and what seems to hold the child's interest longest. This is important as you begin to help your child deal with problem behaviors.

If your child is engaged in a behavior that you find particularly difficult to tolerate, it is possible to distract the child without rewarding the negative behavior. Here is an example of redirecting a child's attention to a positive behavior.

"Maggie, I want gum."

"Jason, look at the wheels on this truck! One isn't turning."

"Maggie, I want gum."

"Look, Jason. This wheel stays still when I push."

"Gum, gum, gum."

"Jason, I need you to push the truck wheels. Can you fix this?"

With this question, Maggie puts the truck into Jason's hand. Jason looks at the truck and begins to examine it, redirecting his prior actions.

It is important to realize that active children exhibit certain behaviors that tolerant adults should ignore. Some children develop habits such as tapping their fingers, wiggling their feet, humming, etc., and others seem to whine or nag constantly. By ignoring these behaviors, you are not rewarding the behavior. (You should not, however, ignore behavior that is dangerous to your child or someone else.)

Explain New Situations

You often can resolve behavior problems with active children by explaining new situations before they occur. These children need to have impending changes in their routine described in detail. Tell the child what is coming, offering encouragement before and after the change. Explain, for example, "We're going to have to go to the grocery store. You will sit in the cart. I need you to hold the list. If you do a good job, you can pick out your own fruit from the counter."

Reward Good Behavior

Use praise and rewards generously. Tell your child you are proud of what he or she is doing. When you see the child exhibiting an appropriate behavior without your direction (for example, picking up a tennis shoe off the floor), praise the child immediately: "It is so nice to see what a big helper you are. Thanks for picking up your shoes."

Provide Short Activities

Guide the child in the completion of one activity before he or she proceeds to the next. Provide short activities so that the child can complete the task before moving on to another one.

Give Brief Directions

Use brief, short directions, and ask the child to repeat them to you. This will improve comprehension and attention. Before each activity, tell the child what to expect. Explain, for example, "After we have lunch, we will read a book." Try giving a sequence of directions, then see if the child comprehends or remembers. Some active children will be able to comprehend only one simple direction at a time.

Balance Structure and Free Time

Try to incorporate a balance between structured and unstructured activities. A typical child needs lots of movement but can sustain structure for only a brief period of time.

Keep Your Child Busy

If your child is in a situation that requires being quiet or self-contained, bring along something to keep the child busy, such as a small squishy ball, clay, or a box of paper and pencils. Use bright colors to attract and hold attention.

Parent Articles About ADHD / ISBN 0761667512 / 1-800-228-0752 / This page is reproducible.

Use Positive Statements

When guiding a child's behavior, avoid the word *don't.* Say something positive as you guide the child toward behavior you want. Rather than saying, "Don't put your feet on that table," say, "I want to see your feet on the floor." In giving directions that avoid the word *don't,* you are describing positively the behavior you want the child to exhibit.

Create a Routine

Routines make children feel more comfortable and secure. When children fight the routines, they often are just testing the boundaries of their security. Organize your daily schedule so that certain routines occur at the same time each day. Children respond to positive stimuli, so when they are doing something correctly, praise them and reward them immediately for appropriate behavior.

Clare B. Jones, Ph.D., is an educational consultant and diagnostic specialist at Developmental Learning Associates in Phoenix. The author of three books on attention disorders, she is a nationally recognized presenter in the field of attention disorders and special needs.

Reinforcing Your Child's Self-Esteem and Resilience

Robert B. Brooks, Ph.D.

Parenting a child with Attention Deficit/Hyperactivity Disorder (ADHD) presents numerous challenges and stresses. The very nature of the prominent behaviors of children with ADHD—impulsivity, acting before thinking, being easily frustrated, perceiving things as unfair, and moodiness—often taxes the patience of the calmest parents, resulting in frustration, anger, and yelling.

The Role of Empathy

An essential skill in raising children with ADHD is empathy, that is, the ability to see the world through the eyes of the child. Empathy implies that, as we interact with our children, as we say and do things with them, we think about how they are experiencing our words and actions. If we are not empathic (which is more likely to occur when we are upset, angry, or disappointed with our children), we tend to say and do things that actually work against what we hope to accomplish. For example, parents might exhort their child with ADHD to "try harder" with his or her schoolwork. Whereas the parents feel that they are just being helpful and encouraging with this remark, the child often perceives "try harder" as accusatory and judgmental. The comment backfires and causes the child to be resentful.

The Importance of Self-Esteem and Resilience

What does one discover as one becomes empathic and enters the world of children with ADHD? What are some of the main issues that they face? Given the dominance of these children's negative feelings about themselves, it is important for parents to focus their energy and efforts on how best to reinforce the self-esteem and hope of their children.

We know that many youngsters with ADHD grow up to lead satisfying, successful lives and that they are able to overcome adversity and become resilient. In order to do so, they must have what psychologist Julius Segal calls "charismatic adults" in their lives, adults from whom they gather strength and who help to boost their self-esteem. Charismatic adults do not ignore the problems displayed by children with ADHD, but they look for and reinforce their strengths, their "islands of competence." Charismatic adults understand that simply telling a child with low self-esteem and a pessimistic outlook that he or she will be okay often comes across as hollow words to a child who feels inadequate. We must continue to offer positive feedback and encouragement to our children, but charismatic adults also find concrete ways to identify and reinforce the child's strengths so that these strengths are available for others to see and admire. Focusing on areas of competence creates a ripple effect, prompting youngsters to venture forth and increasingly confront tasks that previously have proved problematic. Success in one arena of their lives can serve as the foundation for success in other areas. We must never underestimate the power of even one adult to guide a child's life in a more productive direction.

Several Strategies for Fostering Self-Esteem, Hope, and Resilience in Children With ADHD

Here are five strategies that can be helpful in reinforcing self-esteem and resilience in children with ADHD. These strategies are not based on false praise but rather on fostering self-esteem and hope in a realistic manner.

Teach Responsibility by Encouraging Children to Contribute to Their World

If children are to develop a sense of pride and accomplishment, if they are to taste success, we must give them opportunities for assuming responsibilities, especially responsibilities that strengthen their belief that they are making a contribution to their home, school, or community environments. Enlist children with ADHD in such activities as doing charitable work (e.g., helping in a soup kitchen or participating in walks for hunger or AIDS), tutoring younger children, painting murals in school, taking messages to the office (this involves permitting the child to move around), and asking the child to set the table for dinner, to help the family. These activities convey the message to these children that they are making a positive difference and thus serve to reinforce their motivation and self-esteem as they witness visible examples of their achievements.

Teach Decision-Making and Problem-Solving Skills

An integral feature of high self-esteem and resilience is the belief that one has some control over what is transpiring in one's life. Because children with ADHD have a great deal of difficulty with being in control, this is an important belief to reinforce but one that will take time. To acquire an attitude of ownership, youngsters with ADHD need experiences in which they can learn and apply decision-making and problem-solving skills. Parents can reinforce some of these skills by holding regular family meetings. During these meetings, the parents and children can discuss issues that are occurring at home or school, and the parents can involve children in developing solutions to these issues or problems. Parents can strengthen the child's ability to make choices and decisions by permitting a finicky eater to select (and eventually prepare) the dinner meal once a week. Parents can ask their child with ADHD whether the child wants to be reminded 10 or 15 minutes before bedtime that it will soon be time to get ready to go to bed. A teacher can tell students that they may decide which six of the eight problems on a homework sheet to do.

Use Discipline to Develop Self-Discipline and Self-Control

A major problem faced by children with ADHD is their impulsivity and lack of self-discipline. Given their difficulties developing self-control, these youngsters require more limits than other children, but they are more likely than their peers to experience rules and limits as impositions, as arbitrary, as unfair. We must remember that the goal of discipline is to *teach* children, not to ridicule or humiliate them. If children with ADHD are to assume ownership for their actions, if they are to perceive rules and consequences as fair, they must be involved increasingly in the process of understanding and even having input in the creation of rules, limits, and consequences. In addition, parents must focus on ways to prevent misbehavior from occurring in the first place.

The family meeting mentioned previously is a useful setting in which parents can discuss rules with children and elicit their response. During a family meeting, parents can ask children with ADHD the best ways the parents can remind them about rules to minimize the feeling of constantly being nagged. One boy with ADHD came up with the novel idea of having his parents hold up a sign to remind him to take his medication. Parents also need to be careful not to set the child up for failure. If a child with ADHD runs wild every time he or she is in a supermarket despite the parents' best preparation, the child probably is not yet ready to handle the supermarket environment. It is also important to remember that consequences should not include hitting or spanking, because such forms of punishment lead to anger rather than learning. We want children to learn from us rather than resent us.

Offer Encouragement and Positive Feedback

Although encouragement and positive feedback are major components of discipline and normally would fall in the preceding section, it is helpful to highlight their importance separately. We nurture self-esteem and resilience when we communicate realistic appreciation to children and help them feel special. When we do this, we become the charismatic adults in their lives. We must "catch" children being good. Also, spending special time alone with children each day or week, writing a brief note of appreciation, attending important events in their lives, and recognizing their accomplishments all serve to convey to our children that they are special and that we love them. This is important for all children but perhaps even more so for youngsters with ADHD, who often receive far less positive feedback than their peers.

Help Children Deal More Effectively With Mistakes

The fear of making mistakes and feeling foolish and embarrassed is one of the strongest roadblocks to developing high self-esteem and resilience. Children with ADHD are often vulnerable to feeling defeated and are likely to retreat from tasks that they perceive might lead to failure. As parents, we must help children realize that mistakes are an important ingredient in the process of learning. Rather than making disparaging comments such as, "You never think," "Do you have any brains?" or "You always rush and get things wrong. Just slow down!" we can respond to children's mistakes by showing them the correct way to solve a problem. We also can share—in a nonlecturing way—some of the mistakes we made as children and how we learned from the situation. In the school environment, teachers can introduce the topic of mistakes at the very beginning of the school year before they assign any work, sharing memories from their own school experiences as children. It is useful to involve students in a discussion of the best ways to avoid being worried about making mistakes or not immediately understanding the material being taught. Bringing the issue of fear of mistakes out into the open typically serves to weaken its potency. When we lessen the fear of failure for children with ADHD, we open up new opportunities for them to succeed and lead more productive lives.

Summary

If, as parents, we are able to use these strategies in a consistent fashion, we can help strengthen the self-esteem and resilience of our children with ADHD. This is truly a wonderful gift we can provide. It is our legacy to the next generation.

References and Resources

Brooks, R. (1991). *The self-esteem teacher.* Loveland, OH: Treehaus Communications.

Brooks, R. (1997). *Learning disabilities and self-esteem. Look what you've done! Stories of hope and resilience.* Videotape and educational guide produced by WETA in Washington, DC, and distributed by PBS Video.

Joseph, J. (1994). *The resilient child.* New York: Plenum.

Katz, M. (1997). *On playing a poor hand well.* New York: Norton.

Robert B. Brooks, Ph.D., is a clinical psychologist in private practice and is on the faculty of the Harvard Medical School. He is the author of a book and videotape on self-esteem and resilience.

Strategies for Home, School, and Life   3.8

Veronica Campbell

The advice of professional experts will be extremely important to you as you plan for the success of your child with Attention Deficit/Hyperactivity Disorder (ADHD). You, as the parent, also must become confident in your own ability to assess your child's needs and coordinate the professionals and resources that will help your child.

As you consider the future of your child, you must realize that you will need to become an expert on ADHD. Your role is pivotal, as would be that of any chief of operations, and your attitude and leadership as the parent will set the tone for the coordination of effort that it will take to help your child. Become an authority on ADHD by heading to the library, bookstore, and local ADHD support group. In addition, you'll find friends and acquaintances who are having success living with ADHD in their own families, and their ideas also will help you.

Think positive! Dwell on your child's potential, not on his or her problems. But be realistic, and don't be hard on yourself when you feel overwhelmed or exhausted. Here are some thoughts, observations, pep talks, and suggestions offered by an experienced parent.

An Informed Parent Is the Best Advocate for the Child With ADHD

- No one knows this child's strengths (and shortcomings) better than you, so you are the expert in that respect. You must serve as your child's greatest advocate, promoter, and defender.

- You also must serve as the coordinator of the multidisciplinary team consisting of the parents, child, physician, mental health professional, and teacher.

- When you are looking for professionals to help you with diagnosis and management of your child, be a smart consumer, and ask questions! "Can you tell me about your experience in assessing ADHD? Will you be willing to talk to my child's teacher and help us all establish goals?" Don't make the assumption that all primary care physicians and mental health professionals are experienced and knowledgeable in this specific field.

- When it comes to dealing with your child, most likely you already have accepted the fact that managing this child's behavior will take more of your effort and patience than anything else you've

ever tried. "Normal" parenting techniques just don't work. That's why you should learn all you can about the management of ADHD and seek professional help through a multidisciplinary team. Because ADHD is complex, this is not a one-person job.

Parents Should Stay Involved With Their Child's School

- Don't assume your child's teacher knows a lot about ADHD. You will need to become a diplomat as you share information and your positive attitude with the teacher—without sounding too "pushy" or threatening.

- Know your rights and responsibilities regarding your child's education and your access to special school services if needed.

- Standardized tests were not standardized on children with attention deficits! Review test results with this in mind. Your child might be eligible to take these tests on an untimed basis or with other accommodations.

- A child's attention deficits can be accompanied by other learning disabilities, including problems with memory, sequencing, or visual perception. Have your child thoroughly tested, to identify and address these problems separately. In other words, don't chalk up all your child's problems to his or her difficulties with paying attention. There might be other learning problems that need to be diagnosed and addressed.

- What level of academic intervention does your child need? The options depend on the severity of the child's learning and/or attention problems. Many children remain in the regular classroom with accommodations. Most children will benefit from tutoring and counseling, and some will need special education placement.

- Become proficient in writing letters to make suggestions to and requests of the teacher. A written communication works well because the teacher can read it when time permits, have time to consider your suggestions and requests, and then respond. You will need to communicate frequently with your child's teacher. Remember, you want to set up a

"We're all on the same team" tone, so avoid confrontation, blaming, and jumping to conclusions after hearing only your child's side of the story.

- Become as involved in your child's school as you possibly can, so you can be in the know and make decisions about which teachers will be most appropriate for your child. Having a good teacher who understands ADHD will make all the difference in the world. An informed, concerned teacher can be the difference between success and failure in salvaging the child's self-esteem and interest in academics. The other benefit of being active and helpful at your child's school is that the administration and the teacher will feel comfortable with you, have respect for the priority you give your child, and therefore will be more personally interested in helping you set the stage for your child's success.

Recreation and a Social Life Are Important, Too

- ADHD will affect not only your child's home and academic performances, but also social situations. Your involvement in your child's activities will need to be more hands-on than most parents'. In order to pave the way for your child's social success, you might want to make sure your home is a place where the kids want to come "hang out." Volunteer to be a troop leader, coach, or room parent. This gives you valuable opportunities to observe and guide your child in social situations. In addition, you become familiar with his or her peers and can help your child develop and promote friendships with compatible children. These kids need best friends and acceptance.

- Do not take physical activity away from your child as punishment. This would qualify as cruel and unusual for a hyperactive child.

- Encourage special interests in your child and give him or her the assistance to shine. Can you work together on a project for the local science fair? Can your child take tae kwon do or karate and progress through the various levels?

Educate Your Child About ADHD

- One theory about the occurrence of ADHD in some people and not others is the hunter/farmer model (Hartmann, 1995). Anthropologic evidence suggests that at the time of the agricultural revolution, two very different human societies could be identified— farmers and hunter/gatherers. Farmers needed to

be patient, to await crop growth, to weed and harvest. Hunters constantly needed to scan the environment for danger and opportunity (in children with ADHD, we call it distractibility) and to act instantly on decisions (we call it impulsivity) to chase and spear wild animals. For a primitive hunter, risk and high stimulation were a necessary part of daily life (to prevent starvation!). It is fascinating to consider that this genetic predisposition for behavior can be a leftover survival strategy! This model lets us view ADHD with self-esteem intact: ADHD could be part of our genetic heritage.

- If your child complains about taking medication, it might help to draw a parallel with other medical conditions. Children with asthma need inhalers, and those with diabetes take insulin regularly. Explain that "Medication is something that helps your body function at its full potential."

- Read to your child about famous achievers who had symptoms of ADHD: Winston Churchill, Thomas Edison, and Ben Franklin.

Closing Thoughts

- Dwell on the positive! This child is full of potential and you will be able to help him or her find success in life! Successful adults with ADHD attribute their success to someone believing in them along the way—parents, a coach, a music teacher. These adults were able to appreciate and enjoy the child's energy, creativity, and spontaneity.

- Avoid parental burnout. This "difficult" child will test you to your very limits. Take time for yourself, plan ways for you and your spouse to have time alone, learn to forgive yourself and your child, and get ongoing outside support.

- Some days are better than others. You'll go for weeks thinking everything is going very well at school and at home. Then everything seems to fall apart. Teachers send notes home, the child has a fight with his or her best friend, and the child is driving you crazy at home. When the stressors pile up, it's time to start over again, analyze the current state of affairs, and put all of the things you have learned back in motion. Go to a support meeting, contact the professionals, and meet with the teacher. But never give up. Your child can have success.

Parent Articles About ADHD / ISBN 0761667512 / 1-800-228-0752 / This page is reproducible.

References and Resources

Bain, L. (1991). *A parent's guide to attention deficit disorders*. New York: Dell.

Hallowell, E. M. & Ratey, J. J. (1994). *Driven to distraction*. New York: Simon & Schuster.

Hartmann, T. (1995). *ADD success stories*. Grass Valley, CA: Underwood Books.

Levine, M. (1987). Attention Deficits: The diverse effects of weak control systems in childhood. *Pediatric Annals, 16,* 117-131.

Maxey, D. (1989). *How to own and operate an attention deficit kid*. Roanoke-Charlottesville, VA: CHADD.

Rich, D. (1988). *MegaSkills*. Boston: Houghton Mifflin.

Silver, L. (1992). *The misunderstood child*. TAB Books.

Veronica Campbell is a senior physical therapist with SSM Health in St. Louis, and a graduate of St. Louis University.

Helping Your Active Child at Night

Magda A. Urban, Ph.D.

3.9

Children with Attention Deficit/Hyperactivity Disorder (ADHD) seem to have time clocks that run backwards. Many children have difficulty activating in the morning and winding down at night. Parents of children with ADHD report increased sleep problems from infancy throughout adolescence. These problems include increased time to get to sleep, snoring, restless legs and arms, and recall of nightmares (Ball, Tiernan, Januz, & Furr, 1997; Chervin, Dillon, Bassetti, Ganoczy, & Pituch, 1997; Hoeppner, Trommer, Armstrong, & Rosenberg, 1996). You can help your children at night by being aware of the problems that can occur with sleep and ADHD and also by being familiar with methods to increase relaxation and sleep.

Consult With Professionals

It is a good idea to consult with your child's physician or mental health professional when your child with ADHD has problems sleeping. Some medications for ADHD, depression, and anxiety can affect your child's sleep-wake cycle. When children with ADHD are tired, many naturally become more active and difficult to calm. Medical and/or psychological professionals can help you identify your child's patterns and break negative sleep cycles.

Keep a Routine

A regular routine before bedtime can help your child with ADHD relax and get ready for sleep. For many children, this routine begins with a relaxing bath, brushing their teeth, putting on sleepwear, organizing clothes and materials for the next day, getting tucked into bed, turning on a nightlight, and having parents give them a goodnight kiss. Some parents close closet doors and peek under beds to assure their child that there is no danger of "monsters."

Massage

Some children with ADHD love having foot and back massages to help them relax and sleep. When 10-year-old Jason has difficulty getting to sleep, his mother Rebecca uses an electric massager on his shoulders and back. Jason likes the hum of the machine as well as the deep vibrations on his muscles. Other parents report success in using wooden back massage tools, available at many bath supply shops.

Story Time

Young children with or without ADHD often look forward to bedtime stories, either read by their parents or played as audiocassette tapes. Keep in mind that stories with lots of action and excitement are for daytime reading and work against the nighttime goal of relaxation and sleep. Choose stories that are interesting yet can be read in a calm, rhythmic way. When children listen to stories, it helps them relax and also increases their language and reading skills.

Gary and Betty, who live far away from their active grandson, Dante, found a way to help him get to sleep. They tape-record stories from children's books or Gary's own stories about "a little boy's adventures." At night, Dante's mother, Laurel, puts the story tape into the recorder and lets it play continuously (the tape player has an "autoreverse" feature). Dante loves to listen to the voices of his grandparents and reports that it usually takes him about seven stories before he falls asleep. Each night the voices of Dante's beloved grandparents lull him to sleep, whether he is at home with his family, travelling, or with a baby-sitter.

Teach Relaxation

Children with ADHD sometimes need to learn how to relax. Teach these relaxation skills by showing your child how to breathe calmly or count breaths, or by talking the child through progressive relaxation exercises.

Mary taught her 12-year-old daughter, Sally, to relax at bedtime, showing her how to breathe slowly and deeply while visualizing her muscles loosening. After Sally concentrated on her deep and regular breathing, Mary talked about the muscles of Sally's feet and how she could see and feel them relax and loosen. Mary described each large muscle group, from Sally's feet to her head, prompting her to relax her muscles and release tension. After a month of Mary's guided relaxation, Sally was able to take herself through the exercise and fall asleep on her own.

Technology

Tape recorders, fans, and environmental noise machines are useful in helping children with ADHD get to sleep. These machines offer background sound also called white noise. Many people with ADHD find that white noise helps them block out the random sounds they hear when the house is quiet and that can interfere with their sleep. Some children with ADHD like to listen to stories or low music as they fall asleep. Machines and commercially available audiocassette tapes that play background sounds from oceans, waterfalls, rain, or forests are popular. Small room fans are inexpensive and produce a continuous audible hum.

Some children with ADHD use visual cues, preferring to look at something relaxing to help them sleep. An inexpensive aquarium with a soothing light offers the child with ADHD lulling visual intrigue as he or she watches the slow swimming movements of the fish and bubbles rising from the air regulator.

Staying in Bed

Despite their best bedtime preparations, parents frequently tuck their child into bed, get to the bedroom door, and find their child following behind them. It is important to have extra patience and offer positive support when your child with ADHD gets out of bed. Let your child know that once he or she is in bed, you expect the child to stay there. You might want to explain, "It's okay for you not to sleep, but you must stay in bed."

Some parents find it helpful to provide a positive reinforcement system for the child's staying in bed. The following is an example of a chart, kept at the foot of the child's bed, that the child fills out each day. The child checks either the "yes" or "no" column under the title "Stayed in Bed"; the parent checks the "yes" or "no" column under "Parent Agrees." After the child stays in bed two to five nights with parents' agreement, the child receives a positive reward, such as extra time on the playground, a trip for pizza or a burger, or a favored and affordable activity. Once you start a chart or graph, check it daily with your child. Be sure to give your child the positive reward as quickly as possible. Children with ADHD learn best when parents give them lots of encouragement along with prompt payoffs for their achievements. Even if the child did not meet the criteria completely, it's still important to give encouragement: "Great, Bobby! You stayed in bed except for one time. You're getting there!" Every little bit of progress you notice helps children learn ways to gain better control of their ADHD, especially when it helps your "active daytime" child become a more "restful nighttime" one.

Day	Stayed in Bed		Parents Agree	
	Yes	No	Yes	No
Monday	❏	❏	❏	❏
Tuesday	❏	❏	❏	❏
Wednesday	❏	❏	❏	❏
Thursday	❏	❏	❏	❏
Friday	❏	❏	❏	❏
Saturday	❏	❏	❏	❏
Sunday	❏	❏	❏	❏

References and Resources

Ball, J. D., Tiernan, M., Januz, J. & Furr, A. (1997). Sleep patterns among children with Attention Deficit/Hyperactivity Disorder: A reexamination of parent perceptions. *Journal of Pediatric Psychology, 22,* 389-398.

Chervin, R. D., Dillon, J. E., Bassetti, C., Ganoczy, D. A., & Pituch, K. J. (1997). Symptoms of sleep disorders, inattention, and hyperactivity in children. *Sleep, 20,* 1185-1192.

Hoeppner, J. B., Trommer, B. L., Armstrong, K. J., & Rosenberg, R. S. (1996). Developmental changes of parental-reported sleep disturbance symptoms in children with attention deficit disorder. *Journal of Clinical Psychology in Medical Settings. 3,* 235-242.

Lewis, S., & Lewis, S. K. (1996). *Stress-proofing your child: Mind-body exercises to enhance your child's health.* New York: Bantam.

Thalgott, M., & Furst, M. (1988). *Mindscape: Mix-and-match imagery exercises.* San Luis Obispo, CA: Dandy Lion.

Magda A. Urban, Ph.D., is an educational diagnostic therapist in Tucson. A contributor to several articles and textbooks, she is a former associate professor at the University of Arizona.

Athletics and the Child With Attention Deficit/Hyperactivity Disorder

David C. Campbell, M.D.

Sending the child with Attention Deficit/Hyperactivity Disorder (ADHD) outside to "run it off" on the athletic field seems like an obvious option, and indeed athletics provide many such children with a chance to shine. But you must consider carefully the choice of a sport and even the choice of a coach, or the chance to shine will become just another frustration and failure. You also must be prepared to get involved, not only in making the initial decisions, but also in working with your child outside the regular practices to make sure he or she understands the rules and expectations (the child might not have been listening when the coach explained them!).

Although there are countless books and articles about the child with ADHD in the classroom, there has been relatively little written about the role of sports participation for these children. Even in what literature exists, there is conflicting data about the role of vigorous physical activity on subsequent ability to concentrate. There are anecdotal reports from adults with ADHD claiming that vigorous athletic activity improves their ability to concentrate afterwards for up to 1½ hours (Hallowell & Ratey, 1994; Hartman, 1995). However, Craft (1983) found that after 10 minutes of pedaling a bicycle, hyperactive preadolescents showed little improvement in cognitive performance on standardized tests.

Selecting a Sport for the Child With ADHD

The selection of a sport for the child with ADHD is a very individualized process (as it is with any child). Some sports are generally more suitable than others. The song "Right Field" performed by Peter, Paul, and Mary (Welch, 1986) talks about the child relegated to playing right field, "watching the dandelions grow." Add to that chasing the butterflies, turning in circles, and rolling in the grass, and you'll have a picture of the typical child with ADHD playing the outfield on a baseball or softball team.

The first step in selecting a sport is to find something the child likes, is interested in, and is thus more likely to be "tuned into." Attending an area high school game of soccer or baseball with the child is easy and inexpensive and might give some preliminary indication of the child's excitement about participation. Similarly, providing opportunities to participate in individual activities such as swimming or tennis will allow you to judge the child's level of enthusiasm.

At the same time, you also should try to assess the child's physical abilities and limitations objectively. No one is able to catch a pop fly, hit a ball with a bat or racket, or dribble a soccer ball gracefully down the field on the first attempt. However, you should try to discern whether your child shows some facility with the gross and fine motor skills associated with each activity. Working with the child at home before placing him or her onto a team can help the child avoid embarrassment and a sense of failure if he or she simply is not capable of achieving the skills and coordination required for a given activity.

In general, the child with ADHD has difficulty with unsupervised "sandlot" or "pickup" games. Because these children characteristically have difficulty taking turns and can be impulsive, they might have a bad experience in such settings. This observation should not necessarily lead you to rule out the sport involved, but realize that your child probably will do better in a situation with adult coaching or supervision.

Team or Individual Sport?

You also will have to decide between a team sport or an individual sport. Most team sports require concentration by all players even when they don't have the ball. Children who are inattentive in team sports such as soccer or basketball can cause the rest of the team to suffer. This experience can result in the inattentive child's being criticized or harassed by his or her peers.

Team sports also require following rules and taking turns. Although these things can be difficult for the child with ADHD, this also might be a chance for the child to improve his or her social skills in these areas if they are introduced in the right setting (including a patient and supportive adult supervisor or coach).

You also should talk to the coach directly about your child's strengths and weaknesses. Within the team structure, there might be certain roles or positions for which your child is best suited. In baseball or softball, for example, the child with ADHD might not do well in the outfield, but pitching or catching could encourage the child to stay very focused if he or she has the necessary physical skills. There is nothing a coach wants to hear less than a parent pushing for his or her child "to be the shortstop," but if you establish a rapport, the coach might be more willing to place your child in roles where he or she can excel.

Many children with ADHD might do well to consider individual sports. Swimming, track, and other individual sports allow the child to perform at his or her personal best without inattentiveness affecting the outcome of the game. Some have suggested that the martial arts are an ideal activity for the child with ADHD (Kennedy, 1997). Martial arts incorporate physical activity with a mental discipline that can have an important carryover into other aspects of the child's life.

Medication and Sports Participation

The final consideration for parents as their child becomes involved in organized athletics is whether or not to use medication. Stimulant medications, such as methylphenidate, have a clear beneficial effect on attention span and impulsivity in the classroom setting. However, some parents might be reluctant to have their child use these medications to facilitate sports participation, given that the National Collegiate Athletic Association (NCAA) and the United States Olympic Committee have banned their use in collegiate and Olympic events.

Although the decision to use stimulant medication is an individual one, there is some research to support its benefits in sports. Pelham, et al. (1990) studied 8- to 10-year-old children playing baseball. The drug had neither a positive nor a negative effect on the children's skills (hitting and throwing), but it did improve their ability to pay attention to the game. Considering the perils that lack of attention can have in a team sport, and considering that one of the goals of athletic participation is to improve self-esteem, parents need not withhold medication, even if it means giving an afternoon or weekend dose prior to team competition.

Summary

Vigorous physical activity and participation in organized sports are important for a child's well-being. They also can be extremely valuable for the child's self-esteem. Sports participation offers an opportunity to improve gross and fine motor skills as well as social skills. Parents need to be careful to assess the child's abilities so as to select the proper sport or activity. Parents also should be sure that the adult supervisor is knowledgeable and sensitive to the child's special needs.

References and Resources

Craft, D. H. (1983). Effect of prior exercise on cognitive performance tasks by hyperactive and normal young boys. *Perceptual Motor Skills, 56,* 979-82.

Hallowell, E. M., & Ratey, J. J. (1994). *Driven to distraction.* New York: Simon & Schuster.

Hartmann, T. (1995). *ADD success stories.* Grass Valley, CA: Underwood Books.

Kennedy, R. (1997, September supplement). Attention Deficit Disorders. *Sports Illustrated for Kids,* 48-49.

Pelham, W. E., Jr., McBurnett, K., Harper, G. W., Milich, R., Murphy, D. A., Clinton, J., & Thiele, C. (1990). Methylphenidate and baseball playing in ADHD children: Who's on first? *Journal of Consulting and Clinical Psychology, 58,* 1-4.

Welch, Willy. (1986). "Right field," recorded by Peter, Paul, and Mary on *Peter, Paul, and Mommy, Too.* Playing Right Music; based on Willy Welch's book, *Playing right field,* published by Scholastic Books, 1995.

David Campbell, M.D., M.Ed., is a board-certified family physician and the director of the Residency Program of Family Medicine of St. Louis.

Helping Siblings Understand Attention Deficit/Hyperactivity Disorder

Laura Falduto, Ph.D.

Helping a child understand a sibling with special needs can be a unique task for many parents. Inevitably, people raise their children based on their own growing-up experiences. And unless you've had some personal experience with the sibling relationships of children with special needs, it can be tough to develop a model for ways to help your children cope. This article addresses some basic strategies for helping your other children deal with the child who has Attention Deficit/Hyperactivity Disorder (ADHD).

Modeling

One aspect of helping siblings adjust depends on how you model the way you cope emotionally with your child with ADHD. Of course, the challenges faced by your children depend greatly on the dynamics of your family system. *Family dynamics* refers to the ways that family members experience themselves and subsequently relate to other members of the family. The dynamics of the family system can be influenced enormously by external and/or structural factors such as relationships in the extended family, birth order, proximity in age, and gender. Adding a child with ADHD to the family also can have a profound influence on these dynamics. Your attitudes and behavior, as the parents, set examples and guide your children's attitudes and behavior. Thus, when you deal with their own feelings about having a sibling with ADHD, you already have taken the first and most important step in helping your other children.

Naturally, family dynamics include a wide range of positive and negative feelings that can vary in intensity from very subtle to excessive. In dealing with the feelings in a family that includes a child with ADHD, it is essential to cultivate understanding, acceptance, love, and support. This process begins in the relationship between the parents. Given the strong influence of heredity in ADHD, parents often have to cope with their own feelings about family genetics and the disorder. Many times one or both parents have had to live their lives coping with their own (or a sibling's) symptoms of ADHD in the absence of proper diagnosis or treatment. Relevant issues are likely to include genetics, experiences in their families of origin, self-experience, and interpersonal relationships, particularly marital and co-parenting relationships. Parents who develop a healing attitude about addressing their own life experiences with ADHD eventually will find that, although difficult, this process ultimately will result in enrichment and marital and family health.

It is important to recognize and honor individual differences in each of your children. Parents who establish a sense of appreciation for each child's unique giftings and challenges are providing a foundation for healthy self-esteem. True self-esteem comes from an appreciative awareness of self. There exists within families a rare opportunity to cultivate an environment of love that will help your children maintain a positive sense of self that can endure the inevitable bits of pain in life. When family members are aware of each other's endearing qualities as well as trying qualities, healthier dynamics develop that support coping and adaptation skills. Most of this depends on establishing good family communication. Communication is essential in creating an atmosphere in which parents and children can develop an emotional balance in daily family life.

Family Communication

So much of helping children to communicate their feelings is really modeled and taught by parents' interactions with family members. This begins very early in childhood as parents encourage younger children to use words, rather than behaviors, to express themselves. The capacity to communicate feelings progresses developmentally: As children get older, good communication between parents and children increasingly depends on listening. This is particularly true during adolescence. To listen well, you must be authentically interested in understanding what your child has to say. Parents often find this task challenging, especially when they disagree with what the child is saying! Parents who ask for clarification, verbalize their understanding, and empathize with their child's feelings help the child feel validated, even when the parent's opinion is different. It is important to remember that good communication skills are at the heart of facilitating children's coping skills. Each child's reaction to having a sibling with ADHD is unique and likely to vary enormously from child to child. Therefore, a powerful form of parental assistance is to be aware of and attuned to individual differences and reactions, by talking to each child about how he or she feels.

One way to model good coping skills is to talk with your children about your feelings and also about the nature ADHD. You need to gear such communications to your children's developmental levels and be sensitive to time and setting as well as to their level of interest and emotional tolerance. Some parents mistakenly feel that if they don't say anything to the children about their own negative feelings, the children are unaware of these negative feelings. The truth is that children often are keenly aware of the emotional states of their parents. However, this awareness does not mean your children understand why you are feeling that way. In fact, children can misunderstand parents on an emotional level and act out their confusion and uncertainty by exhibiting problematic behavior. Sharing your feelings and information about ADHD can do wonders to dispel the imagined problems that children naturally generate when coping with the uncertainties about the emotional lives of their parents.

Facilitating Healthy Sibling Relationships

Many times, the most common struggles faced by children who have a sibling with ADHD involve the discrepancies between their own capabilities and those of the child with ADHD. For example, the child without ADHD who demonstrates organization, responds to parental interventions, follows the rules, and has good self-control might begin to disparage the child with ADHD who does not have these skills. Avoid the trap of developing the "good-kid/bad-kid" split in the family system. The child who establishes a favored position in the family on the basis of not messing up as much as the child with ADHD might be vulnerable to the need to establish superiority by identifying shortcomings in others. A child whose idea of self depends on others' failures lacks true self-awareness and self-esteem.

Another problem arises from the fact that the child with ADHD appears to get more parental attention in the form of medications, doctors, and trips to the counselor. Your other children cannot see the "invisible" disability of ADHD, and they might conclude that their sibling is being "bad" all the time. Unfortunately, they might develop problem behaviors to get some of the negative attention that the child with ADHD appears to be enjoying. Alternatively, they might complain that the child with ADHD "gets away with everything!" Children can feel resentful and jealous, complain about the security of parental love, and protest about "fairness."

Parental emphasis on individual differences and strengths can help a lot. Modeling how to cope with difficult feelings and demonstrating your empathy can be tremendously helpful for your other children. You could respond to complaints about fairness by saying, "I see how difficult it is for you when your brother is having a hard time and you want some time with me." Follow your expression of empathy with a commitment to give this child positive attention whenever you can. Promise to spend extra time with the

child before bed, or arrange a special outing. Also, minimize the negative effects on your other children. For example, take separate cars to events that might be difficult for your child with ADHD. This way, one parent can provide the natural consequence of removing the child with ADHD from the event without spoiling the fun for the rest of the family.

It is also important not to attribute poor sibling relationships to typical "kid stuff." Having conflict with and intense feelings about siblings are both quite natural occurrences in families, but poor sibling relationships are not. ADHD can complicate matters even more. Parents who have become used to hearing siblings complain about one another might be overlooking situations where one child is having to cope with something that goes above and beyond usual sibling conflicts.

Sibling relationships within a family are often a testing ground for developing the interpersonal skills your children will have for the rest of their lives. The foundation for good sibling relationships lies in early experience. You can affect these experiences profoundly by the manner in which you talk to your children about their ways of relating to their brothers and sisters. Help your children develop empathy for each other by asking how they would like to be treated by their siblings. Ask them to describe qualities they admire in sibling relationships, and begin to identify how they can develop or improve those qualities, even in the small things they do. Help older children realize how much younger children look up to them. This helps them understand that younger siblings might stop pestering them if they give the younger ones some time and positive attention.

Growing up in the same family gives your children a common experience they will never share with anyone else throughout their lifetimes. Help them to see this as a unique opportunity, but acknowledge that they also might be called upon to learn and demonstrate unusual depths of tolerance and patience. Supportive guidance from parents can go a long way in the development of healthy sibling relationships in a family with a child with special needs, particularly when the children are young. However, as children grow older and begin to leave home, sibling relationships become less subject to parental influence and more the responsibility of each child. These family relationships can nurture a bond that can bring a great deal of enrichment and happiness and carry siblings through the rougher spots they inevitably encounter.

Laura Falduto, Ph.D., completed her postdoctoral fellowship in child and adolescent psychology at the Menninger Clinic in Topeka, Kansas. She is a clinical psychologist at the Institute for Developmental Behavioral Neurology in Scottsdale, Arizona.

Individual Psychotherapy and Counseling for the Child With Attention Deficit/Hyperactivity Disorder

Honore M. Hughes, Ph.D.

What Is Psychotherapy or Counseling?

Individual psychotherapy is an opportunity for a person (child or adult) to talk or play with an objective, trained professional about the individual's feelings, behaviors, or thoughts that are troublesome or not understood. You might wonder, "How could talking (or playing) help?" A therapist would explain that people often behave in certain ways because of how they feel, and therapy/counseling can help them learn about the connections between feelings and behavior. Also, after talking, people can understand and manage their feelings better. Talking isn't always the preferred way to communicate for young children, so therapists use play activities and drawing to help these children share their feelings and concerns. This process can help children feel better and might help them alter their behavior.

The basic goals of therapy for children are to (a) relieve the child's feelings of distress, (b) decrease behavior problems, and (c) improve the child's overall adjustment and self-esteem.

What Types of Psychotherapy or Counseling Are Available?

Treatments vary based on how much structure the therapist provides, how the counselor communicates with the child, and the specific goals of the treatment. Two types of therapy commonly used with children who have Attention Deficit/Hyperactivity Disorder (ADHD) are psychodynamic therapy and cognitive-behavioral therapy.

Psychodynamic therapy is a more traditional approach and often includes play therapy. In this type of treatment, the child forms a special bond with the therapist that is different from the child's relationship with a parent or teacher, and the focus is mostly on emotions. The goals of this type of therapy (along with the goals mentioned above) are to figure out the causes of particular feelings and talk or communicate about them. Negative feelings often diminish considerably when the child communicates these feelings through talk or play, which helps the child feel better about him- or herself.

In cognitive-behavioral therapy, the therapist typically uses more talking along with play and gives the child concrete tasks to accomplish during and between treatment sessions. Cognitive-behavioral treatment consists of a combination of techniques, including focusing on thoughts (the "cognitive" part) and actions (the "behavioral" part), as well as feelings. Therapists help children work actively to change their thoughts, behaviors, and feelings.

What Types of Problems Can Individual Psychotherapy or Counseling Help?

Therapists most frequently use psychodynamic therapy (play therapy or talking with a therapist) to treat distress that is emotional or expressed more internally (such as sadness, anxiety, and low self-esteem). Therapists usually address problem behavior such as aggressiveness or disobedience by teaching parents and teachers techniques to handle the behaviors. Group therapy might be helpful for children with ADHD who have difficulties getting along with peers. However, when children reach 11 or 12 years old, cognitive-behavioral techniques that build problem-solving skills, impulse control, and sensitivity to others work well.

When Is Individual Psychotherapy or Counseling Useful?

Before seeking treatment, parents need to ask themselves: Does my child seem upset, lonely, sad, or scared? Is the child overly self-critical? Does the child lack confidence? Although all children have these feelings occasionally, parents and teachers should be concerned if the child has these feelings more often and to a greater degree than the average child of the same age. A related issue is whether the difficulties are interfering with daily life at home or school. Perhaps the child's impulsiveness gets in the way of completing schoolwork or doing it correctly. Children also might be having problems with peers because it is difficult for them to wait their turn, or they blurt out what is on their minds without thinking. Behaviors that are a concern at home include not following reasonable rules, aggression, and being unable to do chores without constant monitoring and reminding.

Many of these difficulties are transient and do not last longer than 2 to 3 weeks. If problems persist substantially longer, from 3 to 6 months, it would be wise to seek the opinion of a professional. Most problems children with ADHD experience do not differ from those of other children, but they are likely to be more frequent or severe than

Copyright © 1999 by Communication Skill Builders, a division of The Psychological Corporation. All rights reserved.
Parent Articles About ADHD / ISBN 0761667512 / 1-800-228-0752 / This page is reproducible.

67

for the average child. Seek professional assessment if you think your child's difficulties are more severe than usual for his or her age. Intervention is more successful the earlier it starts, especially for aggressiveness and disobedience, and can prevent more serious problems from developing later.

When Is Individual Psychotherapy or Counseling Useful With Children Who Have ADHD?

Children with ADHD are likely to have other difficulties in addition to their primary ADHD symptoms. The core problems with self-control can lead to other difficulties because children with ADHD have such a hard time inhibiting impulses to do or say things. Other problems the child might experience include learning difficulties, aggressiveness or disobedience, sadness and fears, and low self-esteem.

For many of these symptoms, individual therapy is not as appropriate as other interventions. When children are younger than 9 or 10 years, the most helpful approach is to teach behavioral interventions to parents and teachers. Individual counseling probably will not be very helpful until children are approximately 10 years old. Individual treatment usually is most effective when combined with medication and behavioral interventions in the home and school. Psychodynamically oriented treatment can be helpful for children with ADHD who have experienced trauma such as physical or sexual abuse or the death of a close family member. Individual cognitive-behavioral interventions along with behavioral management at school and home seem to be most useful for older children and those with acting-out types of problems.

What Should I Expect if My Child Is in Counseling?

Many parents wonder how long therapy should last. Usually, the child will see the therapist once a week. It is important that these weekly meetings be consistent. Therapists also will have contact with the parents, usually once a week or so, for 10 to 15 minutes. The counselors want to hear from parents about how things are going at home and school. Also, every 10 to 12 sessions, many therapists will meet with parents for a longer time to evaluate how the treatment is going and set future goals. Overall, research on individual therapy indicates that the vast majority of children who participate show improvement, with children who engage in treatment over a longer period of time showing greater gains.

Honore M. Hughes, Ph.D., is a professor of psychology at St. Louis University. She currently teaches graduate courses in clinical child assessment and therapy. Dr. Hughes conducts research and has published a number of articles and book chapters on family violence and its impact on children.

Section 4

Early Childhood

The Developing Child

Clare B. Jones, Ph.D.

How Can We as Parents Make a Difference Right From the Start?

Parents of young children always have known how important they are in their children's lives. Children who receive warm and responsive care from their families along with the essentials find it easier to cope with difficult times when they are older, despite possible learning challenges. L. Alan Stroufe, Ph.D., and his colleagues at the University of Minnesota have found that children who are securely attached to their caregivers get along better with other children and perform better in school than children who are less securely attached.

You can help your child in the early years by following these 10 guidelines established by the Reiner Foundation's parent awareness campaign, "I Am Your Child."

- Be warm, loving, and responsive.
- Respond to the child's cues and clues (the sounds they make and their facial expressions).
- Talk, read, and sing to your child.
- Establish routines and rituals.
- Encourage safe exploration and play.
- Make television watching selective.
- Use discipline as an opportunity to teach.
- Recognize that each child is unique.
- Choose quality child care and stay involved.
- Take care of yourself!

Many people make a list of things they want to do each year as a way to set goals. This simple list-making task can provide the same sort of springboard to future plans and ideas for spending positive time with your child. Post the list on your refrigerator, desk, family bulletin board, or bedroom mirror. This list can provide a wonderful source of inspiration and gentle reminders every day.

Emotional Development

One area in which you can make a powerful impact on your child's life is emotional development. Emotional development contributes to one's attitude about oneself, one's self-esteem. As a parent, you help form your child's attitudes about him- or herself and others because you are such a critical and ever-present model.

Research indicates that there are three areas in which children develop: intellectual, emotional, and social. Of the three, emotional development is the area in which parents have the strongest influence. It is important to make your children feel secure and loved from the very beginning. Children's feelings can be hurt easily, and children can read and interpret their parents' and others' emotional clues quickly. Children respond to positive stimuli, so when they are doing something correctly, praise them. Smile and reward them immediately for their appropriate behavior. Then, when the day is done, put up your feet, relax, and think back over the positive things that have happened in your child's day. This time will help you celebrate what special pleasures your children also bring to the world.

Gathering Information

Sometimes parents of children with Attention Deficit/Hyperactivity Disorder (ADHD) refer to the challenges with their children as "tough love." They feel they have to learn different ways to cope with their challenging child. You will need to learn a variety of parenting techniques, and as you learn, your education becomes your tool for success in raising your child.

As the parent of a child with ADHD, you will need to be your child's advocate. Not everyone will understand your child's behavior, and some might question your parenting skills. Be informed, know what works with children who have attentional problems, and stay true to the behavior plan you design. Ignore negative comments from ill-intentioned and uninformed observers. Join local support groups such as Children and Adults With Attention Deficit Disorder (CHADD), and meet other families like yours. Seek friendships among families who understand what you are doing and why.

If you have access to the Internet, search in the area of attention deficit disorder for the extensive collection of information including "chat rooms" where you can talk with other parents of children with ADHD. The Internet will give you immediate access to current information about medications and new research.

Your local public library will have a selection of books on all topics that concern attention deficit. In addition, many libraries also have special-needs sections devoted to printed materials and videos about disabilities that will be an excellent resource for you.

If you are positive, consistent, and begin to use the suggestions here, you will help your child and your family learn acceptable ways to be successful.

References and Resources

The first years last forever. Booklet published by the Reiner Foundation, 1010 Wisconsin Ave. NW, Washington, DC, 20007.

Clare B. Jones, Ph.D., is an educational consultant and diagnostic specialist at Developmental Learning Associates in Phoenix. The author of three books on attention disorders, she is a nationally recognized presenter in the field of attention disorders and special needs.

Early Childhood Identification

Clare B. Jones, Ph.D.

Early identification of children who are at risk for attention deficit disorders helps both the child and the parents because it can prevent many further difficulties. Early intervention will benefit the child's behavior and development. Parents will need to develop a variety of strategies to help the child between the ages of 2 and 4 years learn to manage his or her attention and activity.

Help Your Child Within Your Home Environment

A child with attention disorders needs a well-managed, structured, consistent environment. Plan your daily schedule to include predictable times, transitions, routines, and rituals. Try to have meals at a regular time, and wind down play or activities as designated meal times approach.

Arrange your child's environment so that it is safe and well maintained. Place toys and belongings in drawers and boxes and on shelves. Circulate toys, and bring out only a few at a time to help maintain alertness and interests.

Childproof Your Home

The impulsive behavior of children with Attention Deficit/Hyperactivity Disorder (ADHD) makes them prime candidates for accidents. It is important to create an environment for such children that is secure and predictable. Protect a young child from hurtful objects such as scissors, knives, and letter openers. Put away cherished glass items, statues, and expensive collections until your child has demonstrated personal control.

Use Color to Help Organize Your Home

Use color coding, pictures, and words to label storage containers so the child begins to know where similar objects belong. Label and color code personal belongings such as clothes and toys. Find a color theme that will be easy for your child to remember. For example, the white box holds socks, the brown box holds shoes, the yellow box holds shirts. This consistent color-code system will help your child begin to organize his or her own personal belongings.

Plan Your Day

Plan highly routine schedules with a regular time each day for such activities as nap time, lunch, story time, etc. Cue your child that you are approaching specific times: "After we play this game, we will wash our hands and make lunch." Review several interesting or motivating aspects of what is coming next. Active children find it difficult to leave an exciting activity for one they find less interesting. Offer transition so the child can wind down from a very busy time. For example, if the child has been playing on a tricycle, do not announce quickly, "Time for your nap!" Rather, encourage the child to leave the bike to color with chalk on the sidewalk, followed by a story and then nap time. This provides a smooth transition and takes the child through a step-by-step process that often reduces conflict and reaction to change.

Help Your Child Understand His or Her Challenges With Attention

Your child needs to be aware of his or her own personal challenges and learn acceptable ways to cope with these difficulties. One helpful technique is bibliotherapy, selecting a book to read to the child that tells a story about similar challenges. Books that deal specifically with problems the child might experience can help the child feel accepted and understood. Collect age-appropriate books that tell about personal triumphs over difficulties. There are a variety of books for younger children that help them better understand their attention deficit, such as *Shelley, the Hyperactive Turtle,* by D. M. Moss; *Otto Learns About His Medicine,* by M. Galvin; *The Don't Give Up Kid,* by Janet Gehart; and *Jumping Johnny, Get Back to Work,* by Michael Gordon.

Help Your Child Understand Which Behaviors Are Allowed and Which Are Not

As a parent, you need rules in your home. When your child is impulsive and out of control, you need to maintain a calm but firm manner. Work with your child to establish the punishment for infractions ahead of time, before an incident. Time outs (removal from the area) often are helpful. Some doctors recommend that time out for an active child be less than a minute at a time. As the attention span increases, the time increases. If the child hurts another's property, he or she should be expected to make some repayment and attempt to clean up the property, fix it, or put it back together. If your child is 3 years or older, an apology is also in order.

Many 3- and 4-year-old children with ADHD respond well to a token, poker chip, or point system whereby good behaviors earn tokens the children redeem for special privileges. The parents post a menu of reinforcers, and the child "buys" the privileges with the designated amount of tokens (for example, with five tokens, the child may pick the video for the family's Friday night viewing).

If you are positive and consistent and use the methods suggested here, you can help your child with ADHD learn self-management from an early age. The time and guidance you spend now will make your life and your child's more successful as you age together. Finally, be good to yourself. You are invaluable in your child's life. Each intervention you employ is propelling your child toward success.

Clare B. Jones, Ph.D., is an educational consultant and diagnostic specialist at Developmental Learning Associates in Phoenix. The author of three books on attention disorders, she is a nationally recognized presenter in the field of attention disorders and special needs.

Using Time-out to Guide Behavior

Linda M. Levine, Ed.D.

What do you dream about when you make wishes for your child's future? One thing most parents mention is a desire for their child to become a happy and competent adult. They want their child to act properly in many different situations. They often say, "We want our child to *know* the right thing to do, and then to do it!" What these parents want their child to develop is called self-discipline. This type of built-in responsibility takes a while to develop in a young child.

It is normal for all young children to be active, impulsive, and impatient. But when these behaviors happen often, last a long time, and are disruptive, parents must use many different ways to help the child learn to exercise self-control. If talking it out and giving praise for good behavior isn't working to stop the disruptive behavior, parents might need to remove children to a quiet place where they can calm down, think about their actions, and get themselves under control. This popular behavior-management technique has been described variously as thinking time or time alone, but most often it is referred to as time-out. For all young children, but especially for those who are impulsive, inattentive, impatient, or hyperactive, using time-out is a good way to stop unwanted behaviors and help children learn to take responsibility for their actions.

What Is Time-out, and Why Does it Work?

Time-out is a technique that temporarily deprives children of attention from adults and other children. It is an opportunity to help children develop internal controls for their out-of-control behavior. It is a way to give them time to calm down and think about how to act appropriately. It is also a way to help children begin to understand that they have the power to decide how to act. The message they get from time-out is that adults *expect* them to develop self-control and use it every day.

When the behavior of a young child is disruptive and continues to be troublesome, adults often try quick solutions such as yelling, threatening, or punishing to stop the behavior. These solutions stop the behavior for a little while, but the inappropriate behavior usually returns very quickly. That happens because the adult, rather than the child, is exercising control. Adults need a way to help children know what to do and then do what they know!

Children need adults to set limits and make rules to help them live in harmony with others. Paying attention to children's behavior, good *or* bad, is called *reinforcement*. Adults can reinforce good behavior by giving praise, a smile, a hug, or a reward. Good behavior that is reinforced is likely to happen again. When adults pay attention to bad behavior by yelling or nagging, that is also reinforcement and encourages the bad behavior to repeat itself. Some children seek adult attention, even if it is negative attention, by doing unacceptable behaviors. Using time-out can help an adult change this pattern and get the child to listen to requests and heed warnings. This technique works because it isolates the child from reinforcement and gives the child some thinking time. It's a way of teaching the child, showing the child respect, and trusting the child's ability to start building the skills to exercise self-control.

Using Time-out as Part of a Behavior Management Plan

Children need discipline that teaches them how to develop self-control. They need discipline based on good teaching and parenting practices. Following these good practices means making up reasonable rules and allowing children to experience consequences when they find it hard to stick to the rules. Changing the behavior of a child, especially one who is impulsive and lacks patience, is not an easy job. All children learn that certain strategies work for them every time and often use nagging, whining, acting out, or temper tantrums to get their needs met.

How to Use Time-out

When a child has violated the rules, is being disruptive, or is having a tantrum, tell the child, "You are not controlling yourself. You've decided to be in time-out." Set a kitchen timer to help the child understand that time-out is for a brief period. When the timer rings, time-out is over, and the child understands he or she needs to be back in control and ready to return to the group or the family. Here are some helpful hints when you use time-out with young children:

- Be brief and firm but *not* angry.
- State the rule the child has broken: "No hitting. Hitting means you have chosen time-out."

- Place the child in a time-out chair or in another room and say the rule again: "Remember, no hitting. Time-out is over when you hear the bell."
- Try not to give the child attention or eye contact during time-out.
- After the child returns, offer a hopeful comment: "Oh, good, you're back. You must be ready to join us again," or, "I'm glad to see you are in control again."

How Long Should a Child Stay in Time-out?

Time-out helps children establish self-control. Because young children find it difficult to understand the concept of time, time-out should last for only short periods of time. To a young child, 5 minutes can seem as long as an hour. A good time rule for time-out is that the number of minutes should not be greater than the child's age in years. For a 3-year-old child, for example, 3 minutes is the right amount of time to be excluded from the group or from the adult's attention. Five minutes should be the longest amount of time a 5-year-old child stays in time-out.

If the child does not return automatically when the timer bell rings, go get the child and ask, "Are you ready to return? Do you need to stay longer?" You might need to put the child who refuses to sit in a chair for time-out into another room. And you might need to hold the door shut until the timer bell rings. It's fine if the child plays in the room or becomes busy with an activity there. This still accomplishes the purpose of time-out: The child has been removed from a conflict situation or from people and has time alone to think about how to be under control.

Under **no** circumstances should you ever put a young child in a dark room or space without light for time-out. This can be extremely frightening for a child, is disrespectful, and will defeat the purpose of developing self-control.

What Should You Say When Using Time-out?

In the middle of an argument or confrontation with a child, it's sometimes difficult to remember to say the right thing. But saying the right thing is a very important part of the time-out process. The idea of time-out is that *the child has chosen* to be there, not that you have decided to put the child there. This is a small but important distinction. It is the way children learn that *they* are the ones who have the power to act appropriately or inappropriately. If they choose to break the rules or lose control of themselves, their own actions put them into time-out. It's a good idea to practice the right wording before you need to use the time-out technique.

- You should say, "You have decided to be in time-out," or "Your actions have told me you have decided to be in time-out."
- You should not say, "I'm going to put you in time-out."
- Although you should be brief, children sometimes need additional words: "You need to think about how to behave. I'm setting the timer for 3 minutes. When the bell rings, you may come back to the kitchen." You might have to say this several times to children who are very upset and angry, to help them calm down.

What if the Child Asks for a Second Chance?

Providing a second chance is a matter of judgment. If the child has violated an important rule or has broken the rule many times, you might want to insist, "No, you have chosen to be in time-out for 4 minutes. When you come out, you can start all over again." Sometimes a child will promise to behave, and it is certainly to everyone's advantage to give the child a chance to demonstrate self-control. At those times, it's fine to say something like, "Okay, I'll give you another chance to prove you've gotten your act together." If the child can behave appropriately, everyone wins.

Who Can Benefit From Time-out?

Using time-out as a way to develop self-control is an appropriate technique for children of many ages. It is helpful for children who are developing typically, as well as those with moderate or severe behavior challenges. An 18-month-old toddler who is having a tantrum can have a 1-minute time out as the parent removes the child from playing and places him or her in a crib for a minute. An 8-year-old child can go to a bedroom for 5 to 10 minutes to think about appropriate behavior. It is important to remember that all young children are occasionally disruptive. It is normal for them to be loud, active, unsocialized, unable to control themselves, and impulsive much of the time. However, when these behaviors are highly disruptive and persist over time, then they require the services of a professional behavior specialist. Don't hesitate to get this help if it is needed.

Summary

Time-out is only one part of a whole behavior plan. When you are putting any behavior plan into effect, consider three things:

- Patience: Changing children's behavior takes time.

- Consistency: Doing the same thing every time will work eventually. All adults who interact with the child must agree on strategies and when to use time-out.

- Willingness to change: A child's behavior will not change by itself. The only way to make positive changes in the child's behavior is for adults to be willing to change their own behavior and modify what they have been doing in the past.

Linda Levine, Ed.D., is an educational consultant and therapist in Tucson, Arizona. Her specialties include early childhood, advocacy, inclusion, and attention disorders. She is the author of several articles featured in Communication Skill Builders handbooks.

Help at Playtime

Clare B. Jones, Ph.D.

Many children with Attention Deficit/Hyperactivity Disorder (ADHD) find it difficult to keep and make friends. It is hard for their peers to understand their loud, rough, and out-of-control behavior. Other children initially will be drawn to the spontaneity, joy of life, and enthusiasm of the individual with ADHD, but playmates' early interest dwindles quickly when they learn that this child's behaviors include bossiness, anger, and exceedingly selfish attitudes. Who would want to play with a child with these traits?

We can help the child with ADHD learn to play better, and the result should be fun for all concerned. The child with attention concerns responds best to activities that are brief and offer variety, yet have easy-to-understand, well-structured routines and order. The secret to playing with a child who has ADHD is to start slow and proceed in short, brief segments. Begin by offering numerous activities and games. Choose games that have a simple format but encourage variety (for example, patty-cake, clap or pattern games, "I spy" games, finger plays, tic tac toe, preschool Lego®). If you choose board games such as Candy Land®, limit participants to two initially, and set a timer for short breaks during which the child can move, leave the area, and return. When you return after a break, quickly review what has happened in the game so far and what will come next. As the child's concentration increases, you can introduce games that will help focus attention and patience, such as pick-up-sticks, checkers, Advanced Lego®, and Connect Four®. Gradually increase the time and eventually introduce a third player.

Practice Play

Before your child gets ready to participate in larger group games, introduce role playing to deal with possible challenges. Act out "true-to-life" experiences. For example, another child knocks over the board game or Lego® structure. Model with your child the appropriate response. The following language might be helpful: "It is great to know you know how to be a good sport. Show me how you act if a friend gets angry when you win." Another choice could be, "I might win this game, or you might win. Will you cry if I win?" Labeling the behavior and then modeling helps the child see it in a very visual way. It also demonstrates the negative behavior, which should look very silly to the child. Children often will respond by laughing, "No, I won't cry if you win." This eases possible pent-up feelings and makes the game playing more relaxed.

Provide ongoing and immediate feedback as you play with your child: "I know friends will like to play with you. You play nice and are fair." Then *specifically* point out what you saw about the child's behavior that was nice or fair. Also try this: "It is great that you know how to take turns. My turn—your turn—you follow game rules." It helps to use physical modeling as a clue to your turn taking. Place your open palm on your chest for "my turn"; face your palm outward and extend your hand toward the child for "your turn."

Help Through Hobbies

Play also can involve collections or hobbies. As a child begins to collect certain items and display them, the child will learn categorization, order, and classification. Hobbies can reinforce skills of tolerance, waiting, or saving for a specific object. They also reinforce patience and order. Some typical collections for younger children include:

- Beanbag characters (new and retired)
- Sport card collections
- Models
- Rocks, shells, different types of wood
- Books about a subject (planes, birds, dinosaurs)
- Action characters and characters from movies or books
- Teddy bears

Learning and performing magic tricks can provide positive play experiences for many children with ADHD. They thrill to the activity of doing a trick and enjoy the special attention it draws from others. Magic is an individually taught skill and gives the child an opportunity to develop a specific talent rather than compete with a peer for a prize, touchdown, or home run. The child moves ahead in magic as he or she personally acquires skills. This self-paced learning complements the typical learning style of children with ADHD.

There are some commercial games for active children age 6 and above that are fun and instructive:

- Electronic Simon®, a battery-operated, color-coded game to enhance memory skills (Coleco)
- Listening Lotto®, an audiotape that encourages matching sounds with pictures on a lotto board (Educational Insights)
- Guess Who?®—a game of details in visual pictures (Milton Bradley)
- Concentration®—a memory game of pictures (Milton Bradley)
- Kat Tracks®—counting and following simple directions (Educational Insights)
- Sesame Street® Games for Growing— beginning reading and sound/symbol games (International Games)
- Nerf® gym balls, bats, and footballs
- Make a Game—a kit to make your own game (Child's Work–Child's Play)
- Somebody—simple anatomy (Aristoplay)

Clare B. Jones, Ph.D., is an educational consultant and diagnostic specialist at Developmental Learning Associates in Phoenix. The author of three books on attention disorders, she is a nationally recognized presenter in the field of attention disorders and special needs.

Managing Your Child in Public Places

Linda J. Jones, Ph.D.

Have you often wished, while standing in the grocery store check-out line with your incredibly energetic and curious child, that you had on a T-shirt that read, "It's not bad parenting, it's ADHD!"? You might lack the energy to explain to all those looking on with such questioning, scornful eyes all the reasons why your child acts the way he or she does. You might want to scream, "It's not the child's fault or mine, either!" That, of course, would not be an appropriate response. You can avoid getting into that frame of mind by being prepared when you go out, so you don't have to suffer through a complete meltdown.

It helps tremendously when you just accept the fact that there will be trying behaviors to deal with when you are in any new environment or in a place with lots of visual and/or auditory stimuli, such as pizza restaurants that have animated characters and activities or indoor playrooms with various amusements. You might decide to avoid any additional difficulty with your child by staying at home and never allowing him or her to experience the outside world the way other children do. Unfortunately, that course of action only causes additional problems for children when they have to figure out how to get along at school and in the community at large, and they haven't had any experiences that require them to learn some self-control strategies.

Most of our responsibility as parents is to educate our children so they are able to live on their own some day. We wouldn't dream of teaching a child how to ride a bike without actually putting the child on a bike, so it stands to reason that we have to take our children into the community so they learn how to function and behave in different public environments.

Plan Outings

The first step in managing children's behavior in public is to know and understand them. What are their likes and dislikes? What will set them off or agitate them? What will calm them and help them feel more secure? How long can you reasonably expect to stay in the store, restaurant, theater, or home where you are going? Because children with Attention Deficit/Hyperactivity Disorder (ADHD) often have inconsistent behaviors, it's best to consider the extremes when you are planning for excursions in public areas.

The second step is to be aware of your personal characteristics and how they influence your parenting style. How important is it to you that your child be quiet or nondisruptive? What will you tolerate? What will you do if things don't go as planned? Are you willing to take a few more minutes to get ready to go if you can circumvent possible problems by having the right "stuff" with you? What is the right stuff anyway? If you know your child well enough, you'll have a bag of the right stuff prepared to take on excursions.

The third step is to know something about the place you are going. Is it a restaurant with a kid's menu and crayons? Will you have to wait to be seated? Will you be able to find a spot for time out in the department store if you need one? Is there an area for children to play, and is it safe for your child to remain there while you shop? Are shopping carts available?

Keep Your Child Occupied

Trips to the grocery store will be much faster and you might be able to avoid the problem aisles for your child if you are familiar with the layout. Children even might be able to help you shop if they are old enough and the store is familiar to them. Even small children can help cross items off the shopping list, count the number of cans, get boxes off the shelf and put them in the shopping cart, and look for the right kind of fruit. Think of ways you can use your child's extra energy and high degree of distractibility to your advantage.

Sandy still puts Jeffrey, an 8-year-old with ADHD, in a shopping cart at the grocery store and will continue to do so until it is uncomfortable for him. He would rather sit in the cart than hold her hand as they walk through the store. It is impossible for him to stay close to his mother with all the distractions the grocery store has to offer. Does he ever get out of the cart? Yes, and she stays close enough to catch him before he runs off, because she is familiar with his actions and also with his lightning speed! Sandy prefers catching him as he climbs out of the cart rather than catching him as he runs up and down the aisles or out the door. His attempt to climb out of the cart is a signal to Sandy that she needs to change his "job" or give him another one of his tactile toys to absorb some of his excess energy. Jeffrey's favorite toys are beads, a necklace, a slinky, a squishy ball, a pompom, and finger puppets. Sandy knows that he loves these things and they help keep him calm, so she happily carries them along on shopping trips.

For couples with children who have ADHD, it is challenging to take the time to plan favored family activities, but it makes the activity more pleasant for all family members. Sandy and her husband Mike always have enjoyed dining at restaurants and consider it a valued part of their social life. From Jeffrey's early childhood, they were determined to find ways to include him in this favorite activity. They also vowed not to go only to fast-food restaurants equipped with playgrounds! So how does it work when parents put all these steps together and plan for a successful family dinner at a restaurant? Sandy and Mike think of Jeffrey's needs first, along with the compatibility of the restaurant. As adults, they are easier to please and have learned appropriate restaurant behavior, so their requirements are fewer. Will there be food Jeffrey likes on the menu? If not, they plan to take something along for him. They always bring apple juice because he doesn't like to drink anything else.

Get Creative

Mike and Sandy make reservations when they can, but most places don't accept reservations for small groups, so waiting to be seated is inevitable. Waiting is difficult for Jeffrey, so he brings along his bag of toys and activities. Mike and Sandy keep a bag packed with small cars, books, crayons, or Jeffrey's favorite "toy of the moment" to keep him busy while they wait. It is easy to grab the bag as they walk out the door. However, if they forget or misplace the bag, they've discovered that they're not doomed to restaurant disaster. On these occasions, they invent games to occupy Jeffrey, such as playing "table football" with sugar packets, guessing the items in Sandy's purse, or walking around the restaurant to count chairs, tables, people with glasses, or people with red hair. Games of this sort keep Jeffrey entertained and allow him physical movement without disturbing other tables. Sandy and Mike cannot tolerate nasty stares and comments from other restaurant patrons, so they avoid going to places that aren't child-friendly.

Before any restaurant experience, they discuss with Jeffrey how they expect him to behave, the rewards he can receive, and what consequences will occur if he has trouble with his behavior. They reward him with his choice for dessert, extra reading time before bed, a balloon from the restaurant, computer time, or other things that are easy to give him when he needs to show greater self-control than usual. Consequences for misbehavior or noncompliance mean a time out, a trip to the car (which is a modified time out), no story before bed, no dessert, going to bed as soon as they get home, or some other prearranged consequence.

Extra planning is necessary to manage your child's behavior successfully in public. Once parents have thought it through and planned for the distractions and possible difficulties, everyone will enjoy the outing so much more, and planning for future family activities becomes easier. Be sure your child knows what you expect, and ask the child to explain the rules back to you, using *his or her own* words. Having the child restate behavioral expectations gives parents an opportunity to clarify any misunderstandings or to emphasize what might be different about the place they will be going.

Managing the child with ADHD in public places is more successful and enjoyable when parents remember to modify their planning to meet the changing needs of their child, consider what behavior they will or won't tolerate, and remain flexible and creative in new environments.

Linda Jones, Ph.D., is the parent of an 8-year-old boy with Down Syndrome and ADHD. She is an inclusion specialist/ advocate and educational consultant.

Helping Your Child Improve Attention and Listening

Clare B. Jones, Ph.D.

As a parent, you might be frustrated frequently by your child's difficulties with attention and concentration. Here are some other strategies to add to the interventions you're already using at home and at school that might improve your child's attention and listening skills.

- Encourage your child to be ready to listen and attend. To get your child's attention, call his or her name or touch the child gently. Use key words to enhance focus (for example, "One-two-three," "Eyes here," "Turn to me," "Here we go").

- Whenever possible, eliminate the distractions. Turn off the TV, radio, or water faucet before speaking to the child. Encourage your child to learn to modify him- or herself and/or the environment by making changes that increase and enhance attention. Some children prefer background noise while they are working on homework, particularly during repetitive activities (such as copying spelling words or doing math facts sheets). Other children prefer complete quiet and want to wear earplugs or earphones as they study.

- Use a strong and slow voice. The message will be clearer if the volume level is good. A slower rate of speech gives the child additional time to process the message.

- Make your message more interesting by using inflection, animation, and stress in your voice. People who vary their tone and volume are exciting to listen to. Avoid repeating the child's name over and over again.

- Use body language. Gestures and facial expressions are helpful to a child who has difficulty attending and listening, and they give your child an added visual component.

- Be specific in your instructions. General directions result in limited success. Specific directions make a point and can be followed exactly.

- Shorten and simplify your information. Be direct and simple. Use short sentences and concrete sentence structure. Unique words will grab your child's attention.

- Break up or chunk verbal information, especially directions, into short phrases. Remember to pause between chunks. Specify key points by numbering. For example, you might say, "You need two things before we can leave: one, your library book; and two, your library card."

- Allow extra time to process auditory information. Some children need time to process the first message before receiving additional information. Count silently to 10 before expecting an answer.

- Repeat directions. You might need to restate directions after allowing the child adequate time to process the information. Try to repeat directions in a different way to keep your child from tuning out similar requests.

- Recheck understanding. Have the child repeat the auditory information. This is a positive way to determine if he or she heard the message. Hearing a message more than once will help the child remember it better. Ask the child to "show you" what you asked or expect. Modeling or acting out a direction gives the active child an opportunity to move.

- Give listener breaks. Allow a break from concentration on tasks such as homework or practicing a musical instrument. Frequent breaks prevent fatigue that can occur from the demands of listening. Set a timer to help you and the child keep the breaks consistent.

- Model nonverbal feedback in conversation. Because of their difficulty with concentration, children with attention disorders often will look around and fail to make eye contact. You can help such children by modeling the following behaviors: Demonstrate how to face the speaker, illustrate that eye contact allows people to look interested in what someone is saying, and model facial expressions such as surprise, frowning, confusion, or smiling. Ask your child what he or she thinks you are feeling based on your facial expression. Point out that many people make different facial expressions and that it is important to filter out the difference between an expression and a verbal command.

These suggestions should help your child begin to be more of an active listener and increase his or her concentration in a variety of activities. Remember, your role as an advocate also is to model good concentration and attention. Your child will look to you as the number one role model.

———————————————

Clare B. Jones, Ph.D., is an educational consultant and diagnostic specialist at Developmental Learning Associates in Phoenix. The author of three books on attention disorders, she is a nationally recognized presenter in the field of attention disorders and special needs.

Language and the Child With Attention Deficit/Hyperactivity Disorder

Laura Beth Michon, M.S., CCC-S

If your child has been diagnosed with Attention Deficit/Hyperactivity Disorder (ADHD), he or she also might have difficulty with language. A speech-language pathologist (SLP) can evaluate your child's language. If your child has a language disorder, the SLP might recommend speech therapy. If your child does not have a language disorder but is having difficulty using language effectively, the SLP can offer suggestions to help you and your child communicate more effectively.

How Can ADHD Affect Language?

ADHD can affect your child's language skills negatively in one or more of the three main language areas of form, content, and use.

Form: the rules of the speech sounds (phonology), the rules of word formation (morphology), and the rules of sentence formation (syntax).

Content: the meaning of language (semantics).

Use: the use of language in social contexts (pragmatics).

A child with ADHD can have difficulty with:

1. Attention and distractibility. ADHD can affect one or all five areas of attention:

   Vigilance. The child appears to have disorganized language. The child also might react inappropriately to partial information, then not be ready to hear more information.

   Selective attention. The child appears to misunderstand language. The child "selects" the wrong information from the message, then responds inappropriately.

   Focused attention. The child seems to have difficulty focusing on a topic or a task.

   Sustained attention. The child has difficulty listening and following multiple commands or long discussions.

   Divided attention. The child has difficulty organizing and coordinating two ideas or tasks at once.

2. Overarousal can affect language greatly. The child might not follow the guidelines for social behavior, due to misunderstanding of the social cues for behavior.

3. Impulsivity can affect form, content, and use. As with attention problems, the child might answer questions without having all the information needed to answer correctly.

4. Problems with delaying gratification can have a great impact on language use. The child tends not to wait for confirmation before acting on desires.

Some language problems associated with ADHD include difficulties with:

1. Pragmatic skills. By not focusing on the social cues, the child is not able to monitor behavior adequately.

2. Problem solving. Decreased focus can hinder recognition of important details necessary for basic problem solving.

3. Auditory processing. The child has more difficulty focusing on and interpreting what he or she hears. If your child does not hear all of the information, there is nothing for the child to refer to. Giving visual information can be helpful.

4. Extracting detail. The child has difficulty choosing the information needed for an appropriate response. This can affect the child's ability to sequence information. A person first must recognize all the important details in order to sort them out and put them in the proper sequence.

5. Associative control. The child is not able to control the thought processes necessary to stay focused on language.

6. Topic maintenance. The child has difficulty staying focused on the subject of conversation.

7. Topic switching. The child seems to get stuck on the previous topic of conversation.

Communication Strategies

How you talk to and interact with your child is important. Be a good communicator.

- Talk in quiet places. Turn off the television or radio. Move to a quieter place.

- Get your child's attention before talking. Say, "Listen to me," or "This is important."

- Make eye contact before giving or repeating instructions. Talk at your child's eye level.

- Give hints. Use a key word for your child to focus on, such as, "Chores. Did you do your chores?"

- Get to the main point and stay focused. Talk only about what is important.

- Simplify language. Use short sentences. Give single directions.

- Confirm understanding. Ask a question to see if your child understands.

- Take turns. Only one person talks at a time.

- Have reasonable expectations. Give your child enough time to answer questions and complete tasks.

- Respect your child as a communication partner. Praise your child for trying to listen and talk.

- Reassure your child. Let your child know that it's always safe to try, even if it takes longer to give the message or the other person doesn't hear it perfectly.

Try to avoid:

- Talking over noise.

- Talking before getting your child's attention.

- Looking away when speaking.

- Changing topics in the middle of a conversation.

- Talking in long sentences. Giving multiple directions.

- Walking away without checking to see that your child understands.

- Talking while your child is talking.

- Comparing your child's communication and behavior to others' skills.

- Ordering and/or physically directing your child.

- Pressuring your child to do what you want in the time you want it done.

Remember that successful communication begins with joint attention and focus. Make sure that you and your child both are focused on the same topic. Here are some ways to help your child develop language and thinking skills.

- Have your child talk through a problem or situation out loud. This will help you confirm what your child already understands and will help your child see the situation more clearly.

- Foster independence by creating a system. Use writing and/or pictures posted where your child can see them as a reminder of the child's responsibilities. This will help your child focus on what he or she needs to get done.

- Practice role-playing. Pick a situation where your child acted inappropriately. Act out that situation with your child. Take turns in different roles. Praise

your child for appropriate language and/or behavior. Help your child see what he or she needs to change and what choices the child has in that situation.

- Give clear, consistent choices and consequences. This will help your child learn to predict and take responsibility for his or her actions and choices.

Summary

ADHD can create language difficulties for your child. You can help your child by becoming a better communicator. With your help and support, your child can develop better language skills.

References and Resources

Berk, L. E., and Winsler, A. (1995). *Scaffolding children's learning: Vygotsky and early childhood education.* Washington, DC: NAEYC.

Gonzalez, J. J., Heyer, J. L., Newhoff, M., Peters-Johnson, C., & Silver, L. (1992). The impact of Attention Deficit/Hyperactivity Disorder (ADHD) on the communicative abilities of children, adolescents, and adults. Paper presented at the ASHA Teleconference, Cleveland State University, Cleveland, OH.

Jones, C. B. (1998). *A sourcebook on attention deficit disorder for early childhood professionals and parents.* San Antonio, TX: Communication Skill Builders.

Wallach, G. P., & Butler, K. G. (1994). *Language learning disabilities in school-age children and adolescents.* New York: Merrill.

Laura Beth Michon, M.S., CCC-S, is a speech and hearing therapist in private practice with Excel Communications in Phoenix. She specializes in young children with oral motor challenges and bilingual language needs.

Practical Strategies for Enhancing Social Skills

Terri A. Fong, LCSW, BCD

As Carla watched her 8-year-old son Josh approach the car, she was looking for signs of whether this had been a good schoolday or a bad one. Just the look on his face would let her know what the afternoon would be like.

Josh was moving slowly, his shoulders were slumped, and his head was down. He opened the car door, threw in his backpack, and shouted, "I hate Mike! It's his fault that I got into trouble again." Carla felt her body growing tense. This was going to be a tough afternoon. She was at a loss about what to do. Getting along with others and making friends was not easy for Josh—*how could she help him?*

Children with attentional and/or learning difficulties sometimes have difficulty mastering social skills. This is because the challenges of impulsivity, inattention, distractibility, nonverbal language difficulties, or processing problems also can interfere with a child's ability to figure out social signals and cues and to learn strategies for coping with frustrating social situations. The good news is that social skills are "learned" behaviors. And with a little creativity and patience, parents, teachers, and other significant people in your child's life can help foster good social relationships. Here are some ideas:

- **Identify what social skills you would like your child to learn.** Try to break the skills into specific behaviors. For example, divide listening skills into smaller steps: (a) Look at the person who is talking, (b) think about what they are saying—without interrupting, and (c) wait until the person finishes talking.

- **Build in a sense of mastery.** Start with specific skills the child can master easily. As your child acquires these skills, build upon your child's success and introduce other skills that might be a little more difficult. If you start with the most difficult skills (such as controlling anger), your child might feel less successful and stop trying.

- **Let your child know what he or she did right.** Telling children what they did wrong does not necessarily give them the skills to do what is right. Letting your child know what he or she did right motivates the child to repeat the behaviors you want to see.

- **Take pictures of your child performing the skill you want him or her to do.** Visual reminders can be helpful. For example, take a picture of your child waiting quietly while you are on the phone. Place the picture near the phone. The next time you are on the phone and your child wants to interrupt, point to the picture. Remember to praise lavishly if your child is able to wait until you are off the phone!

- **Create opportunities for positive interactions with other children.** Have your child invite another child over for a visit. Limit the time spent to what your child can handle successfully (perhaps 30 minutes). Increase the time as your child is able to interact successfully with another child.

- **Create social situations around activities at which your child excels.** If your child is good at making paper airplanes, help your child plan a paper airplane–making event with a friend. Involve your child in planning the activity by reviewing how the child can share his or her special talents with the playmate.

- **Build coping strategies into activities.** Help your child learn how to cope successfully when an activity does not turn out as he or she hoped. For example, Josh would get upset while playing a board game if another player sent his game piece back to "start," and he would retaliate angrily. With some practice, Josh was able to say, "Oh, well," and remind himself that it was just a game.

- **Help your child find the words to describe what he or she is feeling or experiencing.** Children with attentional and learning difficulties often need help in developing the emotional and social language to describe what they are experiencing. Help your child "name" specific emotional experiences. Model this behavior by naming or describing what you are feeling or experiencing.

- **Help your child identify social signals and cues.** Some children have difficulties recognizing other people's reactions to their own behaviors. One way to increase your child's ability to identify social signals and cues is to spend short periods of time observing interactions between other people. For example, as Carla and Josh watched a videotape of the *Cosby Show*, Carla would stop the video and ask Josh to predict how Theo's dad would react to Theo's behavior. Spending time with your child studying another person's body language (facial expression, body gestures, and tone of voice) can help your child recognize the impact of his or her behavior on others and begin to identify his or her own reactions to others.

- **Rehearse special events.** In preparing for special events, such as birthday parties or holiday gatherings, take time with your child to practice the skills you would like him or her to demonstrate. Josh's birthday was approaching, and he wanted to have a few of his friends over to celebrate. Carla and Josh spent time rehearsing how to be a good host, practicing how to greet others, share toys, take turns, thank guests for their presents, etc.

- **Allow time in your child's schedule to enjoy relationships with others.** It is important that children have time to play with other children.

For some children with attentional and learning difficulties, social skills take time to develop. The more opportunities your child has for successfully practicing friendship-making skills, the greater is the likelihood that the skills will "stick."

Terri Fong, LCSW, BCD, is a licensed social worker with Learning Development Services in San Diego. She is also an adjunct professor with the University of San Diego.

Section 5

School Issues

Being an Advocate for Your Child in the School System

Clare B. Jones, Ph.D.

5.1

Finding the Right Environment for Your Child

As parents of a young child, you are concerned about and interested in your child's education. You want to provide for your active child in a positive manner. Under IDEA (the Individuals with Disabilities Education Act), you may contact the local public school to see if they offer a preschool program for children with developmental concerns. Local school district "roundup" or "child-find" programs for children with special needs might be a place to start if your child with attention concerns also has a language disability or other handicapping condition.

The child with attention deficits might not be eligible for a public school program if no other handicapping condition is present. In that case, you would need to seek outside education programs such as private preschools, Headstart, and daycare situations.

Parents of a hyperactive child can have trouble finding the right preschool environment that is conducive to learning and growth. Look for preschools with a developmentally appropriate curriculum. Also, ask the preschool secretary or person in charge if the school has been recognized as providing developmentally appropriate curriculum. The National Association of Early Childhood Programs has a credential program that gives validation or recognition to preschools that meet their rigid criteria for appropriate curriculum. Ask if the preschool you're considering is a part of this program.

Some parents find that their active child does best in a home-centered daycare or preschool with a lower child-to-caregiver ratio, so that the child has more one-on-one experiences with adults. This is a helpful way to guide the child slowly into larger group activities. The active, spirited child will need more than the usual amount of structure and modeling of appropriate behavior during the toddler years.

Throughout the community, there are various opportunities for helping you learn more about your child's behavior and the symptoms of Attention Deficit/Hyperactivity Disorder (ADHD). Some of these resources include: (a) local Children and Adults With Attention Deficit Disorder (CHADD) group meetings (see the References and Resources list at the end of this article), (b) community college courses on active children, (c) commercially offered parenting classes (such as Active Parenting), (d) parent classes offered at mental health clinics and facilities, and (e) parent classes offered at religious centers, public schools, and Headstart centers.

Obtaining Services for Your Child

Children with attention disorders might be eligible for services and support under varying laws for children with handicapping conditions. Two important federal regulations that support the service plan for the child with attention concerns are Federal Law 94-142, now called IDEA and Section 504 of the rehabilitation law of 1973. Federal regulations require a written individual education plan (IEP) for each area in which the child is deemed eligible to receive services. The IEP the school creates for 3- and 4-year-old children must be designed specifically for their individual needs and requires parents' participation in the development of the plan. The needs of the child and parents, as well as other resources available to the school, will dictate the type and amount of additional parental involvement and adult support.

Depending on how much the different therapists and educators work together in a given school, each professional might develop an IEP for the child, or the team might develop a joint IEP. The team develops an IEP when the child with ADHD has been identified as having an additional handicapping condition such as a learning disability or significant language delay or if the team feels an IEP is the best way to provide services for the child. The 504 plan is developed when additional documentation of another handicap is not necessarily available but the team is interested in ensuring that the child with attention concerns does not fail in the learning environment. The team members provide a series of interventions that should accommodate for his or her present weaknesses in attention, impulsivity and hyperactivity. Section 504 protects all students with disabilities defined as having any physical or mental impairment that substantially limits one or more major life activities, including learning.

Accommodations for young children include clustering activities into short chunks, eliminating distracters in the immediate play area, designing a structured environment in the classroom, and providing immediate reinforcement. The plan also might describe a specific behavior plan for caregivers, teachers, and aides to follow when the child exhibits excessive impulsivity. The value of such a formal document is that it encourages the team to put in writing specific strategies to implement for this child. This helps to guarantee the child's right to a free and appropriate education based on individual needs.

The accommodation plan is a simple, one-page document that presents the nature of the concern and the basis for the determination of the disability. It then describes how this challenge affects one or more of the child's major life activities and designs some reasonable accommodations within the schoolroom. The team members give their suggestions, decide on the plan, sign it, and place it in the child's cumulative file.

Summary

When your child enters any type of formalized learning experience, be it daycare, preschool, or elementary school, you begin to be part of an educational process that will continue for more than 18 years. Most parents of school-age children never will have the experience of being on a multidisciplinary team that focuses on their child, nor will they need to be aware of IDEA and 504. For you, however, as the parent of a child with specific needs, it will soon become matter-of-fact.

References and Resources

Children and Adults with Attention Deficit Disorder (CHADD)
8181 Professional Place, #201
Landover, MD 20785
(301) 306-7070
Home Page Address: www.chadd.org

Clare B. Jones, Ph.D., is an educational consultant and diagnostic specialist at Developmental Learning Associates in Phoenix. The author of three books on attention disorders, she is a nationally recognized presenter in the field of attention disorders and special needs.

Developing an Intervention Plan at School   5.2

Susie Horn, R.N.

If you are the parent of a child with Attention Deficit/Hyperactivity Disorder(ADHD), you often worry about what will happen if your child experiences difficulty at school. Will your child receive the necessary help? Will his or her specific problems go unrecognized and untreated? Will the child lose his or her ambition? Parents realize that so much is at stake because children with ADHD are especially prone to behavioral and emotional difficulties. Children who experience too much failure in their lives are vulnerable to a wide range of complications. In managing their children, how can parents put the expertise of private practitioners and school personnel to work for themselves? This article describes the multidisciplinary team your child's school will set up to help you identify successful strategies and modifications for your child.

When a student is experiencing difficulty in school, the school will call on their multidisciplinary team, referred to in most states as the Student Study Team (SST), to intervene. In the case of students with ADHD, the team's goal is to determine how attentional problems are interfering with the child's academic success and social interaction, then to develop a plan to address those needs. Depending on the district's support personnel, the team could include the classroom teacher, special education teacher, school psychologist, administrator, school counselor, speech pathologist, school nurse, and parents. The team develops the plan based on the information shared by the various team members. Parents are a key part of this team and bring valuable information about their child.

The Student Study Team

The diagnosis of ADHD historically has been the responsibility of medical doctors. In recent years, however, this process has shifted so as to obtain information from multiple sources. This method ensures that the diagnosis is accurate and helps the team plan the most comprehensive approach to managing the complex needs of this particular child. The school can do a formal assessment that includes (but is not limited to) a review of school records, a psychosocial/developmental history, behavior observations by at least two professionals other than the classroom teacher, academic productivity measures, behavior checklists completed by parents and teachers, and statements from the teachers describing the areas of difficulty. Although the child might not need a complete set of psychoeducational tests, develop-

ment of the educational plan requires some evaluation of the child's learning abilities.

Whether or not the student receives a formal diagnosis of ADHD and/or learning disabilities (LD), the team can begin to formulate a plan of intervention. Typically, the team will meet again 4 to 6 weeks after putting the plan into action, to evaluate the plan's effectiveness and change it if necessary.

Federal law protects children's rights. These protections fall into two categories for students with ADHD: Section 504 of the Rehabilitation Act of 1973, which requires a free and appropriate education for students who have a disability that substantially interferes with a major life activity, and the Individuals with Disabilities Education Act (IDEA) for students who have a learning disability and or attentional problem to such a degree that it requires special education.

Working Together

One of the most important aspects of being the parent of a child with school challenges is to provide the best educational situation for the child. One of the most effective ways to accomplish this is to develop a collaborative relationship with the school. Collaboration refers to several parties working together toward a common goal that they cannot achieve alone. "ADHD is a problem shared by child, parents, school, and pediatrician. Optimal management requires communication, and input, ownership, and 'buy-in' from all" (Altemeier & Horwitz, 1997, p.738).

One of the first things you can do to collaborate with your child's school is to find the person at school who cares and knows about your child. This person often will advocate for your child and be able to help you deal with the other school professionals. Identify the professionals—the school counselor, nurse, resource specialist, or school psychologist—who are most knowledgeable about ADHD, and meet with them early in the school year. The school can provide ongoing information about your child's learning and behavior, which is extremely valuable to the physicians and therapists working with the child. You'll need to be willing to give permission for the exchange of medical, academic, and behavioral information so that the school, family, and community, working in partnership, can develop and monitor an appropriate plan.

When developing intervention plans, both parents and school professionals should come to the table with a positive attitude. Here is a suggested format for the meeting:

1. Pinpoint the problem. What is happening in the schoolroom?

2. Analyze where the breakdown comes. When does the child appear to struggle most?

3. Divide up the responsibility for change. Assign each team member a responsibility.

For example, if a child is struggling to complete homework and is taking a long time to finish it, teachers can modify assignments, post the assignments clearly in the classroom, and assign homework partners so students record the assignments properly. Parents check assignment books, provide a regular time and place to do homework, and communicate with the teacher about the amount of time the student is spending on assignments.

Many children with ADHD are taking medication in addition to the educational interventions. It is important to decide which member of the team will be responsible for managing the medication. Often the school nurse coordinates the administration of the medication, assessing its effects and side effects and communicating the information to the physician and family. In the absence of school nurses, another school professional will fill this role.

There are many examples of successful curriculum modifications for students with special challenges. Your child might benefit from untimed testing or a reduction in the amount of work the student must copy from board to paper. The child might profit from listening to a tape of a textbook while reading along. The student might be more successful with a laptop computer to take notes in class. These changes, or "accommodations," as they are called by the school, allow your child to perform at his or her personal best. Accommodations provide opportunities for students with ADHD to succeed.

Summary

ADHD requires a multidisciplinary team approach for diagnosis, intervention, and management. The multidisciplinary team operates for your child's benefit. Your role as your child's advocate and the leader of the team is to make sure your child has every opportunity to learn and grow. When schools, parents, and community providers work as a team, the child benefits.

References and Resources

Altemeier, W. A., & Horwitz, E. (1997). Working with the school to manage attention deficit hyperactivity disorder. *Pediatric Annals, 26(11),* 737-744.

Hartwig, E. P. (1997). Q and A. *The Special Educator,* Vol. 13, Issue 5, LRP Publications.

Jones, C. B. (1994). *Attention deficit disorder: Strategies for school-age students.* San Antonio, TX: Communication Skill Builders.

Susie Horn, R.N., is the lead nurse for the San Diego Unified School District and the director of the San Diego PARD program, a project to train teachers in the management of ADHD.

Parents as Partners

Clare B. Jones, Ph.D.

Working with teachers on a daily or weekly basis increases the chances of success for your child. When you talk frequently in a positive manner with your child's teacher, you demonstrate your concern for your child's success and your willingness to be a partner with the school to ensure that success.

The average teacher today has received very little information about working with children who have Attention Deficit/Hyperactivity Disorder(ADHD). In fact, if you are a concerned, informed parent, you might know more about attention concerns than the teachers. Unless teachers take special workshops on attention deficits or have their own personal knowledge of it, they might not know how to meet your child's specific needs. So far, only two states (Tennessee and Virginia) have mandated that all teachers in their state receive training in attention deficits. Your child's teacher might appreciate the following information about classroom techniques that are appropriate for children with ADHD. Throughout the year when you see your child benefiting from a particular strategy, take the time to reinforce and praise the teacher. Present yourself as a well-informed, pleasant, caring parent who is sharing new, exciting information that might be helpful for the teacher.

Suggestions, Strategies, and Modifications for the Classroom

Listed here are some suggestions the teacher might want to try if your child has problems in the various areas of classroom behavior and skills.

Getting Started

- Give a cue to begin working.
- Give work in small amounts.
- Explain the purpose for the assignment.
- Provide immediate feedback
- Give suggestions about an appropriate amount of time required for each task.

Staying on Task

- Have the child work at a clean desk.
- Allow the child to hold one object while working.

- Place the student with a child who can provide immediate help.
- Reduce distractions.
- Increase reinforcement.

Staying in Seat

- Make sure the student knows your expectations.
- Ask the student to sit in his or her seat for a set time limit and reward accordingly.
- Move the child's seat away from distracters, such as doors and mobiles.
- Isolate and give time outs as needed.

Following Directions

- Use concrete directions and vocabulary.
- Use fewer words.
- Provide visual examples.
- Repeat instructions in a unique way.
- Have the student repeat and explain your instructions.
- Provide a peer tutor.

Working Independently

- Assign tasks at the appropriate academic level.
- Be sure the child can see an end to the task.
- Give concrete, precise directions.
- Reinforce often. Give praise for concentration.
- Help the student see individual work as a sign of personal responsibility.
- Alternate short, independently completed tasks with tasks on which you give assistance.
- Gradually require more independent work before you give help.

Completing Assignments

- Give assignments that ensure success and completion.
- Collect assignments as soon as the student completes them.

- Reduce size and length of assignments.
- Have a row captain or assigned classmate collect homework and check whether it has been returned.
- Use a special cue for homework collecting time, such as music, a hand clap, or reciting of a poem or verse.

Taking Tests

- Double-space typed tests.
- Allow the student to take tests orally.
- Use multiple-choice tests, well marked and color coded. Allow the student to use a ruler on the scan sheet to separate rows visually.
- Look for alternatives to evaluate students' learning (i.e., project, discussion, report).

Needing a Great Deal of Personal Attention

- Move the student's seat closer to teachers and aides.
- Assign a peer tutor.
- Check with the student as soon as the lesson begins.
- Give positive yet constructive criticism often.
- Try to catch a child doing something right on his or her own without prior direction or correction.

Participating in Class

- Have the student meet with you before class and work together to organize notes and materials. Make a "cue sheet" of important thoughts and points. Later, call on the student, allowing him or her to look at the cue sheet you reviewed earlier together.
- Accept all responses as worthwhile.
- Ask some simple yes/no questions.
- Try not to single out or focus attention on the child in front of his or her peers.

Following Classroom Rules

- Place rules in classroom to review daily. Use variety as you review.
- Set simple rules to follow. Give all children a list of rules to keep on their desks.
- Be consistent in consequences and expectations.
- If necessary, make separate rules for the child. Arrange a "contract" privately with the student, helping the child state the responsibilities and how he or she will accomplish them.

Listening

- Give visual clues to model and follow.
- Tape record important material for the student to review.
- Have the student repeat instructions orally to you or to peers.
- Seat the child in front of the room or close to where you teach.

Copying Notes From the Blackboard

- Have the student copy from another student's notes.
- Let the student copy from your notes. Add visual clues to notes.
- Give the student a preprinted copy of the notes you write on the board.
- Provide an incomplete outline that the student fills in during note taking.
- Make an audiotape of the notes.
- Have the student give a sheet of carbonless paper to a capable student, so the student with ADHD can get a copy of good notes.

Remembering

- Write goals and assignments on the board. Color-cue all assignments. Orally review the assignments. Have students repeat them orally with you.
- Write the exact page and place of the assignment on a board or overhead transparency that remains visible throughout the class session.
- Have a classmate write down the assignments for the student.
- Use a mnemonic or verbal clue to remind students at the end of the period about certain tests, assignments, etc.
- Leave test reminders and other cues on a special voice-mail system so students can call in once they are home.
- Post assignments outside of the room so a student walking through the hall can check the information without entering your room.

Clare B. Jones, Ph.D., is an educational consultant and diagnostic specialist at Developmental Learning Associates in Phoenix. The author of three books on attention disorders, she is a nationally recognized presenter in the field of attention disorders and special needs.

Coaching: What Is It? How Can It Help?

Mark S. Majalca, PPO

Coaching is an instructional activity that helps individuals achieve their goals by building their organizational and time-management skills. Most coaching activities with children who have Attention Deficit/Hyperactivity Disorder (ADHD) involve schoolwork because, regardless of their good intent, students with ADHD often have missing, incomplete, or late schoolwork assignments. And even when students complete their school assignments, their teachers often never see it.

When parents become involved with their children's school assignments and class preparation, the children sometimes view them as "pushy" and are unaware that the parents are offering support. This type of perspective limits the assistance parents are able to give and puts stress on the parent-child relationship. Learning to be a parent/coach for your child with ADHD offers a solution to this common family dilemma.

The Parent/Coach

A parent/coach views the child from a neutral standpoint. When coaching, the parent eliminates all negative or judgmental comments, replacing them with positive and encouraging ones. A coach offers suggestions and support based on what the child wants to accomplish.

Understanding the child is essential for any parent who takes on the coaching role. Your child is not you. Your school experience was different from your child's, and obtaining information about his or her school experience is a critical first step. Allow your child to express his or her needs, wants, and goals. A coach does not say, "Do it this way"; a coach is aware of the task and encourages the child to identify ways to finish the task successfully.

An important component of encouraging task completion is to suggest ways to break down the task into smaller parts the child can complete easily. The coach gives further suggestions and encouragement when the child loses attention, needs information, or asks for help.

- The child expresses his or her choices about what he or she needs to accomplish.

- The parent/coach offers suggestions that might improve on the child's choices.

- The child decides what he or she will accomplish. The parent/coach helps the child identify realistic and successful steps for the task.

- The parent/coach allows the child to do the work, offering encouragement and positive suggestions.

- The parent/coach is the child's advocate.

It is important for any coach to know the player's skill. Initially, many parent/coaches assume they know their child's strengths and areas that need improvement. However, because children with ADHD tend to have low self-esteem, parents sometimes overfocus on the child's problems and have difficulty identifying areas of talent or strength. Ask someone else to watch your child and point out possible strengths or abilities. Share this with your child. Specifically praise your child for these strengths, and help your child begin to acknowledge these strengths verbally.

Coaching involves building skills and talents. Therefore, it is critical to identify areas of strength and focus on these. Building on strong points gives children the solid foundation they need to help them understand the areas for improvement. The coach-child relationship is **positive**. Remember, there are always different approaches to every hurdle your child encounters.

Coaching Your Child

Coaching works when the child is in charge of goal setting, and the coach assists the child with those goals. Respect the goals your child identifies! Refrain from the "parent" desire to choose for the child. Let your child make the choices about his or her goals for achievement in any given subject.

Have your child write down what he or she wants to do and what he or she wants to improve. Make a plan together and set starting dates) progress check dates, and completion dates. Once you've established the dates, look into steps that are needed to accomplish the goal.

1. Identify time lines, potential distractions, and materials and work space the child will need.

2. Type or write down blocks of time allotted for the project, eliminate distractions, obtain materials, and clear work space areas.

3. Start the project one step at a time, checking off blocks of time as the child finishes each portion or project.

4. Review each section as the child completes it. Make corrections together as needed until the child finishes the project.

Remember, you and the child can take any block of free time to move ahead through the process, which then gives the child additional time for other activities. Above all, monitor and discuss progress daily or as often as needed. You need to be there to offer ideas and suggestions when your child is confused or feels frustrated.

Getting a Head Start

You can help your child succeed at school by providing the following equipment. These items can help your child stay organized as he or she moves from one classroom to another.

- D-ring binder with clear plastic pocket on the outside, so students can display their schedules right up front
- Colored clear-plastic double-pouched index dividers for incoming/outgoing homework assignments
- Adhesive dots in assorted colors
- Monthly calendars
- Clear-faced pencil pouch with metal rings
- Sticky-note tabs and 1" x 1½" fluorescent adhesive-backed squares
- Three-hole punch for papers
- Individual journal for each class

Life at Home

Home life can be as challenging as school for the child with ADHD. Starting or completing chores, writing phone messages, and attending to personal hygiene are common difficulties for these children. To assist your child in household duties, review areas that could stand improvement. If your child has a tendency to forget to write down phone messages, place a fluorescent-lettered sign next to the phone that states, "Please write it down," and keep a pad with an attached pencil next to the phone for messages.

Break household chores down into small steps, to help your child understand what the chore involves and what he or she needs to accomplish. The typical strategy of asking the child to "clean up your room" often isn't going to produce the desired results. The child pulls the bedspread over the wrinkled sheets, pushes toys under the bed, opens a desk drawer and scoops everything on the desktop into the drawer, blows the dust off the book case, throws dirty clothes into the closet, and proudly announces, "Mom, I'm done!" Sound familiar? It is more helpful to describe the specific steps this child would need to follow to tidy the room successfully:

- Make bed, straighten and tuck in sheets, straighten bedspread over bed.

- Clear off desk, placing pencils and pens into holder, papers into file folders.
- Put toys into box or on shelves.
- Hang up clean clothes.
- Separate dirty clothes into whites and colors, and place in baskets in laundry room.
- Use duster to dust room, shelves, bookcase, and desk.
- Vacuum carpet and under bed.

It is important to make a timetable of your child's daily routine, from Sunday through Saturday (see sample chart).

Sample Daily Chart

6:30 a.m.	Wake up
6:40 a.m.	Bathe/Shower, brush teeth
7:00 a.m.	Get dressed
7:25 a.m.	Make bed
7:30 a.m.	Breakfast
7:55 a.m.	Brush teeth, floss
8:00 a.m.	School bus/drive to school
8:30 a.m.	School

List all classes attended for the day and after-school activities

4:00 p.m.	Home from school; get snack
4:20 p.m.	Start homework
5:00 p.m.	Break (if necessary)
5:10 p.m.	Resume homework
5:55 p.m.	Clean up for dinner
6:00 p.m.	Dinner
6:45 p.m.	Clear dishes; do chores
7:00 p.m.	Break
7:10 p.m.	Complete homework, study or leisure time
8:00 p.m.	Break; have parent(s) review homework
8:10 p.m.	Make corrections to homework
9:00 p.m.	Get ready for next day: put all school books and homework into backpack, lay out clothes
9:20 p.m.	brush teeth, put on pajamas, tidy up bathroom, take dirty laundry to hamper
10:00 p.m.	Bed

Include personal hygiene tasks in the daily chart. Children with ADHD pay attention to color, so highlight the most important tasks. If your children brush only their front teeth and neglect the rest of their mouth, show them the proper way to brush. Teach them how to use dental floss and mouthwash. Explain the importance of brushing their teeth properly.

When showering or bathing, some children will wash the top of their heads, then rinse, and think their hair is washed properly. Some will stand under the shower without locating or using the soap and feel they have washed properly. Show your child the correct way to shampoo the entire head and how to rinse out all the shampoo. Teach the proper use of a washcloth or body sponge with soap. Again, explain why washing the whole body this way is important.

Once your child has seen the proper way to complete a task, he or she might be more open to taking on new tasks. Above all, talk **with,** not at, your child. Listen to, as well as hear, what the child is saying. You are this child's advocate and he or she does look up to you for guidance.

Mark S. Majalca is a professional ADHD coach (PPO). He coaches children, youth, and adults in private practice in Tucson, Arizona.

Home-School Communication

Candace S. Bos, Ph.D.

"If I can give you one piece of advice about raising a child with attention problems, it is to be consistent at home and school," comments Janice, the mother of a challenging and successful middle-school student with ADHD.

"What a difference it makes for Jon when his parents and I are consistent, coordinated, and communicate regularly," comments Ms. Christiansen, the teacher of a busy second grader with attentional problems.

If you speak with almost any parent or teacher who is working to help children and students with ADHD be successful in school, he or she will stress the importance of communication between home and school. Experts in the field agree that one of the keys to success for students with ADHD, whether during preschool, the elementary years, or during adolescence, is consistency at home and school as well as communication that rewards students for controlling their attention and behavior in both settings (Barkley, 1995; Cohen et al., 1992; Fowler, 1992; Jones, 1991).

Why Is Communication Between Home and School so Important?
Consistent Expectations at Home and School

Home-school communication allows for consistency in expectations both at home and at school. It is difficult for some children with ADHD to adjust to different expectations. Obviously, rules are going to differ somewhat between home and school, just as they do between the playground and the classroom. But guidelines that are consistent in both settings are helpful for children who are working to control impulsive behavior, focus their attention, and complete their work. For example, when Ms. Christiansen and Jon's parents communicate to Jon that they expect him to finish his work at school each day, complete his homework each week, and do work that is thoughtful and neat, Jon is getting one consistent message. When his work for the week comes home on Friday, his parents reward and congratulate Jon for work completed and assist him in finishing work suggested by Ms. Christiansen. The expectations in both settings are the same. If Ms. Christiansen or Jon's parents are concerned about the level of the expectations, then they can meet or talk by phone to discuss what is best for Jon.

Common Language at Home and at School

Home-school communication promotes common language. At every age, but particularly at the preschool and early elementary levels, it is important to use the same language to promote positive behavior. For example, when Sean, an active 4-year-old, was hitting and poking his classmates at school and his sister at home, Sean's parents met with his teacher. They decided to use the same words to remind Sean about his hitting and to reward his positive behavior. Consequently, Sean soon began to hear, "This is not a hitting school" and "This is not a hitting home." At the same time, both at home and at school, Sean was hearing, "You're playing just great with... ." That common language emphasized the consistency of the rules at home and at school and helped Sean improve his social skills.

Monitoring Progress

Home-school communication is important also in monitoring student progress. One frustration for parents, teachers, and students is when everyone realizes too late that a student is not doing well in school. Setting up a home-school report and reward program can help alleviate this frustration (Bos & Vaughn, 1998; Barkley, 1995). When Jon's parents had their first grading-period conference with Jon's first-grade teacher, it was clear that attention and social talking were problems for Jon, particularly during the morning when the students rotated among seat work, art center, math workshop, and reading group. Because Jon could not read easily yet, they developed a pictorial report/reward checklist that Jon and his teacher completed each day and that Jon brought home for his parents to sign (see example).

Classroom Participation Checklist

Name: _Jon_

Day: _Nov. 11_

		Seat Work	Listening	Math/Art	Reading
Listen to directions. Ask an adult for help.		☺	☺	☺	☺
Do my work and finish it.		☺	☺	☹	☺
Talk only when I am supposed to.		☺	☺	☹	☺
How did I do?	?	☆	☆	☹	☆

A good day except Jon had a little trouble concentrating during art.

Sample of Jon's pictorial report/reward checklist

The icons were important because they allowed Jon to read his checklist easily. And Jon's teacher used similar signs to cue Jon when he was not listening or working or was talking too much. Even as early as first grade, Jon's teacher was asking him to make judgments about his own behavior as reflected in the "How did I do?" question. At first the checklist went home daily, and each week Jon and his teacher set a goal of a good report on a certain number of days out of 5. Jon and his parents planned something special for the weekend when he reached the goal. Gradually the number of days for the goal increased, and eventually the checklist came home weekly. Jon's teacher used a similar checklist again in second grade when it was necessary for Jon to monitor his attention and social talking more closely. His art and music teachers used the same behavioral goals and forms. This consistency between home and school and between grade levels and teachers allowed Jon to focus on the behaviors he wanted to improve.

Monitoring Medications

Home-school communication is vital if the child is on medication for attention problems. It is important that the school nurse and teachers be aware of the type of medication, the dosage, and any changes in medication. It is not unusual for the school to give medication, particularly if a child needs a dose during the day. It is also impor-

tant that you provide the appropriate release forms and keep the prescription filled. Additionally, it is essential that you report any changes in medication, because the teacher can be a valuable source of information about how changes in dosages or types of medication affect the child in school. Phone or send a note or an observational report form to communicate with the school about the use and effects of medication.

Homework Support

As students get older, parents and teachers report that it becomes increasingly difficult for students to be successful with homework. There are several reasons for this. First, the amount of homework increases as well as the time needed to complete the homework. Second, the homework becomes more complex and lengthy as teachers require students to read books, write reports, and complete projects. Third, students with ADHD, particularly those who are hyperactive, need time to be active and do activities at which they succeed more easily. As the students spend more time on homework, they have less time for other activities.

What and when should you communicate? Janice, the mother of the teenager with ADHD, reports that communicating at the beginning of the year is one of the most critical times. At middle school, she visited or called each of the teachers and let them know of her son's difficulties with focusing and completing assignments and homework. She asked that they send complex homework assignments well in advance and that the teacher work with her son and the other students to break the project into smaller tasks, with due dates for each part. She also requested a meeting with the teacher and her son to discuss strategies if he had difficulty keeping up with the amount of homework later in the year. Finally, she worked with the teacher to establish a simple written communication system by which she and her son received a weekly progress report on homework and assignment completion. Janice feels strongly that having her son involved in this process is critical for his learning to take responsibility for his schooling. She also feels that having her son meet with teachers when homework becomes a problem provides an ideal opportunity for her son to learn about advocating for himself and setting realistic goals with the assistance of his parents and teachers.

Summary

Home-school communication is one of the keys to helping children and adolescents with ADHD be successful in school. It provides the consistency and open communication that is so important for the ongoing support of children with attentional and behavioral problems. Strategies for promoting home-school communication include:

- Consistent expectations
- Common language
- Home-school monitoring programs
- Medication monitoring
- Homework support

Whatever strategies you use, always set a positive tone. Remember, positive home-school communications are just another way in which you can bring out the best in children and adolescents with ADHD and other attentional problems.

References and Resources

Barkley, R. A. (1995). *Taking charge of ADHD: The complete authoritative guide for parents.* New York: Guilford.

Bos, C. S., & Vaughn, S. (1998). *Strategies for teaching students with learning and behavior problems* (4th ed.). Boston: Allyn & Bacon.

Cohen, M. M., Grynkewich, M., Jaffe, L., Mora, R., Nahmias, M., Powers, G., Daly-Rooney, R., & Schorsch, J. (1992). *Attention deficit disorder: A parent's guide.* Tucson, AZ: Arizona Council for Children with Attention Deficit Disorders, PO Box 3613, 85740.

Fowler, M. (1992). *CHADD educators manual.* Fairfax, VA: CASET Associates.

Jones, C. B. (1991). *Sourcebook for children with attention deficit disorder: A management guide for early childhood professionals and parents.* Tucson, AZ: Communication Skill Builders.

Candace S. Bos, Ph.D., is a professor at the University of Texas at Austin, and the author of several textbooks on students with learning disabilities. She is the former president of the Council on Exceptional Children's Division of Learning Disabilities.

What to Look for in a School Program for Your Child With Attention Deficit/Hyperactivity Disorder

Barbara K. Searight, Ph.D.

Children and adults have different learning styles. The importance of recognizing distinct learning styles is particularly critical for teachers of children with Attention Deficit/Hyperactivity Disorder(ADHD). In many educational settings, the "peg" system has evolved to deal with the large numbers of children needing to be educated. Teachers expect students, whether round or square pegs, to fit into the standard classroom. The "square-peg" students who don't fit into the round holes tend to be labeled as troublemakers, behavior problems, slow, or lazy.

To prevent your child from being viewed as a square peg unable to fit into the round hole, it's important that you take a very active role in his or her education. Before the academic year begins, you should interview your child's prospective teachers to determine if they are a good fit for your child. If a teacher does not appear to be an appropriate match, ask the principal about other options.

As you meet with the new teachers before the school year begins, provide as much information as possible regarding ADHD, other professionals involved with your child, medications and their effect, and past experiences your child has had at school. Develop a system for regular communication between home and school. If possible, include the student in this discussion.

Classroom Structure

Routines

Student with ADHD work most effectively in a learning environment with consistent, structured routines. Students perform best when they can predict the next time period or subject. Teachers should keep the activities within the period short and varied and provide frequent reinforcements (Goldstein & Goldstein, 1990).

The activities within the periods throughout the day should proceed from structured (teacher-directed activity) to unstructured (individual learning labs located around the room). It is best to have the student with ADHD start with the structured activity so that he or she will be more likely to complete the task. The more time the student is left in an unstructured activity, the more difficult it will be for the student with ADHD to return to or begin a structured assignment.

Directions

Observe as the teacher gives directions. They should be short and simple. It is helpful for students to demonstrate their understanding of what they heard by repeating the instructions back to the teacher. The teacher also might choose to assign a buddy whose role is to verify the directions for the student with ADHD.

Rules

Teachers and students should work together to develop the rules of the classroom. Although some rules are fixed, there are others that can be negotiated and allow for both classroom flexibility and student ownership. Because the child with ADHD benefits from visual cues, the teacher should post the rules prominently in the classroom. During the first few weeks of school, the teacher should review the rules every day and then periodically (e.g., every week) in subsequent months.

Space

Because your child probably will be in a regular classroom, it is not always possible to have complete control over the environment. An organized, flexible classroom, however, is much more helpful for the student with ADHD. It is also beneficial to designate a space or area to which the student can go for a short, self-imposed time out. This helps the child develop self-management skills and deal with frustration if it escalates. (Note: The teacher and students should work together to develop the rules for the time-out space. The teacher should post these rules and review them regularly.)

Transitions

Transitions between activities are often difficult for the child with ADHD. It is helpful if the teacher can bridge into the next activity by preparing the student for the subsequent event. Both verbal and visual cues can help the student make the transition from subject to subject, class to class, or activity to activity. For example, when students need to leave the classroom to go to gym, the teacher should coach the child with ADHD through the steps necessary to prepare for departure. A quick reminder of the expected behavior by reviewing the location and activities that will occur in gym and then a short reminder as to the expected behaviors upon returning to the classroom will keep the child on track.

Teaching Strategies
Goals

An effective teacher will establish both classroom and individual student goals for the academic year. Ideally the teacher, the parents, and the student jointly determine the student's goals.

It is also important to encourage students to generate personal goals. These objectives might include planning a work space at home and keeping it organized for the school year, or learning to cue oneself with a stopwatch when it is time to return to a task.

Remember: Keep goals simple and attainable. A good time to review these goals is at report card time. For some students with ADHD, it is best to review these personal goals more frequently, such as at the beginning of the year and then every month.

Reinforcement

Ideally, students should be able to tell themselves they did a good job and be satisfied. However, many students with ADHD have poor self-esteem and don't know how to reinforce themselves. Teachers and parents probably will need to reinforce the child externally. It's a good idea to have the student develop his or her own list of reinforcers.

A behavioral system should begin with low standards for success so that the student receives early reinforcement. At the beginning of the year, a student might be rewarded for staying on task for 5 minutes. The teacher looks at the child, catches the child's eye, nods, then marks a line by the student's name on the chalkboard. The teacher doesn't have to interrupt a lesson to reward the student. As the year progresses, the time interval lengthens. For example, if the student has succeeded with the 5-minute period, the interval then stretches to 7 minutes for the student to receive the reinforcement. This time span continues to lengthen as the student continues to be successful.

Self-Management

Because students with ADHD will become working adults, it is critical for them to acquire self-management skills (Cruickshank, 1979). Teachers should help students acquire the following competencies: (a) organizing their space, (b) planning their day, week, month, (c) breaking tasks down into doable steps, (d) self-pacing, (e) problem solving, and (f) conflict resolution. Because students with ADHD have a difficult time staying focused, improvement in these skills will help them generate their own structure.

The teacher and the student with ADHD should develop a system together by which the student is able to monitor his or her own activity and redirect him- or herself back to the task at hand. The student might use a chart taped to the top of the desk to record his or her activity during specific time intervals. Another option is a tape player with ear phones that beeps every 5 minutes to remind the student to be on task.

Teaching Style

The student with ADHD is best matched with a teacher who is well organized yet flexible. The teacher must have a structured classroom, maintain consistency, and have a good grasp of time management. The student with ADHD works best with an optimistic, friendly teacher who provides frequent positive feedback as opposed to one who is autocratic and rigid. Most importantly, this teacher must be able to judge if the student has the skills necessary to perform the assigned task but is limited by inattention and distractibility or whether the student simply is demonstrating noncompliant behavior (Goldstein & Goldstein, 1990).

Summary

School can be a wonderful opportunity for children with ADHD to reach their maximum potential. The partnership between parents and teachers can give the child with ADHD a chance for success and fulfillment. Understanding what the school can do, knowing the role of the teacher, and learning the strengths of your child will empower you to make that partnership work.

References and Resources

Cruickshank, W. (1979). *Learning disabilities in home, school, and community.* Syracuse, NY: University Press.

Goldstein, S., & Goldstein, M. (1990). *Managing attention disorders in children: A guide for practitioners.* New York: John Wiley & Sons. (Pages 312-327 are particularly useful.)

Barbara K. Searight, Ph.D., received her bachelor's degree in special education from Wayne State University, a master's degree in marriage and family counseling from St. Louis University, and her doctorate in public policy and administration from St. Louis University. She is currently director of the St. Louis Office for Mental Retardation/Developmental Disability Resources.

Encourage Your Child's Written Language Development

Clare B. Jones, Ph.D.

Written language is one of the means by which we send and receive information as well as store it. Approximately 60% of the children with Attention Deficit/Hyperactivity Disorder(ADHD) have difficulties with writing skills. Children who have problems transmitting knowledge and ideas effectively on paper might qualify for adjustments or accommodations in their written language skills at school.

Some simple physical accommodations in the classroom can help if your child is feeling overwhelmed by the writing demands of school.

- Make sure your child uses an appropriate pencil. Pencils with "pillows" or plastic grippers often help relax a writer's grasp on the pencil. Mechanical pencils with a built-in rubber grip are also helpful.

- Suggest that your child place his or her papers on a wooden or plastic clipboard. Sometimes this very firm surface helps an active child whose papers always seem to be sliding and moving.

- Request that the teacher adjust the amount of written work your child is required to do.

- Suggest that your child be allowed to have extended or additional time to complete longer written projects, exams, and reports.

- Share with the teacher that it might be helpful to grade your child's written reports with one grade for mechanics and one grade for content, then average these two grades for the final grade. This rewards your child for creative ideas and doesn't penalize the entire paper for any weakness in mechanics.

- Encourage your child to develop computer skills. Spend weekends and vacation time helping your child learn the keyboard so typing can be more automatic. Look for *Type to Learn*, a software program from Sunburst Publications that helps children grades three through eight learn the keyboard (see the References and Resources at the end of this article).

- When your child is working on a written report, help him or her brainstorm topics of interest. As your child brainstorms orally, jot down on self-stick notes the key words your child mentions. When the child starts the writing process, place the notes right on the desk so your child can refer to and recall earlier thoughts.

- Use semantic web strategies and graphic organizers to help generate thoughts for writing. Place the main topic in the center of the "web"; then, on lines extending out from the center, write the supporting details. Show your child how to use a thesaurus to find alternatives for overused words.

- Your child also might enjoy expressing his or her thoughts for a report into a tape recorder. Later, as the child writes, he or she replays the tape as a reminder of these ideas.

- Teach your child simple shorthand symbols and abbreviations so note taking can be quicker and more efficient.

- If your child is in middle or high school, you might want to request an accommodation plan in the area of note taking. In one such accommodation, an experienced class note taker uses carbonless paper to make a copy during daily note taking. Your child also takes notes but now is assured of a clear copy of notes at the end of class.

- Often the child with ADHD has difficulty starting a written report or paper. Have your child assemble pictures, graphs, maps, and diagrams before he or she begins to write a report. Together, come up with three facts about each visual aid. Jot these down on self-stick notes or a small white erasable board. These notes then serve as a starting point from which your child begins the written report.

- Break writing tasks into manageable chunks. Have the child set a timer when writing and write until it rings, then take a short break for a change of pace and interest.

- Reward completion of written tasks. Let the child know you admire his or her follow-through and finished product.

- Have your child use bright, colorful paper for the rough draft. The writing activity looks different, and the colored paper adds novelty and interest to what the child often feels is a very boring task. Also, it is easier for the students to find brightly colored papers when they are trying to organize their projects.

References and Resources

Levine, M. D. (1993). *Developmental variation in learning disorder.* Cambridge, MA: Educating Publishers' Service, Inc.

LinguiSystems. (1990). *Handbook of exercises for language processing.* East Moline, IL: Author.

Sunburst Publications. (1996). *Type to learn. A new approach to keyboarding.* 101 Castleton Street, Pleasantville, NY, 10570. Order toll-free (800) 321-7511.

Clare B. Jones, Ph.D., is an educational consultant and diagnostic specialist at Developmental Learning Associates in Phoenix. The author of three books on attention disorders, she is a nationally recognized presenter in the field of attention disorders and special needs.

Cursive Handwriting

Christine R. Selger, OTR/L

Parents and teachers alike are aware that the writing process often is difficult for children with Attention Deficit/Hyperactivity Disorder (ADHD). Many of these children do not qualify for or receive special education services either through IDEA (Individuals with Disabilities Education Act) or Section 504 of the 1973 rehabilitation law. It is important to determine why and how the child is having difficulty with writing. The wonderful thing is that as a parent or a teacher you can help this child formulate positive habits that will provide the basis for a lifetime of achievement in writing skills.

Schools teach handwriting and composition so students can communicate their ideas in writing. From the turn of the century through the 1950s, cursive writing was taught using a very structured approach (the Palmer Method of writing), including writing on a vertical chalkboard, repetitive drills, preparation calisthenics, and specific teacher commands. Unfortunately, the art of teaching handwriting has diminished seriously, due in part to the advent of the computer and its widespread use throughout the schools. Consequently, the emphasis on computer literacy has reduced the importance of cursive writing, sometimes replacing altogether the need for writing by hand. It is easy to attribute the lack of cursive writing capabilities directly to the computer, but sadly, this is not the case. Many teachers do not have the preparation or knowledge to understand exactly how children learn to write, how to recognize a problem, and finally, how to implement a solution.

Handwriting is a very valuable skill to develop. It is within your ability as a parent or a teacher to help your child become proficient at cursive writing. For most of us, it will be one of the most fundamental and important skills we will learn. As in any skill, there are many sensory processes and prerequisites that must be in place to teach or learn this skill effectively.

Prerequisites for Written Language

Before any problem can be addressed, it first must be isolated and understood. Once understood, the problem then can be solved using specific teaching strategies. First, let's take a look at the gross (large body movements) and fine (small hand movements) motor skill components or elements of handwriting and some possible indicator signals of problems in the development of each component.

Gross Motor Skills

1. **Component:** Good torso stability and strength. Children should be able to keep themselves in a seated position for an extended period of time (up to 20 minutes) without needing to prop themselves on various surfaces.

   Problem indicators: The child works with the body bent over, head held up by hands, etc.

2. **Component:** Good skill using both the right and left sides of the body automatically. It is also a good sign when children can extend the right arm and move it in an arc from the left to the right side. This indicates that children will have fewer problems with the left-to-right progression needed for reading and writing.

   Problem indicators: Difficulty with hopping patterns, skipping, doing jumping jacks, or jumping rope. Ability to bounce the ball with the right hand while hopping on the left foot is another prime indicator.

3. **Component:** Normal muscle tone and endurance for the child's age, as seen in normal play and physical activities.

   Problem indicators: Delays or avoidance in physical play.

Fine Motor Skills

1. **Component:** Ability to isolate upper and lower arm function.

   Problem indicators: Difficulty in jumping rope backwards, winding toys, turning a key in a lock, and manipulating puzzles.

2. **Component:** Ability to separate the two sides of the hand for purposeful tasks.

   Problem indicators: Difficulty with tasks such as cutting, threading and sewing with a needle, and snapping fingers.

3. **Component:** Appropriate relaxed pencil grip. The wrist needs to be extended with an open web space visible. (This is the open circle made by touching the tip of the thumb to the tip of the index finger.) The child holds the pencil between the thumb and two fingers. Other positions are acceptable as long as the child's hand does not become tired, and the child extends the wrist with the web space visible and actively changing

during the process of writing. To see proper wrist position, have a child write on a vertical surface such as a wall-mounted chalk or erasable board.

Sensory Skills

1. **Component:** Age-appropriate ability in all areas of visual processing.

   Problem indicators: Difficulties with puzzles, coloring within the lines, dot-to-dot pictures, mazes, and hidden-picture books.

2. **Component:** Good tactile discrimination. This refers to children's abilities to process and interpret what they feel with their fingers and hands. Difficulty with tactile processing can cause many problems in the area of handwriting.

   Problem indicators: Cues to difficulty include the child's need to touch everything or play in messy things. The exact opposite is also an indicator: The child avoids glues and paints or washes hands constantly. A child having difficulty with this component also might avoid certain types or textures of clothing or have difficulty with having face and hair washed.

3. **Component:** Ability to motor plan with a tool.

   Problem indicators: Difficulty cutting out complex figures, assembling building toys, or following directions to assemble various arts and crafts.

4. **Component:** Good motor memory for repeated gross and fine motor patterns.

   Problem indicators: Difficulty in clapping patterns, playing "Simon Says," or learning finger plays or sign language.

Solutions

If your child is having difficulties in any of the above components, then you need to reinforce those particular areas of the child's writing program. Bombard the child with experiences in the needed areas to reinforce positive writing habits. For example, if a child seems to have poor muscle tone and endurance for seatwork, it might be helpful to have the child work while standing at a chalkboard or perhaps standing or kneeling at a desk. This will keep the child alert while simultaneously improving upper body muscle tone.

The following is a sequence for teaching writing that addresses most of the concerns listed previously. It is better to start with short, intense sessions and stop while the child is still successful. Do not push the child to his or her limit. Begin with 10- to 15-minute sessions, and expect concentrated effort from the student.

1. Eyes on target! (reminds child to keep eyes on task at hand)

2. Turn on your brain! (reminds child to think about only the task at hand)

3. Take care of yourself! (reminds child to be responsible for self and own learning)

Be certain the child understands these rules and repeats them often, both to you and to him- or herself. These rules also serve as cues to help the child remain attentive and remember to focus on the task at hand. The most important element of any writing program is to be consistent and provide many opportunities to practice.

Cursive Writing Sequence

1. **Warm up!** Use exercises such as cutting, coloring, clay activities, spinning tops, and small manipulative activities to improve the fine motor skills needed for writing.

2. **"Writer" than air!** Demonstrate how to write letters and complete words and sentences in the air. Use your whole arm, including the shoulder.

3. **"Standing" Practice.** Have the child practice writing on a chalkboard, easel, or other vertical surface. First, write with the eyes open, then follow with the eyes closed. This helps train visual memory, motor memory, and visualization. Next, spread shaving cream on a table and have the child write in it while standing (or kneeling, if necessary, keeping in mind that it's uncomfortable to be on one's knees for very long).

4. **Write words.** Remember, cursive writing is a process of connection. Reinforce the process by writing letters and words with chopsticks in salt, sand, and clay trays. Also, form the letter groups with rolled clay or playdough. This helps to increase hand strength needed for an efficient grip and writing.

5. **Play "school."** In classrooms or group situations, have children practice being the teacher and telling the others in the class or group how to write a particular letter.

6. **Move.** Change positions frequently to increase endurance as well as mental and physical awareness. Writing involves full movement from the shoulder. Children need lots of work on improving strength. Isolated movement starts in the torso before children can refine the small details of finger control and separation.

7. **Six Weeks 'Til Paper.** Have children form letters and words with other media for 6 weeks before using lined paper. It is important for children to develop their writing "autopilots" by using their large muscles (air

and chalkboard writing) and small muscles (sand and chopstick writing) before introducing them to writing on paper. This gradual process from large to small allows the muscle-brain connection to develop and be ready to use pencil and paper successfully.

Remember: Have fun! Children will be more alert and get more out of a writing program that they find fun and exciting. Use encouragement and positive words often.

References and Resources

Bell, N. (1991). *Visualizing and verbalizing* (2nd ed.). Paso Robles, CA: Academy of Reading Publications.

Benbow, M. (1990). *Loops and other groups: A kinesthetic writing system.* Tucson, AZ: Therapy Skill Builders.

Schellenberger, S., & Williams, M. S. (1994). *How does your engine run? A leader's guide to the alert program for self-regulation.* Albuquerque, NM: Therapy Works, Inc.

Thorton, T. P. (1996). *Handwriting in America: A cultural history.* New Haven, CT: Yale University Press.

Christine R. Selger, OTR/L, is a developmental teaching consultant in Tucson, Arizona, who also practices as an occupational therapist.

Helping Your Child With Math

Ann B. Welch, M.A., M.Ed.

Many children with ADHD have trouble with math. It is hard for them to remember basic facts, which are the foundation of more advanced skills. They complain that practice is boring, but they need more practice to learn. How can parents help? You can begin when your children are very young. Show your children the practical uses of math, play math games, and look for other interesting ways to practice needed skills. Talk about math in positive ways.

When your preschooler helps to set the table, tell him he is learning to be a mathematician. When your first-grader sorts coins, tell her that money is math. Let your child know you are using math when you follow a recipe, figure out how long it will take to drive to Grandma's, order new carpet for the living room, use a sale catalog, or shop for the best mortgage. Math is everywhere.

Help Your Child Get Off to a Good Start

Even very young children are learning math. Teach your child counting rhymes and songs such as "One, Two, Buckle My Shoe." Count out loud with your child. "How high can we count before the light turns green? How high can we count before your brother is ready?"

Be aware that counting out loud from memory is not the same as counting things. Your child might be able to say the numbers from 1 to 10 without being able to count three cookies. Practice counting real things, beginning with small numbers. Teach your child to touch each object as he or she counts it, then move it to one side. This helps separate the already-counted items from the remaining ones.

Many early math activities do not involve counting at all. Matching and sorting are math. Let your child play with coins, buttons, or other collections of small objects. (Make sure you watch closely until the child is old enough to keep things out of his or her mouth!) Have your child sort the buttons by color, size, or the number of holes. As you line up the buttons, talk about *first, second,* and *third.* Let your child help you sort laundry and match socks. Talk about patterns, shapes, and sizes. All these words are math words.

Teach Math With Card Games

Card games are a good way to learn math skills. This kind of practice is fun! You can begin with matching games like "Go Fish" or "Old Maid." Later, games like rummy, hearts, or cribbage teach more advanced skills. You use an amazing amount of math when you play solitaire. Your child must think about color as well as numbers and count backward as well as forward. Playing solitaire on the computer makes it even more fun. Teenagers might be more interested in games of chance. You don't want your child to think that math is just boring worksheets.

Teach Math With Money

Do you empty your pockets into a change jar? Let your preschooler sort the coins. Elementary school students can count change. Teenagers can keep track of the average amount added each week. Then they can predict how long it will take to reach a goal. It doesn't matter if they are wrong. They need practice making predictions and seeing how close they can get.

Does your child have a piggy bank or a bank account? If not, think about starting one. Recording income and expenses and balancing a checkbook use many math skills. Even if your child needs a calculator, he or she is still thinking about math. Keeping track of his or her own money will be much more interesting than a money unit at school.

Children of all ages need chores. If your teenager helps you with grocery shopping, teach him or her to use unit pricing to find the best value. You then might want to give your teenager some or all of the money saved on the purchase. Money is a great motivator. (Because children with ADHD have trouble with impulse control, you also should make grocery lists and limit your child to only one or two items that aren't on the list.)

Help Your Child Learn Basic Math Facts

Many children with ADHD have trouble learning basic math facts. They often understand more advanced math concepts but make mistakes with simple addition or multiplication. Here are some things you can do to help.

- **Ask the teacher about games and other activities you can do at home.** Are there commercial games or computer programs that would help your child?

- **Add little rewards to encourage your child to practice things that aren't fun.** "After we work on your flash cards for 5 minutes, we can stop for a story." "As soon as you learn the four-times table, we'll celebrate with a special movie."

- **Help your child keep track of progress.** Whether your child is working on addition doubles, subtraction facts from 20, or the six-times table, make a chart showing all the facts the child is trying to learn. Work on only a few at a time. Color the box on the chart when your child has mastered that fact. If you are using flash cards, put the problem on one side and the answer on the other. Half the cards should be review facts your child already knows. Your child then puts tally marks on the backs of correctly answered cards and zeros on the backs of incorrectly answered cards. When a card has five tally marks in a row, add another new fact to the set. This way, your child will have more success than failure. Work on the cards with mixed tally marks and zeros before working on the ones that are all zeros. Can you make up a rhyme to help your child remember a fact? Can he or she draw a picture as a reminder? Is there a game that would help? Ask the teacher for ideas.

- **Once your child has learned a set of facts, work on speed.** You want the facts to be as automatic as possible. Many children find it more fun to work on math facts if you let them play "Beat the Calculator." Turn over a card and see if your child can answer it before you get the answer on a calculator. Sometimes, trade places and have the child use the calculator while you try to beat it. Let your child use a timer to see how many problems he or she can solve in a minute. Frequently, timed tests don't work well for children with ADHD, but children often regard beating the timer as a game, not a test. It doesn't matter how fast your child is at the beginning. The child should work on trying to beat his or her own speed. Of course, if your child becomes very upset with timed drills, you might want to stick to other games. You also should stop timed drills if your child makes too many mistakes.

- **Help your child find ways to be successful even if he or she hasn't memorized the facts.** Your child can find the answers with objects or tally marks, a number line or a number chart, a permanent example or a calculator. Tell your child that knowing how to get an answer in math is always more important than just memorizing it. You can be a good "math thinker" even if your memory is poor. If you want to know the price for 3 pounds of apples, you need to know whether to multiply or divide. If you know what to do, you can use a calculator. If you don't know what to do, it won't matter how well you know your times tables. Even a calculator won't help you!

- **Remind your child of the things he or she has learned.** "Look how smart you are! Just last month you could count only to 5, and now you can go all the way up to 10!" "Remember how hard it was to learn the nine-times table? Now it's a snap!" Above all, if your child is struggling with something, don't say that it's easy. If children can't do a task, they will feel even worse. If they succeed, they won't feel proud. We're proud of the hard things we learn, not the easy ones. Say, "That looks pretty tough, but I think you can do it." Look for ways to help children succeed, then remind them how far they've come.

Summary

Whether you are grocery shopping, cooking, planning a new deck, or hosting a yard sale, you are using math. Talk to your child about math. Find fun activities that include math. Use rewards to help your child stick with things that aren't fun. Work with your child's teachers. Math is a fact of life. How we treat it can make the difference between success and failure.

Ann B. Welch, M.A., M.Ed., is an educational consultant in Virginia and a doctoral student in education at the University of Virginia. She was the 1993 Council for Exceptional Children Teacher of the Year.

Learning Math Facts

Mindy Kobey, M.Ed.

Memorizing math facts can be challenging for many children with Attention Deficit/Hyperactivity Disorder (ADHD). Here are some methods that make practicing math facts enjoyable for you and your children. Use a deck of flash cards to determine which facts your child doesn't know within 3 to 5 seconds. Then, divide the unknown facts into groups of five. Work on one group until it's mastered, using one of the following games.

Dice Game

You will need: one die, two players, two sheets of graph paper with 1" squares, 20 pennies (or other small objects that fit into 1" squares.)

Prepare the game sheets: Write the numbers 1 through 6 down the left side of each sheet of paper, one number per box. Write one unknown math fact next to each number.

1.	8-2=6					
2.	6-1=5					
3.	8-3=5					
4.	9-1=8					
5.	5-2=3					
6.						

To play: Players take turns rolling a die, reading the fact next to that number on the list, then placing a penny in the box next to it. A die roll of six allows a player to mark the next box for any one of the five facts. The winner is the first player to fill one horizontal row of boxes. Repeat the game until you think the child knows those five facts. Then play again, but this time, cover the answers to the facts.

Bang! Game

You will need: two or more players, 30 3 x 5 cards, one tennis ball can (or similar), red paint or paper, one white pipe cleaner (or 6" string), kitchen timer.

To prepare game: Make a deck of game cards by writing each of five math facts (without answers) on a separate card. Write the answer on the **back** of each card. Make five more sets (for a total of 25 fact cards). Then, on the last five cards, write the word "Bang!" Shuffle the deck well. Paint the can red (or cover with red paper.) Knot one end of the pipe cleaner or string and run it through a slit in the plastic lid. (The can should look like a giant firecracker.)

To play: Place the card deck fact-side-up next to the open can. Set a timer for 2 or 3 minutes. Take turns drawing the next card and reading and answering the fact on that card. (The player may look on the back for the answer, if needed, during the first few times you play.) Players keep the cards they've answered in stacks in front of them. When a player draws a "Bang!" card, all of that player's cards go into the can. However, the game continues until the timer rings. The player with the most cards left when the timer rings wins! If the deck is gone before the timer rings, take the cards out of the can and use them to replenish the deck.

Fact Stack Card Game

You will need: two players and a deck of regular playing cards.

To prepare game: Remove the kings, queens, and jacks from the deck of cards. Call aces "ones." Decide whether to practice addition, subtraction, or multiplication facts.

To play: Shuffle the deck and deal out all the cards. Each player places the cards face-down in a stack. On the count of three, both players turn over their top card. Depending on the math operation chosen for the game, the players add or multiply the numbers on the two cards, or subtract the smaller number from the larger number. The first person to answer the fact correctly wins the two cards. If the answer is incorrect, the other player gets the cards. Play continues until (a) one player has won all the cards, or (b) one player has more cards at the end of a designated period of time. **Note: The adult always should count silently to 5 or 10 before answering, to make the competition fair.**

Board Games

Use the deck of fact cards from "Bang!" with any game board you have at home (Monopoly®, Candy Land®, etc.) Just roll a die, move your marker, and answer a fact. See who gets around the board first!

Another Idea

TouchMath® is an alternative to the memorization of facts. It is a published program that helps children compute answers to facts more quickly and accurately than using their fingers. It is based upon learning the "Touchpoints" for each numeral, 1 through 9. Once children can touch and count efficiently, they are ready use the TouchMath® process to add, subtract, multiply, or divide facts (and/or solve problems with several digits).

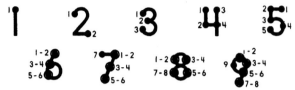

This shows the TouchMath® placement for TouchMath® numbers. Students learn basic computation by touching and counting Touchpoints in a regular pattern sequence. Reprinted by permission.

To subtract, children first learn to **count backward to zero** from any given number between 19 and 1. Then they learn the subtraction rule: "I touch the top number, say its name, and **count backward** on the Touchpoints on the bottom number." Later on, in larger problems, children immediately realize they must "borrow" when they "run out of numbers" before touching all the Touchpoints on the **bottom** number. TouchMath® can help children be more successful on classroom facts tests and with all math computation. (See References and Resources at the end of this article for the address, phone and fax numbers, and website information for Innovative Learning Concepts, Inc.)

Step 1	Step 2	Step 3	Step 4
	↓	↓	
14	67	62	83
-6	-24	-45	-36

This example shows the steps involved in the TouchMath® subtraction process. Reprinted by permission

Facts to Music

Do you remember how you learned the alphabet? Many people have memories of singing the "Alphabet Song" in their early elementary years. Children enjoy learning through hearing tones, rhythms, and patterns.

Children with ADHD who enjoy music can listen to Addition, Subtraction, or Multiplication Rap or Addition, Subtraction, or Multiplication Rock to help them memorize math facts. These audiocassettes from Rock 'N' Learn have lively rap and rock-and-roll rhythms that incorporate math facts into the lyrics. Most children have a preference for either the rap or rock-and-roll version depending on their musical tastes. (See References and Resources for the address of Rock 'N' Learn.)

References and Resources

Innovative Learning Concepts, Inc.
6760 Corporate Drive
Colorado Springs, CO 80919-1999
Phone: (800) 888-9191
Fax: (719) 593-2446
E-mail: info@touchmath.com
Website: touchmath.com

Rock 'N' Learn
PO Box 3595
Conroe, TX 77305
Call (800) 348-8445 for a free catalog.

Mindy Kobey, M.Ed., is a learning disability specialist at Ventana Vista Elementary School in Catalina Foothills School District, Tucson, Arizona.

Helping With Memory Skills

Clare B. Jones, Ph.D.

Children with attention disorder sometimes have problems with memory skills in school, particularly short-term memory. Short-term memory enables us to hold information for a brief period (just a few seconds). We can use such information immediately while it is being developed, or we can forget it almost instantly.

Challenges with short-term memory tend to produce inconsistencies in following verbal instructions; a history of trouble studying math facts, spelling words, dates, and vocabulary; and failure to use strategies of any kind while studying. Short-term memory difficulties also can give rise to confusion with sequential directions and a poor ability to summarize recently presented information.

It is difficult to overstate the importance of a well-developed memory. During our school years, we are required to recall and retrieve more diverse information and material than at any other time in our life. As a parent, you can start early to help your child remember and learn more.

Remembering Instructions

You need to realize that your child with limited short-term memory might not remember directions. Try these suggestions with your child:

1. Give instructions at the time you want them carried out. Avoid giving directions too far in advance of an activity. Rather, give the directions when you want the child to respond. This way, your child won't have time to forget your instructions.

2. When you must repeat your directions, say them in a different manner. State them in a unique way rather than repeating the same thing again and again. Restate your instructions using clear and simple language.

3. As your child grows older, have the child learn how to keep lists and take good notes as a written way of remembering.

4. Help your child act out what you asked for or repeat the directions to you.

5. Use rhythm or a pattern to help your child remember. Use a popular song or poem, and substitute the words you're asking your child to remember. This will help your child recall the information in a song pattern.

6. Point and gesture to give visual cues to your spoken words. The child with ADHD often remembers gestures and visual action such as thumbs up, pointed fingers, an open palm, a smile, hands on hips, etc.

7. Incorporate a reasonable amount of structure in your child's daily routine. Daily routines provide a certain dependability in a child's life. This helps prevent anxiety, stress, and bad situations. As a child feels more confident, he or she will be able to listen more carefully.

In some cases, stimulant medication can enhance short-term memory. Children with attentional concerns who have short-term memory dysfunctions accompanied by weak control of mental energy and processing might benefit from psychostimulant medication. The medication doesn't accumulate in the system, however, so you'll need to time the doses so that the child takes the medication appropriately before studying.

Students with attentional problems can benefit from learning about how their memory works and about the kinds of strategies they can use to make it work better. You can use many daily situations to improve your child's memory. Tell your child that, just like we practice a sport or a musical instrument, we can practice using our memory also. For example, recite a list of three words orally and see if the child can repeat them exactly. Gradually increase the number of words. Have your child repeat a series of numbers to you. Make a game of it. Say, "5-6-3. Your turn!" Don't forget to give praise and reinforcement when the child is able to remember.

References and Resources

Mastropieri, M., & Scruggs, T. E. (1991). *Teaching students ways to remember.* Cambridge, MA: Brookline Books.

Fry, R. (1994). *Improve your memory.* Hawthorne, NJ: Career Press.

Clare B. Jones, Ph.D., is an educational consultant and diagnostic specialist at Developmental Learning Associates in Phoenix. The author of three books on attention disorders, she is a nationally recognized presenter in the field of attention disorders and special needs.

Research Report Writing

Mindy Kobey, M.Ed.

Most students from fourth grade on must write research reports. Often, they do the bulk of the research and writing at home. It usually has been many years since most parents have written a research paper, and teachers often vary in the amount of guidance they give to students. This article describes some useful guidelines for helping your child successfully complete reports.

Procedure

1. **Determine which categories/aspects of the topic to research.** The teacher might provide a list or outline. If not, help your child list three to five categories or aspects of the topic to investigate. For example, the categories for a report about the African elephant might be Appearance (how it looks), Behavior (what it does), Location (where it lives), and Predators (what it endangers and what endangers it). For a report on Magic Johnson, the categories might be Childhood/Family, College Career, Professional Career, and Life After Basketball.

2. **Write each of the categories at the top of separate sheets of paper.** For the above report about the African elephant, the student would make up four sheets, one each for details and facts about appearance, behavior, location, and predators.

3. **Gather information.** Check to see if the teacher requires certain kinds or numbers of sources. Use the school or public library to find books, magazines, encyclopedias, and other reference materials about the topic. Your librarian or the computerized card catalog can help you locate the Dewey Decimal section of the library that contains books about a topic. Search the Internet, then print out the best pictures and articles. Choose as much information as possible at the appropriate reading level.

4. **Take notes.** Model this process for your child:

   a. **Recognize:** Read aloud from one of the sources. As soon as you hear a fact that belongs on one of the category sheets, stop reading.

   b. **Categorize:** Say, "That tells what the African elephant looks like. I will write that fact on the Appearance sheet."

   c. **Summarize:** Write the fact in as few words as possible (not in a complete sentence), for example, "large, leaf-shaped ears."

   Continue with steps a, b, and c, having your child gradually take over recognizing important information, categorizing it, and summarizing it in just a few words. One way to transition your child toward independence is to ask these questions as you read: "Was that an important fact?" "Which category page should I write that on?" "How can I say that fact in just a few words?" You still might need to read or write for the child, but the child should be telling you what to write. Ideally, the child soon will be able to continue on his or her own, but make sure that the child can recognize, categorize, and summarize information accurately before working independently. Write a fact only once!

   Stop doing research when you have listed enough information on each category sheet and you have used as many kinds of sources as the teacher requires.

5. **Combine related information.** Read the information, one sheet at a time, highlighting all the related information in the same color. For example, on the Appearance sheet you could use blue for all the information about the skin, green for all the information about the trunk, and so on.

6. **Draft paragraphs.** The information on each category sheet becomes a paragraph in the report, so the child first needs to decide the order of the categories in the paper. For example, the first paragraph might be about *appearance,* the second about *location,* and the third about *behavior.* Next, the child focuses on the category sheet chosen as the first topic (in this example, the Appearance sheet), numbering each color to reflect the sequence in which to incorporate the facts into the paragraph.

   The child begins with the information highlighted in the color he or she has chosen to be first and creates sentences by combining all the information highlighted in that color into one or two sentences. (Encourage the child to rehearse each sentence orally to be sure it makes sense before writing it down. This can save a lot of revision time later on.) Continue this process, color by color. Then go on to category sheet #2, repeating the process to write that paragraph.

7. **Introductory paragraph.** Help your child develop an introductory paragraph to begin the report. This paragraph might include the importance of the topic, why the child wanted to write about it, what the writer wanted to find out about the topic, the most amazing fact discovered, or questions presented to the reader.

8. **Bibliography.** Help your child list the research sources. Most teachers will provide a format. If not, use the bibliographies of the books you used for the research as models.

9. **Edit and write or type the final draft.** Include some pictures or drawings!

Summary

The most important thing to remember is to pace your-selves! Begin as soon as the child receives the assignment, and work every day for 30 to 60 minutes, depending on the age of your child. You can add interest by using interesting pens and a different color of paper for each category sheet. Best of all, you will enjoy discovering new and intriguing information together!

Mindy Kobey, M.Ed., is a learning disability specialist at Ventana Vista Elementary School in Catalina Foothills School District, Tucson, Arizona.

Independent Reading and Book Report Methods

Mindy Kobey, M.Ed.

Most teachers require monthly book reports or book projects. Getting children with attention difficulties to read on their own often is a challenge for parents and teachers.

Choosing Books

Frequently, the key is finding books at the appropriate reading level that really interest the child. To locate books at the appropriate level with some degree of accuracy, ask your child's teacher for a list of books at the child's reading level for the student to read at home. Many books have the reading level printed on the cover, usually written as grade and month. For example, RL3.4 means a reading level of third grade, fourth month. Another method you can use to test whether a book is at the appropriate reading level is to ask the child to read aloud the first page of a book he or she has chosen. If the child misreads more than five words, it is too difficult.

Children are more successful reading about topics they know about or that interest them. Many children prefer nonfiction books. You can find titles about the *Titanic;* tornadoes; treasure hunters; jets; snakes; Washington, DC; Disney World; and so on. Scholastic Books' "Hello Reading" series offers great nonfiction titles. Ask your librarian or bookstore clerk to point out nonfiction books at the reading level you need.

Reading the Book

Parents often say that their child can't remember a book after reading it. When it is time to write the book report, the child doesn't know how to begin. To avoid this problem, create a setting web (figure 1) and main character web (figure 2) on a sheet of paper.

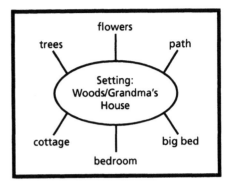

Figure 1. Setting web

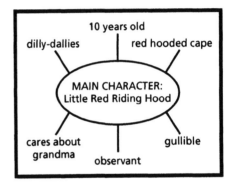

Figure 2. Main character web

While reading, the child enters information on each web. To help the child keep track of the important actions and facts in the book, show the child how to use one of the following three methods while reading: After reading each page, the child (a) uses a cassette recorder to record the key idea, (b) writes a summary sentence or phrase on a self-stick note and attaches it to the page, or (c) writes a summary phrase in the next cell of a "story trail" (figure 3.) For this method, the child might need several of the story trail pages, because each cell represents one page. Choose one of these methods, and use only one method per book!

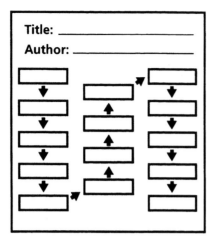

Figure 3. Story trail

Consider your child's learning style in choosing which of the three methods would be best. Children who are visual, like to draw, and notice visual details probably would prefer using the self-stick notes or story trails. Auditory learners (those who remember things they have heard) and children who have difficulty with writing typically prefer the audiocassette recorder method.

You sometimes might need to be the "secretary" for your child, writing what he or she says on the self-stick notes or in the cells of the story trails. You also might need to spend some time modeling what a summary phrase is, such as, "Treasure hunters found gold coins near the *Titanic,*" or "Rattlesnakes have brown diamonds on their back." Children usually get the idea after two or three pages. If the child rambles on and on rather than getting to the point, ask the child to say the important action or fact in **10 words or less.** Model how to do it: Hold up your hands with your fingers extended. As you say each word of the summary phrase, lower a finger.

Each day before the child continues reading, **review** the cassette tape/sticky notes/story trail the child has assembled so far. This will show the child how much the note-taking method helps keep in mind what has happened already in the story.

Book Report

Many teachers will consider the webs, audiotape, story trail pages, or self-stick notes arranged artistically on a poster a great book report. If the teacher requires another format, the work the child already has done contains all the information he or she will need to complete the report successfully. Use the setting web to create a summary of the setting in two or three sentences, use the main character web to write several descriptive sentences, or review the tape, self-stick notes, or story trail and choose five key

actions or facts to write as detailed sentences. The child can finish with a statement about whether he or she liked the book and why. Using the above methods, your child will be consistently successful at writing book reports and might even enjoy them!

References and Resources

Scholastic Books' "Hello Reading" series, available from Scholastic Books, Inc., 555 Broadway, New York, NY, 10012.

Mindy Kobey, M.Ed., is a learning disability specialist at Ventana Vista Elementary School in Catalina Foothills School District, Tucson, Arizona.

Spelling Strategies

Mindy Kobey, M.Ed.

Low test scores on weekly classroom spelling tests often baffle parents because their children seemed to know the words perfectly the preceding night. The following five strategies can help your child remember how to spell words. These novel, vivid materials and methods will help your child enjoy practicing, maintain focus, and remember the words forever!

Screen Writing

Materials

- Newsprint with 1" lines, dotted midline (first-grade writing paper)
- 12" square of window screen with the edges taped
- Crayons (plain, scented, glitter, etc.)

Procedure

1. In pencil, write a spelling word large enough to fit the 1"-lined newsprint.
2. Put the screen under the paper.
3. Have the child choose a crayon and, pressing hard, trace the word you wrote in pencil.
4. Remove the screen and have the child feel the bumpy letters!
5. Tell the child to practice the word several times by:
   - **saying** the word and
   - **spelling** the word while
   - **tracing** each bumpy letter accurately with an index finger.
6. Test the word by covering the model and having the child spell aloud while writing it. Have the child check his or her work.
7. When the child is correct, go on to the next word.

The child could use a battery-operated "squiggle pen" or scented markers instead of the screen and crayons.

Say It Strangely

Materials *(any one of the following)*

- Whiteboard and markers
- Paper and colored pencils
- Chalkboard and colored chalk

Procedure

1. Choose a word that is tricky, not spelled the way it sounds, such as *Tucson, people,* or *where.*
2. Chunk the word into parts and **say each part the way it looks**, pausing between the parts. For example,
   - Tuc – son (pronounce it "tuck" – "son")
   - pe – o – ple (pronounce it "pee" – "oh" – "pull")
   - w – here (pronounce it "w" – "here")
3. Before practicing how to **write** the word, help your child memorize the new way to **say** the word. "When I say 'Tucson,' you think 'Tuck-son.' "
4. To practice, the child:
   - **says the real word,** then
   - **writes the word while saying it strangely, pronouncing each part the way it looks.**
5. Test the word: Cover the model and have the child write it, as in step 4. Have the child check the work.
6. When the child is correct, go on to the next word.

STAR Strategy

This strategy was developed and graciously shared by Donna Buck, M.Ed.

Materials

- Graph paper with 1" squares (You can purchase this in school supply stores or draw your own and photocopy extra sheets.)
- Colored pens, pencils, or crayons

Procedure

1. Print a word, one letter per square, on graph paper.

2. The child practices the word using the **"STAR"** strategy:

   S Say the word

   T Trace and say each letter

   A Arrange the letters (child cuts out the 1" squares, scrambles the order, then rearranges the letters)

   R (w)Rite the word and check it.

3. When correct, go on to the next word.

Rhyming Method

Materials

- Paper
- Colored pens, pencils, or crayons

Procedure

1. Choose a word from the spelling list.

2. Help the child think of a word he or she **knows** how to spell that **rhymes** and has the same spelling pattern, such as *land-and, may-say,* or *took-book.*

3. Say the spelling word and the rhyming word several times to "pair" them in the child's mind.

4. Practice by having the child:

   - write the **rhyming word** he or she knows how to spell, then

   - **change it** into the list word

5. When the child can spell the new word correctly, go on to the next word.

Mnemonics Method

Note: Use this strategy **only** for unique patterns found in several words. For example "ould" works for *would, could,* and *should.*

Materials

- Paper
- Colored pens, pencils, or crayons

Procedure

1. Choose a word with a difficult pattern, such as *should* or *thought.*

2. Make up a phrase in which each word starts with a letter (or sound) of the spelling pattern. For example, a phrase for the "ould" pattern in *should* could be "oh you little doggie."

3. Write the word on paper.

4. To practice,

   - The child says the word (*should*).

   - The child circles the first sound in the word (*sh*).

   - The child says the phrase slowly while underlining the letter that corresponds to each word in the mnemonic phrase.

5. The child practices saying the phrase and writing the pattern several times.

6. Make sure that when child says the word, he or she can recall and use the mnemonic phrase without cueing.

7. When the child automatically uses the mnemonic correctly, go on to another word.

Summary

Children with ADHD will practice their spelling longer when they can use varied methods and materials. The best schedule seems to be two short (15-minute) practice sessions per day for several days. Soon, your child will be able to match a specific method to each word on the list and increase his or her ability to learn spelling words independently.

Mindy Kobey, M.Ed., is a learning disability specialist at Ventana Vista Elementary School in Catalina Foothills School District, Tucson, Arizona.

Homework: The Family Plan

Magda A. Urban, Ph.D.

For parents of children with Attention Deficit/ Hyperactivity Disorder (ADHD), homework is often an area of family tension and conflict. Children with ADHD sometimes feel that they barely survived their schoolday and just want to play and relax at home. Parents can feel that, in addition to their jobs and household responsibilities, assisting their child with homework is above and beyond their capabilities. What are students and parents to do about homework? This article includes sections on why homework is necessary and helpful, suggestions for positive parenting, viewing homework as a team effort, dealing with children who have learning disabilities, and goal setting and self-monitoring.

Why Homework?

The purpose of homework is to give students extra experience with skills or concepts they have encountered in class and to reinforce and increase their independent learning and study habits. The interplay between homework and success in school varies from early elementary, intermediate, middle, and high school years. Researchers have found that completion of homework in middle school and high school substantially raises levels of student achievement (Cooper, Lindsay, Nye, & Greathouse, 1998; Black, 1996). The amount of time spent on homework relates directly to positive attitudes toward school and increased self-esteem and self-control (Ginsburg & Bronstein, 1993; Hagborg, 1991). What are parents to do, then, when their child spends more time watching television or playing video games than doing homework?

Positive Parenting

Parents' attitudes have a significant effect on their children's approach to school and homework. When parents value school and provide positive and encouraging feedback to their children about their schoolwork, children understand that school is important and that their progress in school is noticed and appreciated. On the flip side, parents who are either under- or overinvolved with homework and are negative or critical about their child's progress in school actually undermine their child's potential for school success. Children learn from what they see parents do, not from what they hear parents tell them to do.

Consider your own attitude about school. Do you think school is a worthwhile experience for your child? Do you

encourage your child's achievement? When you have positive expectations about school for your children, they will have them too!

A Team Effort

Parents and children alike can be confused about homework assignments and responsibilities. Here is a brief description of the homework roles and responsibilities of teachers, parents, and students.

Teacher's Role

1. Create assignments that are meaningful and provide independent practice for skills covered in class.

2. Write assignments daily on the board and provide time for students to copy them to assignment calendars, or hand out prepared assignment sheets.

3. Inform students clearly of expectations about accuracy, due dates, and the time allotted for the activity.

4. Provide prompt feedback to reinforce or correct student performance.

5. Have a system for alerting students and parents of upcoming assignments and late or missing work.

6. Keep the student's unfinished class work separate from homework, unless it is the student's only homework for that class.

Student's Role

1. Record the homework assignment on a homework calendar, or be aware of an assignment on an assignment sheet.

2. Complete the homework in a timely way.

3. Ask for help from a teacher or parent when necessary.

4. Remember to hand in your homework, and hand it in on time!

Parents' Role

1. Understand school homework policies about schedules, assignments, due dates, time for assignment completion, amount of parental assistance expected, etc.

2. Provide a quiet place and materials.

3. Monitor and assist your child as necessary.

4. Obtain extra help when necessary from the teacher or an outside tutor.

5. Accentuate the positive! Encourage your child by noticing all the "right things" she or he has completed. You might say, for example, "Kathy, you have completed eight math problems already. Wonderful! I notice you are really staying with your homework!" or "Sam, you really are improving your spelling, especially words ending with 'ing'!"

Remember that positive attitudes and encouragement from parents are essential elements in setting the stage for work at home and also for homework completion.

Children With Learning Disabilities (LD)

Many children with ADHD also have learning disabilities (LD). When a child has a learning disability along with ADHD, homework becomes much more difficult to understand and complete. Therefore, parents and teachers might need to make additional refinements to help the child complete homework assignments.

Teacher's Role

1. Keep assignments short and simple.

2. Give positive and corrective feedback to students immediately.

3. Increase home-school communication so students and parents are aware of long- and short-term assignments.

4. Modify homework: For example, cut spelling lists in half, assign only even-numbered math problems, allow tape-recorded responses, or highlight important information in textbooks.

Parents' Role

1. Understand the ways your child prefers to learn and also the conditions at home that assist his or her learning.

2. Set a regular time for homework.

3. Model "study time" yourself by turning off the TV and doing quiet work (e.g., paying bills, writing letters, reading).

4. Stay in close proximity to assist and encourage your child when he or she becomes confused or frustrated.

5. Offer breaks when the child has finished a section or is tired.

Parent and Teacher

Communicate with each other! Teachers often are unaware of family stress, especially in families with children who have ADHD. Parents who feel overwhelmed about homework and how to help their child should inform the teacher(s) about the areas of frustration. Teachers have positive attitudes toward parents and students when they communicate and share common goals. Parents and students have positive attitudes toward school when teachers show respect for them. When parents and teachers maintain communication, each will identify many creative ways to assist the child with ADHD.

Goal Setting and Self-Monitoring

When you have used the preceding suggestions consistently and positively, yet homework remains a problem, how can the child with ADHD succeed? Students with ADHD use huge amounts of effort to pay attention, stay focused, and complete tasks. Goal setting and self-monitoring can help students increase their productivity with homework.

Goal Setting

Students who decide how much of an assignment they want to complete and how accurate they want their work to be can sustain effort for longer periods of time, especially when they can see their increased success on a graph or chart. For example, John wants to complete half his homework and, of that 50%, get 80% correct. John has made an important commitment to himself and intends to use the effort necessary to accomplish this goal. Some teachers and parents might be horrified about his goal because the idea should be to complete the entire assignment. However, partial completion is better than no completion at all! Students with ADHD often complete only part of their work, so John's goal of completing 50% of his homework is an admirable one. However, the point is for John to choose a goal and complete it.

Self-Monitoring

After the teacher grades John's work, John writes his goal and performance percentages on a chart. This helps him see how his performance matches his goal. Goal setting and self-charting increase student motivation and involvement in completing tasks.

What Else Helps ?

Games

Parents and children with ADHD can be productive *and* have fun with homework by playing games. Make up games to practice spelling, learn vocabulary, identify geographical areas, or improve math calculation. Children with ADHD are creative and can invent interesting and instructional games with help from teachers and/or parents. Homework games provide a fun, interactive way to reinforce and practice school learning in the context of an enjoyable family activity.

Study Buddies

Study buddies are children who are paired with each other to support and encourage schoolwork. The buddy could assist the child with ADHD by playing games to increase academic skill, writing down assignments, or organizing materials. The child with ADHD also can phone the study buddy if questions come up at home. Study buddies are best suited when children with ADHD can contribute to the relationship from their own areas of strength (brainstorming ideas, solving puzzles).

Summary

Homework is a part of any child's school experience and helps the child acquire independent study and learning habits. Parents play a supportive role by maintaining positive attitudes toward school and learning, scheduling and modeling family study times, and encouraging their child to set goals and chart progress.

References and Resources

Black, S. (1996). The truth about homework. *American School Board Journal, 183,* 48-51.

Cooper, H., Lindsay, J. J., Nye, B., & Greathouse, S. (1998). relationships among attitudes about homework, amount of homework assigned and completed, and student achievement. *Journal of Educational Psychology, 90,* 70-83.

Ginsburg, G. S., & Bronstein, P. (1993). Family factors related to children's intrinsic/extrinsic motivational orientation and academic performance. *Child Development, 64,* 1461-1474.

Hagborg, W. J. (1991). A study of homework time of a high school sample. *Perceptual & Motor Skills, 72,* 103-106.

Magda A. Urban, Ph.D., is an educational diagnostic therapist in Tucson, Arizona. A contributor to several articles and textbooks, she is a former associate professor at the University of Arizona.

More Relief for the Homework Headache

Jill Bamber, M.A.

For parents and teachers of students with Attention Deficit/Hyperactivity Disorder (ADHD), homework can be one of the biggest headaches of a child's academic career. Whether the challenge with your child's homework is getting it home, getting it done, or simply getting it over with, you're not alone. Put yourself in the position of the student with ADHD, whose schoolday is spent fighting focus and frustration: staying on task, staying in one's seat, keeping one's mind on work completion, surviving transitions, following oral instructions and directions, and the list goes on. Finally, it's time to go home—to homework.

The following guidelines will help make homework time less frustrating and more productive.

Set up a Specific Homework Area in the House

Help your child establish a special homework place. The location should be well lit and free of distractions. Have your child make a "Do Not Disturb" sign to post while doing homework. This not only will indicate to other family members that work is in progress, it also gives the child a visual cue and reminder that he or she has entered the "study zone." Gather all supplies the child might need to complete homework and keep them together, organized, and ready to use so the child won't waste time scavenging through the house in search of homework materials (Canter & Hausner, 1987).

Develop a Homework Schedule

Build homework into your child's schedule. As the child becomes older and more responsible, encourage him or her to keep an assignment book that tracks all long- and short-term assignments and helps in scheduling daily homework time. Write out daily and weekly schedules of activities (e.g., sports, music practice), family times, homework, and free time. Post the weekly schedule in a central place (e.g., the refrigerator). Use a kitchen timer to monitor work time or to help the student focus on an assignment for a reasonable length of time. Younger elementary-school children probably will need help in estimating the time necessary to complete various assignments. By their midteens, students should be able to schedule their work independently.

If necessary, set up a mandatory homework time during which students must use the entire time for homework or other academic activities such as reading, studying, doing corrections, or practicing math or other skills. Providing a mandatory homework time teaches your child that rushing through work or "forgetting" work at school does not buy extra free time (Canter & Hausner, 1987).

Work Toward Greater Independence

Homework is your child's responsibility, and you must encourage independence. Express confidence in your child's ability, help break down difficult tasks, and provide support in the steps along the way. Encourage your child to try all tasks independently first, but be sure to let the child know that he or she can come to you with any and all questions.

Praise Works Better Than Criticism

As parents, your words are more powerful than you can imagine. What you say (or don't say) is the key to how children see themselves and their abilities. Remember to praise your child's efforts constantly and specifically, describing what you like about what the child is doing (or has done). Offer rewards (additional TV time, going to a movie) to help motivate your child, then slowly phase them out as your child develops more responsibility and independence.

Challenge your child with games, goals, and "bets" to complete tasks. If needed, use a homework contract to encourage your child to accept the responsibility of an agreement. The homework contract includes points or stars for completion of assignments that the child can redeem for concrete rewards (Canter & Hausner, 1987).

Don't Do Children's Homework for Them

Calmly and clearly tell your child of your expectations surrounding homework. Many parents unwittingly end up doing their children's homework for them. This shift in responsibility often occurs because parents give in to their child's complaints that the work is "just too hard." Additionally, parents who have had a series of power struggles with children over homework completion often will find themselves doing their son's or daughter's assignments to avoid conflict. Taking on your child's academic responsibility does more harm than good. In the short run, it makes parents resentful and children doubting of their own ability. In the long run, children become less independent and do not develop skills necessary to tackle challenges and overcome adversity.

Don't get drawn into debates with your child over homework. Children often are particularly skilled at getting parents off-track and into an argument about something entirely different from the topic at hand. A discussion about homework can deteriorate into an all-out debate about the unfairness of parental rules. Consistently state and restate your expectations like a broken record. Then, if a child does not follow through with homework, carry out the consequences. The best consequences are those that are natural and logical, such as no TV or use of the phone until the child finishes the homework.

Communicate Often With Your Child's Teacher

Children benefit most often when there is a true partnership between parents and teachers. You can do your part by communicating regularly, by phone or with notes or comments in your child's assignment book. Your child's teacher might have some good ideas about how to address the homework problem. However, teachers might not know about homework difficulties unless you inform them. If work consistently seems difficult and the child appears to be giving his or her best effort, notify the teacher.

Summary

Homework habits are all about children making choices that will affect their academic careers. By laying out ground rules, organizing work space, and setting goals, you will help your child deal successfully with homework, make academic achievements, and build better self-confidence and self-esteem.

References and Resources

Canter, L., & Hausner, L. (1987). *Homework without tears.* New York: Harper Perennial Publisher.

Sawyer, V., Nelson, J. S., Jayathi, M., Bursuck, W. D., & Epstein, M. (1996). Views of students with learning disabilities of their homework in general education classes: Student interviews. *Learning Disabilities Quarterly, 19,* 70-85.

Jill Bamber is a middle-school teacher at Clayton Academy in St. Louis, Missouri. She has a master's degree from the University of Missouri in St. Louis and a bachelor's degree from Emporia State University, both in special education.

How to Select a Tutor for Your Child

Sandra L. Geraghty, M.Ed.

Tutoring can be an important part of your child's educational day. Experts are unanimous in acknowledging the benefits of tutoring for any academic problem. Most students like the idea that they have a tutor to help them stay on top of their daily work and view tutoring as a privilege. Selecting the type of tutor your child needs can be a confusing task. The following information can help you make an appropriate choice.

There are three broad categories of tutors. Read over the descriptions below to see which one best fits your child's needs.

- **Homework coach:** A homework coach models how to organize and follow through on assignments. This type of tutor helps the student with daily homework and test preparation.

- **Tutor/Teacher:** This type of tutor helps the student understand and complete homework in a specific subject. These tutors are experts in a specific topic or curriculum (such as Spanish or math) and teach skills required to master the subject.

- **Academic therapist:** An academic therapist teaches specific remedial skills the student needs to catch up and stay successful in school but does not necessarily help with homework.

Each of these tutors provides instruction in organizational strategies, time management, and study skills.

Once you decide on the type of tutor your child needs, you must find and interview prospective tutors. You can find names of tutors in your area by checking the following sources:

1. Contact your child's school and see if they have a list of tutors.

2. Call your local university or community college department of education for students who tutor.

3. Check "Tutor Services" in your local Yellow Pages.

4. Contact your local Children and Adults With Attention Deficit Disorder (CHADD) chapter (see the References and Resources at the end of this article), and ask if they have a list of available tutors.

5. Call the specialist who diagnosed your child with attention disorders for information regarding resources in your area.

6. Talk to neighbors and parents of children in your child's class for information regarding tutors.

Tutors typically charge on an hourly basis, and prices vary within communities. Tutors who have advanced degrees and certification in a specific area such as learning disabilities will charge more.

An important question to ask of a potential tutor is, "What type of instruction do you use when tutoring a student?" Ask the tutor to explain the methodology. Most tutors with experience can spend at least an hour explaining their approach in great detail. Ask the tutor to explain how he or she would individualize your child's instruction.

A tutor should be well trained in various teaching methods and understand that individuals learn differently. You will want to make sure that the work your child will be doing with the tutor matches your child's learning needs. The tutor needs to make modifications for the differences in your child's learning style as well as guiding the student to feel good about himself and what he is learning. The tutor should be able to describe a typical tutoring session and what you can expect your child to be doing during the tutorial period.

The prepared tutor will place an emphasis on organized lesson planning that includes: (a) structured teaching procedures, (b) multisensory teaching, (c) logical and sequential instruction, and (d) prolonged review (linking new learning to old).

Planning leads to a successful, well-focused lesson that utilizes the student's strengths, needs, and time. Your child should then feel and believe, "I can learn this."

A good tutor will pace the activities. While focusing on the goals of the session, the tutor will change activities in order to extend the student's attention span and avoid tiring her. This interesting, segmented format allows for individual variation.

Some tutors work with more than one student at a time. This is usually less costly but can be very distracting for an inattentive child. Most children with attentional concerns do better with a tutor on a one-to-one basis. They need direct, individualized instruction and reduction of stimuli and distractions to learn.

The rapport between the student and the tutor is very important. Look for a kind and understanding personality, someone who maintains order and sets standards for each student. Children with attention deficits generally respond to teachers who use positive facial gestures and are animated and enthusiastic in their teaching style.

Ask tutors to provide letters of recommendation from former or present clients and professionals in the field of education.

Once you select the tutor, it is important to give the tutor updated information on how the child is doing in school (report cards, notes sent home, etc.). It is also helpful to provide the names and phone numbers of classroom teachers if you wish the tutor to speak directly with your child's teacher.

"How Will I Know This Is Working?"

A good tutor will evaluate the student's performance informally on an ongoing basis in order to make instructional modifications when appropriate. You should expect periodic reports on your child's progress. It is appropriate to request a conference with the tutor to ask questions and obtain an update on your child's skills. With your child's permission, you occasionally might want to sit in on a lesson for a short period of time. Keep in mind that the tutor and the student might be working in areas of academic difficulty, which could make your child feel less than successful initially. Your child might not feel comfortable having you watch this process of acquiring a difficult skill. Let the child decide whether you can sit in.

Tutoring can be a positive experience for your child as he or she begins to develop new skills that will be tools for lifetime studying and success. As your child gathers confidence in schoolwork because of the preparation with the tutor, be sure you offer praise and reinforcement for the effort they both are putting forth.

It is important to keep the tutor informed of any changes at home that might influence your child's attitude or manner on a particular day. Model punctuality and organizational skills for your child by being on time for the appointment and by communicating regularly with the tutor. Make tutoring appointments a priority in your child's daily plan. Purchase or make a large calendar and mark the tutor appointments on it with your child. Place the calendar in a prominent place for all family members to see. This helps the child see how important you think the tutoring sessions are.

Working with a tutor can help your child feel prepared and confident in school. Take time to select a tutor you respect and your child will like. The rewards will be evident for years to come.

References and Resources

Children and Adults with Attention Deficit Disorder (CHADD)
499 Northwest 70th Ave., Suite 102
Plantation, FL 33317
(305) 792-8944
Website: www.chadd.org

Sandy Geraghty, M.Ed., is a former classroom teacher and director of reading for New Way School and is now in private practice as an educational therapist with Developmental Learning Associates in Phoenix.

Using a Computer

Clare B. Jones, Ph.D.

Parents and teachers working with children who have Attention Deficit/Hyperactivity Disorder (ADHD) often report that these children are extremely interested in computers (or, for that matter, any video-related activity) because of their variety, color, and excitement. Parents relate that although their children have difficulty sitting still in school for a variety of tasks, they are capable of sitting with sustained attention in front of a video game or computer screen for much longer periods of time. Computers, interactive CDs, and video games might interest children who have attention deficit for several reasons:

1. Children with ADHD respond best to activities that provide *brevity, variety,* and *structure.* Video games provide brevity because they contain short sequences with a minimum of delay. Novel and highly interesting software provides variety. At the same time, computer software operates within a structured format with clear operating routines and a beginning and end to each activity.

2. Children with attention deficits often are visual learners who respond well to the highly visual stimuli of video games and graphics programs.

3. Children with attention deficits need constant and immediate reinforcement. Certain software offers immediate reinforcement for a child who is learning a new skill. The programs are set up to review the same material until the child has mastered the task. If the child needs more time to review the material on the screen, you can adjust the response time. Software offers self-paced activities that guide children to develop independent work skills and motivate them to persevere.

4. The highly tactile involvement of finger to key can be rewarding to some children who need kinesthetic reinforcement.

5. One researcher suggests that many children with attention deficits maintain an illusory view of the world in which they are all-powerful. These children typically have a variety of related fantasies of self-protective strategies. Video and computer technology—especially video games that interact with CDs—provide a fantasy world in which the child can be in control and feel invulnerable.

Many parents agree that young children approach the computer-learning experience with confidence and enjoyment. Research indicates that young children working in pairs on the computer show a greater enjoyment in task involvement but don't actually show better achievement than those working alone. Such findings suggest that parents continually need to monitor children's time on the computer and provide other activities consistent with their children's competency to ensure a balanced day.

Selecting Software

Choosing software for your child is an important part of creating a child-oriented experience on the computer. Appropriately designed software can promote social interaction, academic skills, and a positive attitude about using computers. When selecting software for children with attentional concerns, look for programs that provide variety, self-paced activities, and immediate reinforcement. Software that is open-ended and controlled by the child creates different environments for learning than does fixed and lecture-type software. The operating procedures of the software should be straightforward and consistent. Programs that target skills such as sequencing, problem solving, visual memory, and selective attention are particularly useful.

Resources for Software Information

A. I. Media Company
For resources on videos, computers, and ADD/LD
PO Box 333
Chelsea, MI 48118
Phone (888) 797-1997

Computer Catalog for Special Times
Cambridge Development Laboratory
214-3rd Avenue
Waltham, MA 02154
Phone (800) 637-0047

Highscope Survey of Early Childhood Software
600 North 1st
Ypsilanti, MI 48197
Phone (313) 485-2000

Innotek, a division of the National Lekotek Center
2100 Rich Ave
Evanston, IL 60284
Phone (312) 328-0661

Clare B. Jones, Ph.D., is an educational consultant and diagnostic specialist at Developmental Learning Associates in Phoenix. The author of three books on attention disorders, she is a nationally recognized presenter in the field of attention disorders and special needs.

IDEA and Section 504: Plans and Accommodations

Gary S. Grynkewich, J.D.

In the last several years, the United States Congress has passed substantial legislation aimed at leveling the playing field for persons with disabilities. For example, almost everyone has been affected to some extent by the Americans With Disabilities Act (ADA). The ADA has recognized and, in some instances, created numerous rights for persons with disabilities and has defined the remedies available for violations of those rights.

Congress has not ignored education. The Individuals with Disabilities Education Act (IDEA) and Section 504 of the Rehabilitation Act of 1973 (known simply as "504") might be applicable for students with Attention Deficit/Hyperactivity Disorder (ADHD) so they can obtain appropriate educational plans or accommodations in the schools.

As with almost any federal legislation, the interpretation of specific provisions of these statutes can spark considerable debate. It's helpful to have a general understanding of how this legislation might apply to your situation. Being knowledgeable about these acts can be very helpful in parent/school meetings, particularly when communicating the reasonable need to accommodate a student with ADHD.

In a negotiation, a little knowledge can be a dangerous thing, and a total lack of knowledge almost inevitably spells disaster. Exhibiting comprehension of one's rights can be a powerful negotiating tool. This article provides a basic understanding of IDEA and 504, to assist you in advocating effectively for your child's education.

Both IDEA and 504 require that school systems make available a "free and appropriate public education" for students with disabilities who meet eligibility requirements. The school must provide special education and related services to any student having a qualifying disability that impairs the student's educational performance. However, there are differences between IDEA and 504. Being aware of these distinctions can be useful when negotiating to receive assistance for a child with ADHD. Additionally, it helps to have some knowledge of what educational assistance might be available under these laws when discussing your child's needs with administrators.

IDEA Qualification Criteria

To qualify for services under IDEA, students with ADHD must have at least one of the disabling conditions listed in the statute, and they must need special education and related services that address that condition to benefit from their education. ADHD is not listed as a separate disabling condition. Some students with ADHD meet IDEA qualification standards because they have a Specific Learning Disability (SLD) or Serious Emotional Disturbance (SED). However, not every child with ADHD also has an SLD or SED. If the student does not meet the criteria for any of these specific disabilities, IDEA still might apply to a student with ADHD who falls under the rather broad category of Other Health Impairment (OHI). In this circumstance, a diagnosis of ADHD alone might support the need for services under IDEA. It depends on the severity of the individual's ADHD, the impact on his or her education, and/or on the school district's policy.

IDEA Educational Assurances

Students who qualify for services under IDEA are entitled to many assurances and rights. These involve identification and evaluation of the disability, nondiscriminatory assessment of the degree of the disability and appropriate services, multidisciplinary teams, placement and services, individualized educational programs (IEPs), and legal due process. Because school districts receive funds from the federal government to provide these services, parents as well as the school district might prefer to qualify the student with ADHD under IDEA.

Section 504 of the Rehabilitation Act of 1973

Section 504 is a broad civil rights law. Its purpose is to guarantee individuals with disabilities access to a free and appropriate public education in schools receiving federal financial assistance. Section 504 protections reach further to assist students with educational disabilities than does IDEA because, under 504, the need for special education is *not* an eligibility requirement, as is the case under IDEA.

504 Qualification Criteria

Under 504, if a student has an impairment that "substantially limits a major life activity... such as... learning... or... social development," then he or she might qualify for assistance in school. If a student is limited in learning and/or social development, the child might be considered for special education *or* related services. Children might be entitled to appropriate assistance under 504 if they need classroom modifications or appliances to benefit from their education.

Section 504 requires a school district to evaluate a student if that student is believed to have a disability and is believed to be in need of services. Under 504, students with ADHD are eligible for evaluation and special education and/or related services even if they do not qualify under IDEA. This distinction might offer many students with ADHD additional educational assistance. Although many school districts have limited 504 accommodations to regular classrooms, students in special education settings also should be eligible to receive these services.

504 Educational Assurances

Section 504 is written rather broadly. The same assurances set forth under IDEA are not included in the language of 504, which has led to confusion in many school districts. However, 504 does include broad general guidelines about notice, identification, evaluation, placement, review of records, and impartial due process hearings.

The Office of Civil Rights administers compliance with 504. A district that violates the requirements of 504 is subject to possible curtailment of federal funding and may be sued by the student for money damages and attorney's fees. For this reason, parents should not overlook 504 in negotiations with a school district when they are seeking accommodations for a student with ADHD.

Accommodations

Many students with ADHD receive their education in general classrooms from general educators who are responsible for making appropriate and reasonable accommodations for these students' educational needs. Typically, children with ADHD who are educated in general classrooms receive assistance under Section 504 rather than IDEA. Therefore, it is important for parents to have a general idea of classroom accommodations that might assist their child with ADHD and therefore should be included in a 504 plan.

Accommodations can include alterations in the student's classroom surroundings, such as providing a "study buddy" for the student or placing the student nearer the teacher, away from doors, or near a fan or other device in order to block out certain noises. The teacher also might modify classroom work by giving the student study guides or outlines, assigning a note taker to provide duplicate notes, having the student reverbalize any directions to show understanding of those instructions, or using computers for drill and practice or for note taking.

Accommodations also might address independent work and tests. The teacher might allow extra time to complete projects, reduce the amount of class and homework assignments to ensure that the student understands the work, let the student record test responses into a tape recorder instead of writing them, or provide a reader to give directions on items. Accommodations for behavior might include making special note of effort and encouraging the student, providing reinforcement with breaks or special privileges, and using physical or verbal cues to stay on task.

Being aware of the types of accommodations your child could receive under these different laws will help you become a better advocate for your child and provide a more appropriate environment for your child's education.

References and Resources

A.D.D. Warehouse, (800) 233-9273. This warehouse has a free catalog of materials that include selected items and articles featuring information on Section 504.

Aleman, S. R. (1991, *CRS report for Congress: Special education for children with attention deficit disorder: Current issues.* Washington, DC: Congressional Research Service.

Cohen, M. D. (1997). Section 504 and IDEA. *Attention!, 4,* 23-27.

Latham, P. S., & Latham, P. H. (1992). *Attention deficit disorder and the law: A guide for advocates.* Washington, DC: JKL Communications.

Public Laws:

Education for All Handicapped Children Act. Public Law 94-142, November 29, 1975.

Individuals with Disabilities Education Act of 1990. Public Law 101-476.

Rehabilitation Act of 1973. Section 504, Public Law 93-112.

Gary Grynkewich is a senior partner in the Tucson, Arizona, law firm of Whitehill, Linden, Grynkewich, & Halladay, PC, 5210 East Williams Circle, Suite 500, Tucson, AZ, (520) 745-8000.

After-School Activities

D. Steven Ledingham, B.S., LNHA

The good news is we have discovered that the behaviors that drive parents crazy are the same things that drive children with Attention Deficit/Hyperactivity Disorder (ADHD) to explore everything in the world. Knowing about ADHD will give you many new options for creating an environment that is healthy for you and productive for your child with ADHD. With a positive and empowered perspective, you can promote activities that make good use of your child's time, teach essential life skills, provide educational content, use surplus energy, are fun, and improve self-esteem.

Current medical research suggests that hyperactive behavior might be due to a lack of inhibition in the ADHD brain. In practical terms, this means that the ADHD brain is free to wander without restriction in any direction, especially toward what seems interesting at that moment. When tempted toward a distracting activity, many of us without ADHD would stop and ask ourselves, "Is this practical?" or "Does this make sense right now?" **before** we stop what we are doing and start a new activity. The ADHD brain does not stop to ask these things. In fact, such questions probably don't even occur in the minds of children with ADHD. Their thought process is more like, "That looks interesting. I want it now!"

Below are eight concepts you can capitalize on to announce to a child, "Ah—now that is a great and interesting thing to do": novelty, immersion, reward, peer modeling, appropriate challenge, distracting the busy brain, allowing for "cool down" time, and the need to have fun. Understanding these concepts can help you select an appropriate and interest-building activity for your child.

- **Novelty:** The ADHD brain is constantly craving novelty. Remember, to the child with ADHD, all perceivable events and sounds receive the same value and attention. The child with ADHD has difficulty isolating any single event from all the others in the environment. Individuals with ADHD compensate by focusing on the loudest, most exciting, or most *novel* event. (If you don't believe this, watch your child channel-surf the television, stopping only for the next gunshot, explosion, or commercial.)

- **Immersion:** Children with ADHD have been described as "a-historic," that is, they have a poor sense of past and future. *The child is focused primarily on the "now,"* with everything in the present tense. If the child has had a great week but

experienced a problem 10 minutes ago, the child remains focused on the problem and the bad feelings, not on the successful week. Conversely, if the week was filled with frustration and failure but ends with success, the child focuses on that, making it difficult to learn from failure, a crucial skill. Activities that require total concentration and total involvement (listed at the end of this article) will build on this "living-in-the-now" attitude and help focus the child's concentration on the current activity.

- **Reward:** The ADHD brain might be experiencing "Reward Deficiency Syndrome," which means the child is not getting or producing enough dopamine. This neurotransmitter works to satisfy the brain's natural need to feel safe and rewarded, resulting in a feeling of being basically OK. Without enough dopamine, the child feels driven to obtain recognition, praise, and reward. (Contrary to popular myth, the child with ADHD *is more driven to succeed* than the child without ADHD.) Frequent praise and short-term recognition in the form of awards or healthy treats are valuable tools in motivating the child with ADHD.

- **Peer modeling:** Gaining acceptance and a sense of belonging are powerful motivators for the child with ADHD. With a history of getting into trouble and having few friends, the child begins to believe that maintaining friendships is impossible. Children learn by watching each other and observing how to look, talk, and act. When children have no such role modeling, they tend to isolate and withdraw. Team and group activities play a very important role in building healthy self-esteem and important social skills. Group activities need to be prominent in the child's life.

- **Appropriate challenge:** Often the child with ADHD is clumsy and has trouble verbalizing thoughts accurately, controlling anger or moods, reading and following directions, and behaving appropriately. Isolation, angry outbursts, and refusal to participate are common ways the individual tries to cover up these difficulties rather than deal with them. Caring and knowledgeable adults need to be present during the activity to see through these coverups and assist the youth in a positive and caring manner.

Remember, the child is craving praise and support, so provide reassurance and compliments frequently.

- **Distracting the busy brain:** Hyperactive children feel driven to keep some part of their bodies moving, *so let them do it!* Physically involving activities are essential and also help the ADHD brain to "normalize" in a way that increases the ability to focus, remain calm, and stay on task. Allow these children to fidget with building blocks, puzzles, or some other device (even a pencil) while you talk or read to them. Don't make them stand perfectly still and look directly at you.

- **Allowing for cool-down time:** Remember, the child will lock or hyperfocus on the current task, event, or feeling. If the child is upset or angry, create a distraction: Point the child to some other activity or conversation for a few minutes. This is often more effective than negative criticism or correction. With luck, in a few moments the child will have forgotten what caused the original upset. The goal is to minimize the negative and build on the positive. *Remain positive.*

- **Need to have fun:** Children with ADHD usually need more time to complete homework and household tasks than children without ADHD. They even might feel like they need to work all the time just to keep up, while other kids get to have fun. Be sure to put frequent fun activities in the schedule, such as going to the movies once a week, scheduling a trip to the burger place, or going for ice cream.

What Are Some Good Activities for the Child With ADHD?

Team Sports

Baseball, basketball, football, soccer—nearly any team sport that is highly physical and requires total involvement gives the child a good chance to learn social skills and be exposed to appropriate peer modeling.

Karate or Tae Kwon Do

Martial-arts activities involve positive role modeling, peer interaction, clear directions and rules, and require total mental and physical involvement and immersion.

Scouting

Scouting is an excellent activity for both young men and women with ADHD. For this to be most effective, you'll need to participate actively in the troop meetings and inform the scout leaders about ways to work with the child.

Acting or Plays

Stage and theater are excellent activities for children with ADHD. Being able to act out different characters and scenes is a terrific outlet for the creative ADHD imagination.

Model Building, Carving, Woodworking, or Mechanical Activities

Youth with ADHD often love to solve problems or puzzles. Learning how to turn ideas into concrete realities and successfully completing projects can be extremely rewarding for anyone, but especially for the child with ADHD. Once the task is done, the child has a *solid and visible message for success* that says, "I can do it! I did it!"

Swimming

This is a total-immersion activity requiring physical effort and total concentration, and it is fun.

Art Classes or Music Lessons

Encouraging self-expression in children with ADHD is essential, and art and music are two great ways to do this. Remember, this isn't just about art classes or music lessons; the goal is to increase self-expression and self-esteem.

Activities to Avoid

Excessive Television

Current medical studies suggest that the effect of viewed violence, as well as the frequent advertisements on television, can have a negative effect on the skills and values development of the child with ADHD. We know that the repeated messages used in advertising have a measurable impact on consumers. The ADHD brain appears ill-equipped to block out negative information and select only positive, healthy, or important messages, so the child takes in all messages, both good and bad. Also, as with video games (see below), television watching is a passive, isolated activity that takes time away from the patterning and development of important learning skills, social interactions, and physical exercise that children need to grow into healthy adults. In effect, television actually might make it more difficult for your child to improve learning and social skills.

Video Games

Research is showing that, in the ADHD brain, video games actually reduce baseline brain activity. The result can be that the hyperfocused brain (acting as a result of Reward Deficiency Syndrome) becomes "ADHDicted" to this activity, making it difficult for the child to set reasonable boundaries. The ADHD brain is seeking the reward of doing well in the game, to compensate for diminished dopamine levels that normally give the child a sense of well-being.

Long Waiting Periods

The child with ADHD seldom will demonstrate the patience necessary for games or activities that involve long periods of inactivity or a long sequence of steps. If the child must wait in line or if a game is slow-moving, provide snacks and small "fidget" items. Be prepared to play a talking game or tell a story.

Summary

Children with ADHD can be exciting, interested in life, intelligent, and capable. Everything in life can be interesting and engaging to them if presented in the right context. These children want success, and you can provide them with the opportunities!

References and Resources

Amen, D. G. (1996). *Windows into the A.D.D. mind.* Fairfield, CA: Mindworks Press.

Barkley, R. A. (1998). *ADHD and the nature of self-control.* New York: Guilford.

Cherkes-Julkowski, M., Sharp, S., & Stolzenberg, J. (1997). *Rethinking attention deficit disorders.* Cambridge, MA: Brookline Books.

Csikszentmihalyi, M. (1996). *Creativity-flow and the psychology of discovery and invention.* New York: Harper Collins.

Ledingham, D. S. (1996). *The scoutmaster's guide to A.D.D.* Tucson, AZ: Positive People Press.

Steven Ledingham, B.S., LNHA, is the creator and manager of ASK about ADD, a website dedicated to providing quality information about learning disabilities (http://www.azstarnet.com/~ask).

Section 6

Adolescence

Attention Deficit/Hyperactivity Disorder in Adolescence: Common Dilemmas for Parents and Teens

H. Russell Searight, Ph.D.

We've only just begun to appreciate that Attention Deficit/Hyperactivity Disorder (ADHD) is likely to be a lifelong condition for many people. There are often unique issues for adolescents who have ADHD. The teen years present new challenges even for individuals who were diagnosed in early childhood and have been treated for a number of years.

Medication

Children who have been very cooperative and compliant about taking medication on a regular basis sometimes rebel when they enter adolescence. Taking medication often makes teenagers feel different from their peers. They sometimes become acutely self-conscious about taking medication and feel that it makes them "defective" in some way.

One area of sensitivity is disclosing to peers, in particular to a boy- or girlfriend, one's ADHD diagnosis and need for regular medication. In early teenage years, most adolescents tend to go through a period where they feel they are invulnerable. This view of themselves as self-sufficient and protected from all harm can result in teenagers with ADHD feeling that they don't need the "crutch" of medication. It is often helpful to talk with these teens about other common conditions their peers might have, such as poor vision that requires contacts or eyeglasses (Robin, 1990). Similarly, inattention and distractibility are correctable with medication.

Additionally, many adolescents become acutely sensitive to any medication that is supposed to affect their mind and erroneously feel that they are "under the control of a drug." In talking with teenagers who have ADHD, it is important to emphasize that the medication does not take away their control or individuality but only optimizes their ability to achieve personal goals.

Parents, Independence, and ADHD

It is normal for teenagers to want greater independence from parents. However, teenagers who achieve a healthy separation come from families with parents who provide optimal levels of support while encouraging the adolescent's age-appropriate independence. Although teenagers should be permitted privacy proportional to their maturity (for example, requiring that anyone knock before entering their bedroom), it is important for parents to remain in control of issues such as curfew, academic standards, and knowing their children's whereabouts.

Teenagers with ADHD sometimes feel that their parents are overly focused on their ADHD. Some teenagers view ADHD as a "kid's disease" and think they should have outgrown it. Parents tend to contribute to this pattern by excusing the teenager's behavior and in particular by excusing behaviors that are not related to core ADHD symptoms. Non-ADHD behaviors include stealing, lying, and aggression. The most helpful approach is for parents to talk openly with their teenager about the ADHD-related inattention and concentration problems while emphasizing that there are a number of coping skills for managing and overcoming these weaknesses.

Schoolwork and Teens With ADHD

Many adolescents with ADHD will continue to struggle with academic work. In school, these students usually are entitled to such accommodations as extra time for tests. Teachers and parents can be of greatest help to these students by teaching them to "learn how to learn." Students at this age can develop a sophisticated understanding of ADHD and help generate strategies to compensate for their weaknesses in attention and concentration. Such strategies include making lists, using electronic schedulers, and working in short time intervals punctuated with brief breaks.

As tests in high school gain greater importance, it is crucial for students to learn effective test-taking strategies. For example, students taking multiple choice tests should recognize that when they come across a specific test question that they can't answer, they should move to the next question rather than catastrophizing ("I don't remember anything about this question; I can't think of anything about the next one either—Oh no! I'm losing my focus!! I shouldn't bother trying to finish this test!").

Parents might need to monitor homework. Teenagers should have a specific time and place set aside for homework. Although parents should not hover over the adolescent who is doing homework, they should check the work for completeness. In addition, the teenager might benefit from verbal review and quizzing for exams. Parents should allow teenagers some autonomy for homework, but the parents generally should be in the household and aware that homework is taking place (Robin, 1990).

Parental Standards and Support

It is important that parents have a strong alliance with one another. Teenagers are particularly skilled at "splitting" parents. Mother might be the "bad guy" and Father the "good guy." Teenagers also are particularly skilled at going around one parent to the other. Thus, parents need to be in constant conversation with each other about their rules for teenagers.

Parents also should pick their battles wisely (Robin, 1990). It usually is not helpful for parents to "come down" strongly on core ADHD symptoms such as fidgetiness, restlessness, and inattention. However, it is appropriate for parents of adolescents to expect respectful behavior and common courtesy.

Parents need to take time for themselves. It is important for parents to have a strong support network of friends, spouse, and extended family. Married couples should schedule regular time for themselves so that the marital relationship will continue to be strong. Individually, each parent should have time for exercise, relaxation, and quiet activities such as reading. By taking care of themselves and their adult relationships, parents will have greater patience and consistency with their teens.

References and Resources

Robin, A. L. (1990). Training families with ADHD adolescents. In R. A. Barkley (Ed.), *Attention deficit hyperactivity disorder: A handbook for diagnosis and treatment* (pp. 462-497). New York: Guilford.

H. Russell Searight, Ph.D., is the director of behavioral sciences for the Residency Program of Family Medicine of St. Louis. He is the author of several textbooks and an adjunct associate professor in the department of psychology and Community and Family Medicine at St. Louis University.

Strategies for Middle School Through High School

Clare B. Jones, Ph.D.

Middle school and high school often can be disconcerting for parents of children with ADHD. Parents are overwhelmed just thinking about whether the child will be able to handle multiple classes, cope with the great variety of teachers' styles, and deal with a busy middle or high school campus. Middle and secondary schools provide a unique set of learning opportunities and challenges for these students and their parents.

Helping Students Transition to the Complexities of Secondary Schools

For students emerging from elementary schools in which their instruction and curriculum were integrated and centered within one classroom, making the transition to secondary schools is a challenge. Students who have been successful with the continuity between instructional areas and having one or just a few teachers often have difficulty dealing with several different teachers and compartmentalized instruction. Most middle and high schools are organized on a departmental or subject matter basis. Therefore, children benefit from a strong transition program to ease them into the secondary school. It is important for the elementary teacher to collaborate with parents and secondary school teachers and provide modeling experiences prior to the student's entering secondary schools.

Secondary schools typically are large places in which students are expected to function independently, and students with attention deficits often seem overwhelmed by such a complex system. The traditional format of instructional delivery in secondary schools might not correspond at all times with your child's preferred learning style. For example, children with ADHD who have difficulty remembering information presented verbally might find that their grades suffer in courses where teachers use a lecture style. Likewise, if your child needs additional time to process information, the short class period could make it difficult to do so. Be encouraged, however: Many students with ADHD enjoy secondary school because they like the variety of teachers and the brief academic periods.

It is important for parents of students entering secondary school to visit the campus with their child before school starts, taking the opportunity to walk around the campus, to see how doors are numbered, and to walk a typical day's path from room to room. This will help the child begin to understand the organization of the school. Students with ADHD are more successful when they know what to expect. Learning how to work locker combinations, discovering the routes from one building to the next on a large campus, and locating the offices (and restrooms!) are all parts of this learning experience.

Staying in Touch With Your Child's Teachers

If your child will benefit from a 504 plan or needs to be part of an Individual Education Plan, it is your responsibility as a parent to schedule a meeting prior to school to review with teachers your child's expected individual needs. This is a long-term strategy that you should employ before the beginning of every new school year, and it will benefit not only you and your child but the school team as well.

Speak openly and to the point with teachers about your child's needs. Ask for input throughout the year, but particularly at the beginning of the school experience. Provide your phone number and times you can be reached to help teachers see that you are sincerely committed to being a responsible parent.

When you meet with the school team prior to the school year, discuss reasonable accommodations they might offer in the classroom for your child. Such accommodations for your child might include:

- Advance notice of tests and assignments
- Extended time on standardized tests
- Use of compensatory strategies
- Reduction of written tasks
- Designated places for materials
- Copies of good notes from class note taker
- Permission to audiotape class

You might need to provide additional outside support for your child in the form of tutors, organizational/academic therapists, and computer-assisted instruction. Budget now for mechanical aids that can be helpful for your child at the secondary school level, such as a hand speller, calculator, tape recorder, computer, and printer.

Be involved. Don't wait for the 8-week report from the school to find out that your child is failing. Visit the school and teachers on a regular basis, starting at the beginning of the school year, to stay in good communication. Some

Parent Articles About ADHD / ISBN 0761667512 / 1-800-228-0752 / This page is reproducible.

secondary-level schools will set up a daily assignment sheet to be initialed by each teacher and then sent home to you, brought home by your student, or faxed to your workplace. Ask about this daily assignment sheet and see if it can be part of your child's day until he or she learns to be accountable for class assignments on a regular basis. When you are involved in your child's school life, then you will be aware of what is happening on a daily basis in school.

Secondary school can be a positive, worthwhile, and exciting experience for children with ADHD and their parents. With advanced planning and organization, you can enable your student to meet the challenges of secondary school.

References and Resources

DePaul, G., & Stoner, G. (1994). *ADHD in the schools.* New York: Guilford Press.

Jones, C. B. (1994). *Attention deficit disorder: Strategies for school-age students.* San Antonio, TX: Communication Skill Builders.

Clare B. Jones, Ph.D., is an educational consultant and diagnostic specialist at Developmental Learning Associates in Phoenix. The author of three books on attention disorders, she is a nationally recognized presenter in the field of attention disorders and special needs.

Study Tools

Clare B. Jones, Ph.D.

Students with attentional concerns will have difficulties with study skills. They need help in improving organization and sequence. This article describes a variety of techniques that are appealing to the diverse learner. These tricks of the trade seem to benefit students who employ them.

Study Tools for Students With Attention Deficits

Clipboard

A clipboard gives a sturdy base to a writing activity. For children who move around frequently, the clipboard presents a strong but mobile surface for writing. It also provides a sense of order and structure for the student with attention challenges. Clipping papers to the board makes it easy to put work immediately into the book bag and pull it out quickly. For an additional benefit, tie a pencil to the clipboard.

Electronic Hand Speller With Dictionary

Research indicates that children with attention disorders often are poor spellers. They leave out important details and repeatedly misspell similar words such as *girl* and *bird*. A handheld electronic speller supports a visual learning style, and the student might remember the words more readily because of the visual imprint. Hunting for a word in a dictionary often can be tedious for someone with poor spelling and phonics skills; thus students with ADHD will find it difficult and boring. The handheld dictionary is more efficient and more motivating for them to use.

Self-Stick Removable Notes

Colored, self-adhesive notepads should be in every student's backpack. These self-stick notes come in different sizes and are helpful for writing quick messages, adding to homework lists, marking pages in books, and numerous other uses. Look for the pads that mount directly into a notebook for easy use.

Self-Adhesive Removable Tape Pop-Ups

Colorful self-stick tabs help the student flag important pages, note homework assignments, mark pages for a test, etc.

Three-Ring Punch

Many of the papers students receive during the day haven't been punched, and disorganized students tend to jam them into a notebook rather than sorting and filing them appropriately in the three-ring binder. Having a hole punch on hand encourages students to punch and organize their own papers. Try to find one that fits into the notebook.

Super-Large Three-Ring Notebook With Colored Dividers

Buy the strongest notebook you can find. It also helps to color-code the dividers to go with subjects and classes. Folders with pockets tend to end up being clutter holders, and the volume of paper stuffed indiscriminately into the folder eventually exceeds the folder's capacity. As an alternative, use clear plastic pockets that allow the student to see the materials easily.

Lightweight Mechanical Pencil and Fine-Tipped Pens

Writing is the least-favorite task for some students with attention deficits. They press so hard when they write, they are constantly having to sharpen their pencils. A disposable mechanical pencil is lightweight and produces a more fluid stroke. When these students first start using a mechanical pencil, they break the lead frequently because of the pressure they exert. Eventually they learn to compensate and actually prefer a mechanical pencil or a fine-tipped pen for writing. It helps to make their writing look crisp and legible.

Colorful Stick-On Dots and Color Coding

Students can stick colored dots on their personal calendars or on wall calendars at home to remind themselves of important upcoming dates. It is helpful to coordinate the colors to the different subjects. For example, if the math book is red, a red dot on the calendar is a reminder of math homework. Likewise, the student will use a red folder for math.

Small Handheld Tape Recorder

Students should have a tape recorder and supplies for audiotaping classes. The preferred model has a number counter, so as the student is recording a lecture and the teacher states, "This is important, it will be on the test," the student can jot down the counter number. This helps the student find the exact spot on the tape later. Tape recorders also are very helpful for foreign language classes. As they begin to learn the language, students can practice pronunciation, then listen to their own efforts.

Colorful Highlighting Markers

Different colors of highlighting pens are handy for marking notes and directions on worksheets.

Index Cards in a Variety of Colors

Students can use colored index cards to organize information quickly. For example, social studies students can write down all of the countries in Africa on cards of one color and all capitals on cards of another color. This adds an attention-focusing cue to the memorization task.

Memory Tape Disc

Some students like to use credit-card-size handheld memory tape discs that hold 3 to 5 minutes of tape. They typically cost less than $30. Students who are reluctant to write daily assignments carry these in their pockets and record their assignments after each class.

Large Colored Paper Clips

Colored paper clips are helpful for students who find it difficult to read one chapter without daydreaming or who constantly count the pages to see how many are left. They use the paper clips to divide the chapter into chunks, then read to the paper clip, put down the book, take a break, and come back ready to read the next section. This helps students stay focused through a long or tedious chapter.

Personal Organizational Planners

A daily schedule calendar or day planner book is important for any student. Let your child select one and encourage him or her to carry it to class (and use it!) every day. These planners also are available now on the computer and as part of software management.

Additional Study Strategies
High-Carbohydrate Snacks

Students with ADHD often experience cognitive fatigue when they remain too long on an activity requiring sustained attention. Proper amounts of sleep and good diet are paramount. A carbohydrate snack late in the day after medication wears off can help. Some students also find it useful to take half a dose of medication immediately after school to help with study times.

Background Noise

Music, television, or a ceiling fan on in the background can help some students with attention deficit concentrate while they work. This background or "white noise" helps them tune out many distracting sounds and concentrate on only one. Students have reported success using tapes of environmental sounds or classical music as background noise. Some students turn their room ceiling fans on high, finding the constant whirring helpful in tuning out other sounds.

Short Study Periods

Studying in small chunks of time, rather than long study periods, appears to be more beneficial for the student with attention concerns. Planning the study period to include enjoyable breaks can be motivating to the student. As your child sets up a schedule, encourage him or her to allot time for all types of activities, schedule time for relaxation, and set priorities for tasks based on their due dates.

Class Schedules

As they get older and can participate in choosing their own class schedules, some students benefit from scheduling their core courses (basic skills) in the late morning, putting high-interest classes later in the day. This tends to fit their personal time clock and make their day more productive.

Note-Taking Strategy

Students with ADHD can recruit the aid of excellent note takers in their classes, asking them to insert a sheet of carbonless paper beneath the top page on which they take their notes. The student with ADHD also takes notes but now is assured of a clear copy of notes at the end of class.

The student with ADHD will continue to need a variety of strategies in the classroom. These suggestions are just part of the tools that students with attention deficit will need all their lives.

Clare B. Jones, Ph.D., is an educational consultant and diagnostic specialist at Developmental Learning Associates in Phoenix. The author of three books on attention disorders, she is a nationally recognized presenter in the field of attention disorders and special needs.

Working Toward Homework Success for the Adolescent

Sydney S. Zentall, Ph.D.

Homework stands as a window through which parents can watch their children's ongoing education and express positive attitudes toward their children and their education. Yet this home-school connection is fragile and easily broken for families with children who have ADHD, because completing homework is so difficult for these children. Here are a number of ways to make homework more productive and positive for both parents and teenagers.

Importance of Homework

As children get older, homework and the amount of time spent on homework increase in importance. At the elementary level, students need high levels of feedback and/or supervision so they can practice their assignments correctly. In-class study time or homework with parent feedback produces better outcomes than homework completed without feedback.

For students in middle and high school, however, greater benefits come from the actual time spent working on homework. Average high-schoolers in classes that require homework perform better on standardized tests than about 70% of their classmates in classes that do not require homework. For junior high students, the difference is about 35%. Given the importance of homework at the higher levels, it isn't surprising that teachers assign more of it. The numbers that follow give some general guidelines about how much time you should expect students to work on homework:

- Elementary school: 15 to 45 minutes
- Junior high: 1 to 2 hours
- High school: about 2 1/2 hours

Common Reasons for Homework Difficulties

The amount of time a student actually spends on homework is a result of the student's abilities and motivation to achieve and the quality of instruction. Although you have less control over instructional quality, you can negotiate with teachers to alter some assignments. You might want to see if your child is more successful when the teacher reduces the length of assignments. You also should request high-interest activities or topics for elementary children and greater variety in the type of assignments at

the older age levels. As teachers in today's classrooms recognize that problem solving and experimentation are important in a world with rapidly changing information, they are giving students different types of assignments. In contrast, practice-oriented assignments involving almost all practice (worksheets, memorizing material) reflect the traditional role of schools as helping children learn a fixed body of information.

In summary, teaching quality, which includes the types of assignments teachers give, influences your child's desire to start and finish homework. Your child's abilities and learning style also will be important. Children with ADHD resist homework when it involves boring activities, such as worksheets, repetition of daily lessons, or long assignments. Older students become even more bored during homework. Children with ADHD who also have learning problems consider homework as just another opportunity to fail. Even children with ADHD who are gifted dislike homework greatly, especially when their teachers believe that children who can't do the basics (e.g., practice tasks) certainly can't do higher-level assignments. However, challenging and unusual assignments will motivate students with ADHD, and this motivation will trickle down to help them learn rote skills. They will be more likely to edit or rewrite one of their own poems to put in their portfolio rather than to do a similar activity with a worksheet.

Parental Involvement

Parental involvement—taking a general interest in your child's education—can take the form of keeping track of the student's whereabouts after school, supervising homework, or asking questions at the family table ("What did you learn today?" "Do you have any interesting or tough assignments tonight?"). When parents are involved in these ways, their children generally spend more productive time on homework.

You also can be involved at a broader level through volunteer activities in your child's classroom or school. School involvement, whatever its form, contributes to better achievement because it communicates to your child that you believe schooling is important.

You also can involve yourself in your child's schooling by overseeing conditions at home (space, siblings, noise, light, resources, TV) and regulating homework time in relation to other time commitments.

1. **Provide choice in working conditions.** Because your child grows and changes, as does the nature of the assignments, let your child select the settings for homework. Have your child try out different places for different tasks: (a) in the kitchen, bedroom, dining room, or on the stairs; (b) on the bed, floor, chair, couch, or in a tent; (c) with music, TV, or silence.

   Perhaps because of the boring nature of many assignments, junior high students seem to be more likely to do homework when there is music. During the performance of practice tasks, students with ADHD perform significantly better with music than speech or silence. Some children with ADHD can work effectively with conversations or TV in the background, especially if they are older, don't have learning problems, and are engaged in easy tasks.

2. **Plan a daily schedule.** Set and consistently reinforce a family rule (for example, "We work on homework between 5 and 6 p.m."). Use a checklist or tape-recorded list of homework, chores, and preferred activities and snacks to communicate the daily plan. A number of shorter homework periods in the late afternoon separated by preferred activities and/or chores is best, especially for children with ADHD, whose abilities to sustain attention are limited.

3. **Plan ahead positively for the month.** Use erasable or magnetic boards to break bigger projects into parts or to keep track of upcoming tests, quizzes, and reports. Help your child understand that homework isn't like medicine—it doesn't have to taste bad to be good for you. The more pleasant you can make the study conditions, the more likely your child will be to do homework.

4. **Develop a routine for returning homework.** Have your child select one or two places in the house where the backpack will stay. This makes it easier to file completed homework and return it to class the next day.

Parental Assistance With Homework

If you and your child are struggling each evening to complete homework, you might need to provide some adaptations and assistance. Students who are young, have low levels of achievement, or are learning new skills will need more assistance.

1. **Set priorities on types of assistance.** Don't allow a child's poor skills to interfere with gaining knowledge or showing what he or she knows. If your child has reading problems, read the social studies material with your child. This lets your child focus on learning about history. At a separate time, work on developing reading vocabulary with a flash card game. Similarly, it might

be important for you to come up with a different way for your child to demonstrate his or her knowledge. If the child has difficulty writing, as do most children with ADHD, he or she might draw a sequence of pictures showing the events in the story or tape or type the events to demonstrate understanding. If your child is young, you might write down the child's ideas.

2. **Don't do homework for your child.** Even though you might make an assignment easier by writing, typing, or reading for the child, rarely should you do the homework yourself. It is better for your child to do just a part of an assignment well. You can help your child to:

   a. **Get started.** Provide additional attention or show the child how to figure things out. Fathers of children with ADHD report success here.

   b. **Understand the directions.** Ask your child either to tell you what the directions mean or to use highlighting markers to underline important parts of directions. The child can use colorful markers to focus attention on important parts of the lesson (for example, highlighting addition, subtraction, multiplication, or division signs in mixed-problem computations).

   c. **Provide choice and incentives.** Mothers of children with ADHD report success with strategies that provide incentives, choice, and discussions or activity breaks between assignments. Colorful folders and supplies can be motivating and help with organization.

3. **Use outside resources.** If your child does not want help but needs it, you might want to hire a tutor, especially if the child needs to be monitored after school or has specific learning disabilities, mild mental handicaps, or oppositionality.

4. **Avoid excessive correction.** Too many corrections reduce motivation and increase feelings of low self-worth. Listen to what your child has to say about homework, and be sensitive to feelings of frustration and success. Accept the child's feelings of frustration but redirect the child to the task at hand and how best to do it.

5. **Help the child learn independence.** Eventually, it will be important to move away from adult assistance to self-help by encouraging choices and use of resources, which might include homework buddies, reference books such as encyclopedias and dictionaries, checklists, taped reminders, or step-by-step lists of components to include in each paper. It is particularly important for children to begin learning independence

prior to adolescence, when parents need to find a more delicate balance between assistance and interference.

References and Resources

Abikoff, H., Courtney, M. E., Szeibel, P. J., & Koplewicx, H. S. (1996). The effects of auditory stimulation on the arithmetic performance of children with ADHD and nondisabled children. *Journal of Learning Disabilities, 29,* 238-246.

Bryan, T., & Nelson, C. (1994). Doing homework: Perspectives of elementary and junior high school students. *Journal of Learning Disabilities, 27,* 488-499.

Cooper, H., & Nye, B. (1994). Homework for students with learning disabilities: The implications of research for policy and practice. *Journal of Learning Disabilities, 27,* 470-479.

Hall, A. M. (1997). *The effects of a homework station on the completion of math homework for middle school students.* Unpublished doctoral dissertation, Purdue University.

Jenson, W. R., Sheridan, S. M., Olympia, D., & Andrews, D. (1994). Homework and students with learning disabilities and behavior disorders: A practical, parent-based approach. *Journal of Learning Disabilities, 27,* 538-548.

Kay, P. J., Fitzgerald, M., Paradee, C., & Mellencamp, A. (1994). Making homework work at home: The parents' perspective. *Journal of Learning Disabilities, 27,* 550-561.

Larson, R. W., & Richards, M. H. (1991). Boredom in the middle school years: Blaming schools versus blaming students. *American Journal of Education, 99,* 418-443.

Miller, D. L., & Kelley, M. L. (1991). Interventions for improving homework performance: A critical review. *School Psychology Quarterly, 6,* 174-185.

Murphy, J., & Decker, K. (1989). Teachers' use of homework in high schools. *Journal of Educational Research, 82,* 261-269.

Polloway, E. A., Epstein, M. H., Bursuck, W. D., Madhavi, J., & Cumblad, C. (1994). Homework practices of general education teachers. *Journal of Learning Disabilities, 27,* 500-509.

Zentall, S. S. (1993). Research on the educational implications of attention deficit hyperactivity disorder. *Exceptional Children, 60,* 143-153.

Zentall, S. S. (1995). Modifying classroom tasks and environments. In S. Goldstein (Ed.), *Understanding and managing children's classroom behavior* (pp. 356-374). New York: John Wiley.

Sydney S. Zentall, Ph.D., is a professor in special education at Purdue University. A leading researcher in the field of attention disorders, she is a recipient of the CHADD Hall of Fame Award.

Working at Home to Manage Attention Deficit/Hyperactivity Disorder

Michael W. Cohen, M.D.

The potential impact of behavioral management in the overall treatment of a child or adolescent diagnosed with Attention Deficit/Hyperactivity Disorder (ADHD) is enormous. Long-term treatment goals include maintaining self-esteem, enhancing academic functioning and social interactional skills, and fostering effective communication within families. It is possible to reach these goals because of the pivotal emotional role of parents and because most youngsters truly want to satisfy parental expectations.

Because youngsters with ADHD are more different than they are alike, the following treatment recommendations, based on the principles of behavioral management, are general in nature.

- Provide **structure** with flexible boundaries.
- Define **expectations** regularly and consistently.
- **Subdivide tasks** into their component parts.
- Teach by **modeling.**
- Use **multisensory communication:** Provide simultaneous visual and auditory input.
- **Reward** effort in addition to outcomes or product.
- Provide **frequent positive reinforcement** even for behaviors you generally take for granted.
- Respond specifically to a youngster's **behavior,** not to the child's self-worth or value.
- Be **consistent.**
- Learn to **accept** the child for who he or she is.
- Be **patient** with the child.
- Remain **emotionally neutral** as much as possible.
- Have **patience,** because you might not see results from your behavioral efforts for months or years.

Successful intervention requires intensive strategies throughout the child's day. However, most parents find that successful strategies require no greater expenditure of energy or time than their previous attempts to manage, which generally didn't work.

Promoting Self-Esteem

- Reward effort rather than always focusing on outcome or product. This ultimately will help increase your child's willingness to attempt future endeavors.

- Always begin a new challenging task by defining expectations in a way that allows your child to experience initial success in a realistic, age-appropriate fashion.

- Highlight the difficulty of a task while expressing confidence in your child's ability to complete the task.

- Help your child recognize and identify his or her emotional reactions to the outcome of any effort. Label your child's feelings ("That sounds frustrating" or "You sound sad"), talk about them, and receive the feelings as an honest expression. Don't supply automatic, artificial reassurance ("You'll do fine").

- Always be aware of your child's strengths, guiding him or her toward activities that express those strengths, and allow the child a maximum feeling of competence.

Enhancing Responsibility at Home

- Use nonverbal reminders or cues, such as checklists or self-stick notes placed in areas the child frequents (e.g., the refrigerator). Preadolescents and teenagers often tolerate and receive nonverbal cues much better than verbal reminders ("nagging").

- Gently determine whether your child understands your instructions. Watch the child's face or actions for clues.

- Provide step-by-step guidance for new tasks until the child succeeds, even if the task is simple.

- Limit to two or three the number of chores you expect the child to accomplish in a day, and reduce the number of spontaneous requests you make. It is also helpful to provide some sort of incentive system. For example, the child earns a star for each job completed and displays the stars on a calendar. Two stars earns a specific reinforcer; five stars earns a special treat. The calendar helps keep a visual record of the stars the child has earned.

- Discuss with the entire family the tasks and roles *all* members must share for the family and household to run smoothly. Make a list of family rules and post them on the refrigerator.

Increasing Self-Control

- Attempt to respond to your child in an emotionally neutral manner despite your own levels of frustration, disappointment, or anger.

- Use "I" messages for identifying how your child's actions affect you rather than criticizing the child for expressing his or her emotions.

- Express belief in your child's competence at regaining self-control, and reinforce his or her effort while suggesting strategies to accomplish this goal.

- Apply consequences (rewards and disciplines for behaviors) immediately, consistently, unemotionally, and in a predictable manner.

- Don't compare this child's behavior or performance to that of peers or siblings.

Succeeding at Homework

- Encourage your child to complete homework as early in the day as possible to avoid fatigue's adverse effect on concentration.

- Work together with your child's teacher to set up a time-limited approach to homework: This allows the student to get full credit for work he or she completes during a specific time period.

- Set up a time-management plan that lists all the necessary and desired activities for each evening. Display them on a chart of clocks, giving the child a sense of ownership of his or her own schedule and confirmation that there is enough time for both work and play.

- Provide a consistent, nondistracting work place with available materials for all youngsters in the family.

- Prediscuss or negotiate with your child the degree to which he or she wants you to be involved in the homework process. Stick with the agreement for a defined period of time before changing anything.

- Have your child use an assignment book, signed off by teachers and parents, to ensure that the child remains aware of homework and projects.

- Reward your child's effort to complete homework, and accept his or her frustration as a reasonable reaction to difficult work.

- Let your child try headphones with quiet music while doing homework. This approach actually limits some children's general distractibility.

- Solicit input from a special education professional (such as an academic therapist or an educational consultant) to help your child develop individualized learning strategies that match his or her own processing strengths and weaknesses.

Improving Social Skills

- Encourage social interaction with a limited number of children at any given time.

- Anticipate difficulties regarding social interaction, and discuss alternative approaches with your child prior to the experience.

- Play "what if" with your child: Review social situations and the effects of the child's actions on others.

- Consider a formal social skills group for youngsters with ADHD. This type of group creates communication opportunities and allows a professional to help the participants learn new interactional approaches.

Increasing Enjoyment of Recreational Activities

- Select individual rather than team sports.

- Consider the timing of recreation or sports activities, and schedule experiences for the child's peak times of behavioral control.

- Find recreational and sports activities that fit a youngster's profile of strengths.

- Inform activity leaders regarding a youngster's diagnosis of ADHD and provide strategies for successful management.

Michael W. Cohen, M.D., is a behavioral pediatrician with 30 years of experience. He is the director of the Attention Disorder Center in Tucson, Arizona, and is a clinical professor of pediatrics at the University of Arizona College of Medicine. This article was adapted with permission from the author's 1997 publication, The attention zone: A parents' guide to ADHD, *published by Brunner/Mazel (New York).*

Anger and Aggression Management

6.6

H. Russell Searight, Ph.D.

Children with ADHD sometimes have angry outbursts, including verbal and physical aggression. The difficulty children with ADHD have with inhibiting their impulses plays a major role in this problem. Angry and aggressive children often find themselves with few friends, which in turn serves to intensify their disruptive behavior. Anger often begets more anger in a vicious cycle.

What Causes Anger?

Anger is usually a response to an actual or threatened loss. The child might be facing the loss of an important role (e.g., basketball team player, choir member) or relationship (e.g., girlfriend). The child might fear loss of self-worth or self-esteem from teasing, criticism, and put-downs. Criticizing a child or teenager in front of peers or other adults is particularly likely to elicit anger. In these situations, the child has two agendas—responding to the criticism and saving face in front of others. It is also important to recognize that many children have grown up in situations where the adults around them modeled explosive, sudden, angry outbursts.

Aggressive behavior among teenagers is associated with exposure to violence, being victimized (being assaulted or robbed), and being subjected to severe physical punishment in the home while growing up. A child exposed to chronic violence will be more likely to act aggressively toward others. It is important to recognize this pattern because adults sometimes respond to adolescent anger with angry outbursts themselves. This response only inflames the teenager further.

Although these external situations contribute to anger and aggression, there are also internal processes that play a major role in the anger-aggression cycle. Emotional arousal—being tired, stressed, or overwhelmed—leads to lowering one's guard and increases the likelihood of verbal or physical aggression. Emotional arousal makes it more likely that the child will misinterpret others' actions, seeing a joke as a put-down or a friendly pat on the back as intrusive touching. The teenager's own thought patterns or self-statements also can inflame the individual further (e.g., "He has no right to talk to me like that," "She can't ignore me, she has it coming," "I don't deserve this kind of treatment"). These self-statements typically fuel other repetitive thoughts and increase angry feelings.

How Can Teenagers Control Anger?

Anger is the typical response in the following chain of events:

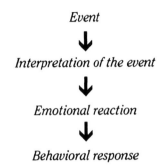

Event

↓

Interpretation of the event

↓

Emotional reaction

↓

Behavioral response

The key to anger management is to insert a step in the chain between the emotional reaction and the behavioral response. This step consists of a new coping skill, such as self-statements, deep breathing, or counting to 20.

What Are Anger Management Strategies?

The first stage in teaching older children and teenagers to modify angry responses is to help them recognize early warning signs of anger. At first, many people are unaware of these warning signs. Children and teenagers commonly report that anger just erupts suddenly, and they can't label any physical sensation or feelings preceding the outburst. When asked specifically about their experience of getting angry, they say they simply "go off," "pop," or "snap."

Over time, through questioning and giving them examples, children can learn to recognize anger in its early stages. For example, many report that their face feels hot or that they clench their fists, grit their teeth, feel their heart pounding, or feel like smashing something. Teenagers might say that they "see red" or that everything seems like a blur. One question that is often helpful in detecting anger cues is, "When you get up in the morning, do you know it's going to be a day when you're going to go off?" If teens have difficulty describing their own anger cues, ask if they can determine when other people are angry and how.

The next, and probably most important, step is helping the child build in a delay between the interpretation of an event, the angry emotional reaction, and the aggressive response. Deep breathing or progressive relaxation training helps to facilitate this delay. The child should try to use his or her anger cues as a warning sign to use these strategies.

A Step-by-Step Approach for Anger Control

Break down the potentially angry exchange into substages. In the first phase, preparing for the provocation, children should learn the types of encounters that are likely to provoke their anger. For example, being singled out by the teacher for arriving late to class might arouse anger associated with loss of esteem in front of friends. Encourage the child to be aware of these situations before they occur ("This is going to upset me, but I know some ways to deal with it. I don't want to let her get to me").

The next stage is the actual exchange itself, impact and confrontation. Children should remind themselves to stay calm, breathe deeply, and not let the other person "get to me." When children do notice emotional arousal occurring—muscles getting tight, heart beating faster—they should use these signs as a reminder to take a deep breath and also to respect the other person. Those children who are oriented toward control and view the situation as a contest might need to tell themselves, "I'll bet he could get me really angry, but I won't let him."

Next, the child or adolescent should become sensitive to situations in which the conflict is not likely to be resolved successfully. Children should remind themselves that conflicts take time to solve and might not be settled at that point. A useful skill is being able to shake it off (Novaco, 1975; Goldstein & Glick, 1987).

Other strategies for anger control include deep breathing, backward counting, and use of imagery. For backward counting, encourage the child to visualize one number per second starting from 20 and counting back to 1. In pleasant imagery, the child thinks of a pleasant scene (swimming, watching television, lying in bed listening to music that is relaxing and soothing).

In addition, the child might need to learn to change his or her internal self-statements. Many children are unaware of how they maintain and increase their own anger. Self-talk often fuels anger with statements such as, "I am going to beat up this guy, he is making me look like a fool in front of my friends," "I hate her," and "She has no right to talk to me that way."

Children also should become aware of the long-term consequences of anger, including harsh punishment (detention) and being suspended from school. Emphasize the contrast between short-term gain (hitting someone who is making fun of them) and long-term consequences, and help children to remember these consequences during situations in which they feel they are being provoked.

How to Teach Anger Management

Teenagers, in particular, often are preoccupied with being in control and not allowing others to have power over them. Because of this view, they can find it difficult to walk away or disengage emotionally if someone is "dissing" them.

Teens will be more likely to use anger management strategies if you emphasize that techniques such as deep breathing are a way of maintaining or regaining control. An angry and belligerent child usually feels helpless and powerless and wants to regain control. You can point out that angry outbursts actually communicate to the other person, "You were able to frustrate me" or "You were able to push my button and get me to react." It is effective, therefore, to frame anger management as a way of improving self-control, which increases your child's power. Strategies such as deep breathing, backward counting, and counting to 10 actually help a child stay in charge of the situation.

Children can learn these strategies in individual and small-group settings and will find these tactics useful in many school settings. Groups sometimes include role playing, in which other children deliberately provoke one of their peers while the therapist coaches the child in anger management skills.

References and Resources

Goldstein, A. P., & Glick, B. (1987). *Aggression replacement training: A comprehensive intervention for aggressive youth.* Champaign, IL: Research Press.

Novaco, R. W. (1975). *Anger control: The development and evaluation of an experimental treatment.* Lexington, MA: D. C. Heath.

H. Russell Searight, Ph.D., is the director of behavioral sciences for the Residency Program of Family Medicine of St. Louis. He is the author of several textbooks and an adjunct associate professor in the department of psychology and Community and Family Medicine at St. Louis University.

Section 7

Associated Disorders

Learning Disabilities

H. Russell Searight, Ph.D.

What Is a Learning Disability?

Learning disabilities (LDs) have been defined in several different ways. It is important to recognize that LD is not simply a failure to do schoolwork or the equivalent of poor grades. A learning disability almost always is defined in terms of performance on standardized tests of intelligence and/or academic skills. One common definition (employed by the American Psychiatric Association) defines an LD as a significant difference between measured IQ and performance on an academic test. Another definition uses extremely low achievement test scores (below the seventh percentile for the child's expected grade level) in specific skills such as reading, spelling, and arithmetic (Barkley, 1990).

Learning disabilities usually affect one of several key academic skill areas: mathematics, reading, or written expression. Children can have learning disabilities in more than one area. As a general rule, though, it is assumed that children with a learning disability are of at least normal intellectual functioning and sometimes have above-average intelligence with a weakness in a specific area.

Professionals typically describe learning disabilities in terms of specific academic skill weaknesses. However, these problems often stem from a more fundamental deficit such as in receptive or expressive language skills, decoding written or orally presented material, or visual/spatial skills (e.g., perceiving and reproducing letters or shapes in the proper orientation). Children with reading disabilities can have difficulty making the connection between written letters and their sounds or being able to combine letters into words and sequences. Problems with arithmetic might be based in visual/spatial problems (keeping numbers in the appropriate columns, particularly when borrowing and carrying) or memory weaknesses (which would be noticeably apparent on tasks such as memorizing the multiplication tables).

How Common Are Learning Disabilities?

It is estimated that about 5% of public school children have a learning disability. However, others report higher rates. For example, problems in written expression affect 8% to 15% of children, with mathematics disability possibly affecting up to 6% of students. About half of all U.S. children receiving special education services have learning disabilities. In the past 20 years, the percentage of children identified with learning disabilities has doubled (Lyon, 1996).

When Should Parents Become Concerned About a Possible Learning Disability?

In kindergarten and first grade, children acquire new material at different rates. Basic reading, writing, and mathematics skills might be easier for a child who has been "preexposed" to this material at home or in preschool. By second grade, a child has had ample exposure to academic material, and it now becomes important to see if the child has been able to master that material. Thus, the diagnosis of a learning disability should not be applied until the child is at least in second grade.

Parents should consider the possibility of learning disabilities when children have had a long history of poor academic performance. Although some children with learning disabilities have had difficulties with particular academic skills such as reading since the first grade, the weaknesses of the child with a learning disability who functions at a higher level might not be detected until later elementary school (fourth or fifth grade). With children who have milder or more subtle learning problems, the upper grades, with their requirements for more independent work (reading independently, writing research papers, or conducting independent science projects) can make a preexisting learning disability finally apparent.

What Should Parents and Teachers Do if They Suspect a Learning Disability?

If you suspect your child has a learning disability, have your child evaluated by a physician to be sure that vision, hearing, and motor skills are all normal. Careful review of report cards, school work, and standardized educational tests also can provide clues about specific areas of academic weakness.

Individual testing by an educational specialist or a school or clinical psychologist is the next step. Testing for a learning disability typically involves an individual intelligence test as well as thorough academic testing. It also might be helpful to have the child's language skills evaluated by a speech-language pathologist and fine motor and coordination abilities assessed by an occupational therapist. The results of the evaluation should specify the area of weakness (language comprehension, mathematical reasoning) and include specific educational strategies to address these skills.

It is important to recognize that children with Attention Deficit/Hyperactivity Disorder (ADHD) are more likely to have a learning disability than students without ADHD. The most common type of learning disability is in reading.

Do All Children With Poor Academic Performance Have Learning Disabilities?

It is important to recognize that not all academic performance problems are related to learning disabilities. Children with untreated ADHD can have academic problems because of difficulties in concentration and retention of school-based information. Children whose ADHD is untreated for a number of years who then receive treatment later in childhood or adolescence actually might have missed out on basic academic material in earlier school grades.

A sudden drop in school performance by a child who previously had good grades should raise the possibility of emotional problems such as depression. It is fairly common, for example, for children to demonstrate declines in academic functioning when there is family distress, such as divorce, a sudden death, or a geographic move. Poor academic performance also might stem from a power struggle between parents and the child. Refusing to complete homework and "forgetting" to turn in assignments might be ways the child is expressing anger and resentment at perceived parental pressure.

Strategies for Helping Students With Learning Disabilities

There are two general approaches to helping students with learning disabilities: (a) early aggressive efforts to treat the area of weakness directly, and (b) accommodations directed toward helping the student develop compensatory skills. The first approach usually is employed with young children and can include language therapy and sensory-motor training. Intensive individualized instruction (such as tutoring in reading) also falls within this category. As children with learning disabilities enter the later elementary and early junior high school years, they will benefit from strategies to compensate for their area of weaknesses.

The specific compensatory strategies used by children with learning disabilities depend on the academic skill involved. For example:

- Allow students who have problems with written expression to answer essay questions in a one-on-one oral format with the teacher or to dictate their answers into a tape recorder.

- Emphasize math concepts (rather than the mechanics of problem solving) for students with a weakness in numerical calculation, and teach them to use a calculator.

- Students with developmental reading disorders might benefit from listening to their textbooks on audiotape.

- Students with a learning disability involving reading or writing often will benefit from extra time on exams.

The majority of students with learning disabilities can perform very well academically if they are permitted accommodations that allow them to express their range of academic knowledge and skills. Students with learning disabilities are *entitled* to these accommodations by federal law up through college and graduate school.

References and Resources

Barkley, R. A. (1990). *Attention deficit hyperactivity disorder: A handbook for diagnosis and treatment.* New York: Guilford.

Lyon, G. S. (1996). Learning disabilities. *The Future of Children, 6,* 54-76.

H. Russell Searight, Ph.D., is the director of behavioral sciences for the Residency Program of Family Medicine of St. Louis. He is the author of several textbooks and an adjunct associate professor in the department of psychology and Community and Family Medicine at St. Louis University.

Oppositional Defiant Disorder

H. Russell Searight, Ph.D.

What Is Oppositional Defiant Disorder?

Children with Oppositional Defiant Disorder are argumentative, negative, and frequently irritable ("touchy"). Preschoolers (3 to 4 years) and young adolescents (12 to 14 years) sometimes have periods of these behaviors, but they tend to be fairly brief. Refusal to interact with children when they are exhibiting these behaviors usually reduces these common tantrums.

Children with Oppositional Defiant Disorder, on the other hand, have a long-standing pattern (for at least 6 months) of losing their temper often, arguing frequently with adults, refusing to comply with adult requests, deliberately harassing or annoying others, failing to take responsibility for their mistakes or misbehavior, and being irritable, reactive, angry, spiteful, and vindictive (American Psychiatric Association, 1994).

These children frequently resist or argue about relatively minor issues. Parents often feel as if they are walking on eggshells with these children. A mother might say, "I quit asking Johnny to pick up his room or feed his dog; I just do these things myself. If I ask him to do it, he fights and argues with me until he wears me down, and the fight just isn't worth it." When confronted with their misbehavior or its consequences, these children frequently deny it or blame others. In addition, children with Oppositional Defiant Disorder instigate arguments and seem to harass and annoy adults and peers deliberately.

Oppositional defiant behavior might not be immediately evident at the beginning of a new academic year with a new teacher or in interaction with adults or peers whom the child has met recently. It is usually most pronounced in interactions with parents and, over the course of the school year, the pattern will become more apparent with teachers. These children tend not to recognize that their oppositionality or defiance is a problem. They typically see their frequent arguing and irritability as a "logical" response to perceived provocation or unfair demands from others.

What Are the Causes of Oppositional Defiant Behavior?

The causes of Oppositional Defiant Disorder are not known precisely. Children who develop this disorder sometimes have difficult temperaments as toddlers. During the early years, it can be hard to soothe these children, and parents

have problems keeping them on a regular schedule of sleeping and eating. In addition, they tend to have difficulty with transitions such as beginning preschool. Oppositional Defiant Disorder also appears to be more common in families in which the caretaker-child relationship has been disrupted, such as when children have been in multiple foster homes. In addition, parenting that is inconsistent or overly harsh or includes extended periods of neglect also has been associated with Oppositional Defiant Disorder. It is not known exactly how common Oppositional Defiant Disorder is in the general population. The literature reports rates between 2% and 16%.

How Does Oppositional Defiant Disorder Develop During Childhood?

This disorder typically begins in early childhood, and behavior problems usually are more pronounced at home until the teen years. By early adolescence, however, Oppositional Defiant Behavior becomes more evident at school.

It is important for parents and teachers to recognize that some oppositionality is common in preschool children and is a normal part of striving for greater independence (the "terrible twos"). There also can be a surge in "normal" oppositional behavior between the ages of 11 and 14 as children enter adolescence. Preteens and young adolescents are notorious for periods of irritability and obstinacy. However, those episodes are short-lived and decline with age.

Children with Oppositional Defiant Disorder generally do not engage in serious legal violations, nor do they typically become physically aggressive with others. They are likely to be verbally aggressive and perhaps even somewhat threatening with others, but this rarely takes the form of physical aggression.

What Can Parents Do to Change Oppositional Defiant Behavior?

Treating oppositional defiant behavior requires a high level of structure and consistency. The most useful responses from parents and teachers are rewards for compliance and punishment (most commonly time out or loss of privileges) for disrespectful or argumentative behavior or failure to follow rules. In the following example, an initial goal for Jimmy might be that he completes his morning routine and is ready for breakfast by 7 a.m. The morning routine includes Jimmy's getting out of bed, brushing his teeth, washing his face, getting dressed, and making his bed. If he performs this routine successfully, he receives a star on a star chart. If he earns enough stars, he gets a reward at the end of the week, such as going to a movie, renting a favorite video, or being allowed extra TV time on the weekend.

Importantly, parents should recognize that when oppositional behavior has been in place for an extended period of time, they might need to modify the standards so that the child can experience some early successes with the behavioral program. For example, if the child hasn't been able to be ready on time every day for the past month without at least five reminders from the parent, an early goal might be that the child complete the morning routine with only two or three prompts. If, in the beginning, this occurs three or four days out of the week, the child would receive the reward. As the child meets the criteria for each successive week, parents can "raise the bar" so that the standard approaches the longer-term behavioral goal.

One of the unique issues for children with Oppositional Defiant Disorder is that parents and teachers often become caught in a vicious cycle of defiance, negativity, defensiveness, and arguing. In particular, if the adults are authority-oriented and believe that children need to respect them, they frequently will find themselves angry and arguing with these children.

It is important for adults to remember that any attention, positive or negative, is reinforcing to children with this disorder. These children have learned that the squeaky wheel gets the grease, and they will squeak long, loud, and hard. A common dilemma parents face is a child who has been sent to his or her room for a 15-minute time out. Five minutes after the time out has begun, the child will start calling out, "I'm hungry; I need to eat." This will escalate to, "I'm starving, I'm going to pass out." Parents should be careful not to respond. Another common situation occurs when, for example, the child is given a half-hour of time out in a room by him- or herself but comes out every 10 minutes asking if the time is up. In both situations, the parents or adults should respond with something like, "You have 30 minutes. I'll talk to you when you have served your time. If you come out before time is up or continue to call out, you will get 10 more minutes." The child often will try to provoke the parents with threats or complaints that seem to require an immediate response. It is important that parents not react to these and continue to state their expectation calmly and neutrally.

Another area where parents often get caught concerns whether or not the child has met the criteria for compliance. For example, the parent tells the child to tidy the room. The parent then inspects the room and finds that the child has hidden most of the toys under the bed. The parent points out that the child really hasn't cleaned the room. The child argues that, indeed, all the toys are out of sight, and the room *is* clean. The parent who continues to argue with the child, attempts to be logical, and tries to persuade the child that the room is not really clean, likely will become increasingly frustrated and diverted from the topic at hand. It is extremely important for parents to catch themselves before this process escalates. Parents should state the expectation and use the broken-record technique of simply repeating the same expectation over and over and not responding to the child's provocation.

References and Resources

American Psychiatric Association. (1994). *Diagnostic and statistical manual of mental disorders* (4th ed.). Washington, DC: Author.

H. Russell Searight, Ph.D., is the director of behavioral sciences for the Residency Program of Family Medicine of St. Louis. He is the author of several textbooks and an adjunct associate professor in the department of psychology and Community and Family Medicine at St. Louis University.

Conduct Disorder

H. Russell Searight, Ph.D.

What Is Conduct Disorder?

Conduct Disorder, a pattern of socially disruptive behavior, can develop along with ADHD. Conduct Disorder also occurs without ADHD. Children with Conduct Disorder exhibit a long-term pattern of disobeying accepted social rules and violating others' rights. Younger children with Conduct Disorder are sometimes cruel to animals, deliberately set fires, or intentionally destroy property. Whereas many young children are aggressive and disobedient at times, the child with Conduct Disorder does not seem to learn from the consequences of punishment, and the behavior becomes more severe.

As they become older, children with Conduct Disorder tend to have little concern about the effects of their behavior on others and have difficulty understanding another person's perspective. Among teenagers, Conduct Disorder takes the form of running away from home, truancy, multiple school suspensions, and illegal behavior such as burglary, theft, and vandalism. Whereas ADHD behavior is typically unplanned and impulsive, adolescents with Conduct Disorder are more likely to be somewhat deliberate about choosing misbehavior. Children with ADHD are likely to feel bad if they have harmed someone impulsively or broken something, but those with Conduct Disorder experience little guilt. Children with Oppositional Defiant Disorder are argumentative and annoying to others, but they usually are not physically aggressive and do not break the law.

How Common Is Conduct Disorder?

Conduct Disorder occurs in 6% to 16% of boys under the age of 18 and in 2% to 9% of girls (American Psychiatric Association, 1994). Researchers have suggested that this problem is becoming increasingly common, particularly in large urban areas. Approximately one of every five boys with ADHD also has Conduct Disorder. This increases to around 40% in adolescence. Boys with Conduct Disorder are more likely to be aggressive and engage in stealing and vandalism; girls are more likely to run away from home, be truant from school, and engage in high-risk sexual behavior.

Does the Child's Age Influence Conduct Disorder?

There are two types of Conduct Disorder, one that begins in childhood (before age 10) and a form that develops later (beginning after age 10). Children with early childhood histories (around 6 to 7 years of age) of disturbed behavior such as repeated fire setting, aggression, and cruelty to animals are very likely to have more serious problems as they get older. Early identification and vigorous treatment of those children can prevent more disturbing behavior from developing. Early intervention is important because children who have been consistently aggressive and destructive throughout childhood are unlikely to change dramatically after age 13 (Comer, 1995). Children who begin developing problems only in their teens and those who have milder behavioral difficulties have better treatment outcomes. Girls usually have later onset (in their teens) and are not typically physically aggressive, nor do they commonly engage in overtly illegal acts such as burglary or vandalism.

When Should Parents Become Concerned?

Children frequently have periods during which they are aggressive and disobedient, particularly during preschool and early elementary school years. Parents should become concerned when children have had several school suspensions, have been involved in multiple physical fights, or have had police contact. In addition, preteen and teenage smoking, alcohol use, and sexual activity often are associated with Conduct Disorder. Many inner-city gang members frequently engage in conduct-disordered behavior. However, gang members are often part of a cultural group that provides them with a sense of social connection. In many respects, the gang has become an alternative family for young people with disintegrating family ties. However, a sizable number of adolescents with Conduct Disorder engage in criminal behavior as adults.

What Causes Conduct Disorder?

Conduct Disorder does not have a single cause. A chaotic and inconsistent family environment is an important contributor to Conduct Disorder. Children in these settings typically have long histories of harsh or rejecting parenting and inconsistent discipline. Parents often have difficulty managing behaviors that emerge as overt, destructive conflict and often include physical violence. Children and teenagers who are frequently without adult supervision are at high risk for developing destructive behavior patterns. Through patterns of poor moral judgment, parents also can fail to teach empathy for others (Comer, 1995).

Treatment of Conduct Disorder

There are several guidelines for treating Conduct Disorder in children. First, intervention should begin as soon as parents or teachers spot a potential problem. Children who have a long-standing history of conduct-disordered behavior are less likely to change as they grow older. Children who are frequently destructive and aggressive throughout childhood and who, in turn, develop more significant illegal and aggressive behavior in adolescence are unlikely to change dramatically after the age of 13 or 14.

Second, parents, teachers, and other adults working with the child must be *consistent*. This principle is far easier said than done and requires a high level of energy and persistence in doing the right thing. There should be a clear, immediate connection between the child's misbehavior and appropriate consequences. Parents will have to ask themselves repeatedly, "Am I being consistent?" "Is the punishment or reward too much or too little for what my child has done?" A combination of rewards for desirable behavior with punishment (such as removal of privileges or time out for a *specific* period for misbehavior) usually will be effective if these are used *consistently*.

To provide this stability, parents need to detach from their strong feelings of anger and frustration. Consider this example: An 8-year-old is on a reward system. If he picks up his room by 5 p.m. for 5 days out of a week, he gets to go out for pizza. The boy has been successful and earned the reward. At 4 p.m. on Saturday, he gets into a shouting match with his mother about whether he has fed the dog. During the argument, he becomes rude and disrespectful to her. If she is acting out of her immediate anger toward the child, the mother is likely to cancel the pizza outing. If the child is out of control, it might be necessary to delay the outing for a period of time until he regains control. However, he has earned the outing successfully, and the parents shouldn't use cancellation as a punishment. There should be a consequence for the refusal to feed the dog (e.g., no video games for the next two days), but the consequence should be unrelated to the reward the child has already earned.

A concern that many parents and teachers voice about reward systems is that children are doing the right thing simply to get something. Parents might be concerned that their child does not have a conscience and is being manipulative to obtain rewards. It is important to recognize that many adults do the right thing as a means of obtaining rewards. Many of us would prefer not to go to work on some days, but we appear at our jobs because we recognize that we won't get paid otherwise. Over time, these children gradu-

ally internalize the standards for appropriate prosocial behavior. Parents can help their children to develop sensitivity and empathy for others by asking them to describe how their actions (grabbing a toy away, hitting a peer) affect the other child. Encouraging the victim to explain his or her feelings to the offender can help children appreciate how their actions harm others physically and emotionally.

As children enter adolescence, the peer group comes to play an important role in development. Although parents still influence important values such as education and religion, the teen's peers affect choices about dress, music, and movies. Because of family distress, teens at risk for Conduct Disorder don't have the moderating influence of parental values. As a result, they can be affected much more readily by the behavior of peers who might be involved in drinking, smoking, early sexual activity, and illegal acts.

Parents should be aware of who their children's friends are, and keep their children away from others who are engaging in illegal and other conduct-disordered behavior. Even parents who monitor their children's whereabouts by phone (which can be the case when both parents work outside of the home) will reduce the likelihood of conduct-disordered behavior. Simply phoning in frequently to check on whether the teenager is at home and what he or she is doing will keep them on track. Encouraging children's involvement in positive social activities such as sports, scouts, choir, and school and church organizations will provide them with a valued role and reduce the influence of deviant peers.

Summary

Although disobedience and testing of limits is common among older children and adolescents, parents should take seriously their children's more grave violations of social rules. Early intervention will prevent antisocial behavior from developing later. Parents should be consistent, persistent, and knowledgeable about their children's friends and whereabouts.

References and Resources

American Psychiatric Association. (1994). *Diagnostic and statistical manual of mental disorders* (4th ed.). Washington, DC: Author.

Comer, R. J. (1995) *Abnormal psychology* (2nd ed.) New York: W. H. Freeman

H. Russell Searight, Ph.D., is the director of behavioral sciences for the Residency Program of Family Medicine of St. Louis. He is the author of several textbooks and an adjunct associate professor in the department of psychology and Community and Family Medicine at St. Louis University.

Helping the Gifted Child With Attention Deficit/Hyperactivity Disorder

Kathryn E. Shafer, Ph.D.

Tim sits by the window, eyes glazed, never having eye contact with the teacher. His feet fidget, and in his pocket are little toy soldiers that he plays with continually. His handwriting is poor, and he frequently blurts out ideas or answers to the teacher's questions without raising his hand. Generally he does not do what the teacher asks him to do. His mind always seems to be elsewhere. At home, Tim never leaves the computer and can answer any question his dad asks about programming.

Is Tim gifted or does he have Attention Deficit/Hyperactivity Disorder (ADHD)? Actually, both are true.

The unique problems of a child who is gifted and has ADHD present parents with a challenge requiring extra effort. Both conditions demand very specialized help often not readily available. Only a small percentage of children are diagnosed as both ADHD and gifted. In this case, Tim had an IEP (Individual Educational Plan) for the ADHD symptoms, but the school was not providing for the giftedness his parents suspected, based on their observations of his hobbies and interests. His teachers insisted that Tim was unable to sit still, pay attention, or complete work and found it hard to believe that Tim could be gifted. Tim's parents didn't know what to do.

What Is Giftedness?

Tim's mother, aware of his abilities and confused about how to get help for his special academic abilities, went to the library. There she found the definition of giftedness used by most schools: Public Law 97-35, passed by Congress in 1981, states that gifted children "give evidence of high performance capability in areas such as intellectual, creative, artistic, leadership, or specific academic fields, and who require services or activities not ordinarily provided by the school in order to fully develop such capabilities" (Sec. 582).

Overlapping Symptoms of Giftedness and ADHD

The government's broad definition assured Tim's mother that, according to school definitions, he was gifted. His high level of knowledge in the area of computers set him apart from other children his age. But even to the most trained observer and many of Tim's teachers, the characteristics of ADHD and giftedness appeared to be the same:

the restlessness, the inattention to things the child is not interested in, the failure to complete tasks. The special characteristics of gifting combined with ADHD make it difficult to identify and serve these bright children.

The recent work of Webb and Latimer (1993) has helped caregivers, teachers, and parents develop a better understanding of the overlapping symptoms of ADHD and giftedness. Children have "poor attention spans, low tolerance for persistence on tasks that seem irrelevant, personal judgment that lags behind the development of the intellect, an intensity that often leads to power struggles with authorities and questioning of rules, high energy levels, distractibility, and disorganization that parallels the behaviors of those children who might be ADHD" (Webb & Latimer, 1993, p. 23).

What Can Parents Do?

Tim's mother knew she was going to have to become more involved with the school so that Tim might fulfill his potential, overcome his academic problems, become more interested in school, and continue getting assistance for his ADHD problems. She already was aware from his ADHD program that one of the most important things she could do was to remain in contact with the school and his teachers.

She asked that Tim be given an additional individual evaluation by the school psychologist. This IQ test, in a one-on-one setting, would give the school additional proof of his abilities. His mother told the psychologist and teachers about his special interests and special abilities. Then, after painting a complete picture of Tim's abilities, Tim's mother requested that the school develop another IEP with his teachers. Here she asked teachers to provide some special modifications for Tim's giftedness as well as his ADHD symptoms.

Tim's teachers agreed that they could set up some independent learning centers where tiered learning could take place. That is, some of the activities would be simple and other activities more complex, requiring higher-level thinking skills. With such centers, all students could proceed at their own level and pace. They even let Tim help pick the topic for the center.

Interest centers accompanied by independent projects with long or no time lines are helpful to the gifted child with ADHD. Such children can work on something they really are interested in and proceed to higher levels of thinking as they complete work. Teachers can let the brighter students skip some of the simpler materials, thus cutting down on the total work the students need to do.

For his class interest center, Tim had the opportunity to choose from a variety of learning resources such as museum visits, personal interviews, photographs, pictorial histories, student-created music, art, films, community lectures, and scientific experimentation to complete assignments. Obviously, these activities required Tim's mom to contribute a lot to the success of this tiered-learning activity.

Knowing of Tim's special interest in computers, his mother began to look for an adult who would be glad to work with Tim and help him advance his gifted interest in computers. In this search for a mentor, she found a rich source of after-school programs, community college programs, and museum programs that offered good opportunities for gifted youngsters to express their talents. These special programs can help a child like Tim overcome the negative self-image created by the behaviors inherent in the ADHD problems.

In Tim's case, the computer was helpful in dealing with Tim's writing and communication problems. Tim's mother convinced the IEP team to provide a computer to help Tim complete his mathematics, writing, and spelling assignments. He also began to work on organizational skills, using the computer to track assignments and keep records.

Another source of help for the gifted child with ADHD is activity-based counseling. Peter DiMezza of the Center for Creative Learning in Akron, Ohio, has found therapeutic martial arts to be a successful method of treatment for children with ADHD (1998). Karate appeals to many gifted children, and this once-a-week physical activity improves self-esteem. The students learn mental and physical skills that transfer to the classroom.

Special modifications for gifted youngsters include programs such as Odyssey of the Mind, Future Problem Solving, and Philosophy for Children, where students in grades 2 through 12 use critical thinking and problem-solving skills to solve problems of interest to them. The higher-order thinking skills developed in these programs are especially useful for gifted children. Many schools take part in one or more of these activities.

Summary

Not all children are as lucky as Tim. In many states, a student might be identified as gifted or ADHD, but not both. If your school does not have a gifted program, or you cannot obtain an individual IQ test or other competency testing to assess your child's giftedness, then seek out a professional psychologist or psychiatrist for an individual examination.

The greatest danger, says Marlene Bireley, author of *Crossover Children: A Sourcebook for Helping Children Who Are Gifted and Disabled* (1995), "lies in overlooking the giftedness in the rush to overcome the disability. If a child perceives himself or herself as disabled, that is what he or she will become. Therefore, the very idea that one has certain abilities or gifts will help the child develop a positive self-concept that will assist him or her in overcoming whatever ADHD problems exist" (p. 37).

The key to your child's education is that the curriculum must be modified for higher-order thinking and special interests and abilities as well as for the ADHD symptoms. You, the parent, must be vigilant and you must be involved. There are techniques for helping the gifted child with ADHD and, as with ADHD advocacy, you must continue to advocate for your gifted child.

References and Resources

Baum, S. (1989). Gifted but learning disabled: A puzzling paradox. *ERIC Digest*, #E479.

Bireley, M. (1995). *Crossover children: A sourcebook for helping children who are gifted and learning disabled* (2nd ed.). Reston, VA: The Council for Exceptional Children Publications.

Clark, B. (1992). *Growing up gifted.* New York: Macmillan.

DiMezza, P. (1998). *The creative gifted child.* Center For Creative Learning, Akron, Ohio.

Jones, C. B. (1994). *Attention deficit disorder: Strategies for school-age students.* San Antonio, TX: Communication Skill Builders.

Webb, J., & Latimer, D. (1993). ADHD and children who are gifted. *ERIC Digest*, #E522.

Kathryn E. Shafer, Ph.D., is a former science teacher and director of gifted services in Lakewood and Hudson, Ohio. She currently is an educational consultant in Akron, Ohio.

Tourette's Syndrome

H. Russell Searight, Ph.D.

What Is Tourette's Syndrome?

Tourette's Syndrome is a relatively rare and unusual disorder characterized by uncontrollable movements and involuntary vocalization. The movements can occur in the head as well as upper and lower arms. Vocalizations frequently include clicks, grunts, barks, snorts, and coughs. Some individuals with Tourette's Syndrome also will verbalize obscenities. Although calling out obscenities has become a well-recognized symptom of Tourette's, it occurs in no more than about 10% of patients with the disorder. Some individuals with Tourette's also demonstrate odd movements during walking, such as touching, squatting, and twirling. One of the first symptoms to appear during the course of Tourette's Syndrome is eye blinking. Throat clearing and stuttering also occur early in the disorder's appearance (Sandor, 1993).

How Common Is Tourette's Syndrome?

Tourette's Syndrome is fairly rare and occurs in an estimated four or five people per 10,000. Tourette's Syndrome typically begins by the age of 7, and it is extremely unusual for onset to occur after age 18. Tourette's is usually lifelong, but people can have periods of time (up to 3 months) in which they are free of tics. Many people with the disorder describe an unpleasant feeling preceding the tic that seems to be relieved by the movement or vocalization itself. Persons with Tourette's Syndrome can stop the tics by consciously focusing on suppressing the movements, sometimes for several hours. However, there can be a rebound of more severe tics after these periods (Sandor, 1993, 1995).

Tourette's Syndrome appears to exist on a continuum from fairly mild tic-like behavior to more severe movements, and individuals with Tourette's Syndrome are generally aware of their disorder. Because people with Tourette's Syndrome often do not seek medical assistance, the disorder actually might be more common than available estimates suggest.

What Causes Tourette's Syndrome?

Research suggests that Tourette's Syndrome is genetically based. However, everyone who has a genetic predisposition for this disorder doesn't necessarily exhibit tics and other symptoms. The environment appears to play a role in the development of Tourette's Syndrome, and there are suggestions that these symptoms become more pronounced under stress.

Conditions Associated With Tourette's Syndrome

There is increased evidence that Tourette's Syndrome commonly exists along with other disorders, such as Attention Deficit/Hyperactivity Disorder(ADHD). Some researchers suggest that up to half of those with Tourette's Syndrome also have ADHD. However, the reverse is typically not the case: The majority of children with ADHD do *not* have Tourette's Syndrome.

Recent research suggests that Tourette's Syndrome might be related to and coexist with Obsessive-Compulsive Disorder, a psychiatric condition characterized by repeated intrusive thoughts. These thoughts are typically irrational and center around fears of being dirty or contaminated or of harm befalling the patient or family members. Compulsions often include repeated rituals such as washing, counting, or lining up objects. These actions have no real function except to temporarily reduce the anxiety triggered by the obsessions.

Other behavioral problems that sometimes coexist with Tourette's Syndrome include aggression, mood swings, temper outbursts, and hyperactivity. Not surprisingly, teachers often viewed students with this disorder as "hard to control" (Walkup, Scahill, & Riddle, 1995).

What Is the Treatment for Tourette's Syndrome?

One of the most common treatments for tic disorders is the medication haloperidol (Haldol). Side effects are relatively common with Haldol, including a slowing of motor movements, weight gain, and stiffening of the muscles in the arms and neck. Pimozide also is effective in treating Tourette's Syndrome. Pimozide's side effects are somewhat similar to those of Haldol. A third neuroleptic medication, Resperidone, also seems to be helpful in reducing tics, particularly in the 25% of patients who do not respond to haloperidol and pimozide (Scahill, 1996).

There is currently some disagreement about whether children with both ADHD and Tourette's Syndrome can be treated successfully with stimulant medication such as methylphenidate (Ritalin). There has been some concern about stimulants eliciting or making tics more pro-nounced in persons with a predisposition for Tourette's Syndrome. Although this issue is not settled, alternative medications to treat ADHD symptoms in individuals with Tourette's Syndrome are the tricyclic antidepressants such as imipramine and desipramine (Walkup, Scahill, & Riddle, 1995).

Behavioral intervention, particularly cue-controlled relaxation training, can be helpful with some children. In cue-controlled relaxation, the child uses slow, even, deep breathing alone ("inhale... exhale") or while tensing and relaxing different muscle groups (shoulders, arms, stomach). A technique called habit reversal, in which the person practices a response that competes directly with the tic, has been very helpful. With this technique, the person learns to contract the opposite muscle associated with the tic. For example, the person counteracts a tendency to wrinkle the nose by attempting to stretch the skin of the nose. In school settings, tics are likely to emerge when the child is under stress. Giving students with Tourette's Syndrome extra time for examinations and helping them organize large projects, such as term papers, into a series of smaller tasks will reduce the pressure that they experience (Packer, 1997).

References and Resources

Packer, L. E. (1997). Social and educational resources for patients with Tourette Syndrome. *Neurological Clinics of North America, 15,* 457-71.

Sandor, P. (1993). Gilles De La Tourette Syndrome: A neuropsychiatric disorder. *Journal of Psychosomatic Research, 37,* 211-226.

Sandor, P. (1995). Clinical management of Tourette's Syndrome and associated disorders. *Canadian Journal of Psychiatry, 40,* 577-583.

Scahill, L. (1996). Contemporary approaches to pharmacotherapy in Tourette's Syndrome and Obsessive-Compulsive Disorder. *Journal of Child & Adolescent Psychiatric Nursing, 9,* 27-43.

Walkup, J. T., Scahill, L. D., & Riddle, M. A. (1995). Disruptive behavior, hyperactivity, and learning disabilities in children with Tourette's Syndrome. In W. J. Weiner & A. E. Lang (Eds.), *Advances in neurology* (pp. 259-272). New York: Raven Press.

H. Russell Searight, Ph.D., is the director of behavioral sciences for the Residency Program of Family Medicine of St. Louis. He is the author of several textbooks and an adjunct associate professor in the department of psychology and Community and Family Medicine at St. Louis University.

Childhood and Adolescent Depression

H. Russell Searight, Ph.D.

Can Children Really Become Depressed?

Depression among children has been recognized only recently as a serious mental health problem. Researchers now accept that even infants can become clinically depressed. One of the problems in knowing whether or not a child is depressed is that the symptoms are not as clear-cut as they are for adults. With adults, there is typically an episode of sadness or a general loss of satisfaction or pleasure in usual activities. There also are several other symptoms that commonly include disruptions in sleep, changes in appetite and weight loss/gain, decrease in energy level, slower motor movements, thoughts of death and/or suicidal thinking, and difficulties with attention and concentration.

How Common Is Depression Among Children and Adolescents?

Clinical depression occurs in 10% to 15% of adults, and experts estimate that depression occurs in only about 1% to 2% of preadolescent children (Pfeffer, 1986). In the midteens, the likelihood of depression jumps considerably, approaching adult levels. It is very possible that the low figures for children are substantial underestimates because, until about age 12, children are not able to describe internal states such as moods or feelings over time with any degree of consistency. The general rule of thumb is that the younger the child, the less depression will look like adult depression. It is possible that children with Attention Deficit/Hyperactivity Disorder (ADHD) are more likely to be depressed.

What Are the Symptoms of Depression at Different Ages?

Among preschool children, indicators of depression include flat or apathetic emotional expression. These children often do not seem to care about much of anything and lack spontaneity and playfulness. Among preschool boys, there can be a particularly high level of aggression. These children typically destroy other children's art work or building-block creations. Around the age of 4 or 5, depressed children who are asked directly sometimes describe themselves as being a "bad" boy or girl. Other signs of depression among young children include failure to eat and gain weight appropriately and an absence of emotional attachment to their primary caregiver.

During the elementary and middle school years, it can be harder to tell if a child is depressed. Some suggestions of depression are a sudden decline in academic performance as well as related problems including refusal to attend school and fearfulness of going to school. Depressed children sometimes find it difficult to sleep, and they tend to have frequent nightmares. In addition, physical symptoms that don't have a medical basis, such as frequent headaches and stomachaches, are very common among depressed children. Although elementary school-age children might not admit readily to sadness, they will describe themselves as incompetent. For example, 8-year-old Jane might not say that her mood is sad, but she will view herself as always "messing up" in school or sports.

Questions for children this age include, "Do you think you are as good as other people?" "Do you think things will get better for you in the future?" In addition, parents and professionals should assess social and recreational activities. When children cannot provide answers to questions about their pleasurable activities or can state only that they watch a lot of TV, parents should be concerned (Hodgman, Kaplan, Kazdin, & Van Dalen, 1993).

Depression increases markedly with the onset of puberty. As teenagers get older, the symptoms begin to resemble those of depressed adults. In younger teenagers, there will be a continuation of physical complaints such as stomachaches and headaches. In addition, there will be considerable moodiness as well as violent outbursts. These episodes sometimes include punching walls or breaking things. Girls, in particular, can become socially withdrawn and not interact with friends or family. Boys can be prone to drinking or drug use. Teenagers also might engage in high risk sexual activity. As teenagers become older, sleep and appetite disturbances, sadness, and suicidal ideation become increasingly common as symptoms of depression. A fairly common form of sleep disturbance in depressed teens is excessive sleeping. Depressed teens sometimes sleep as much as 12 to 14 hours a day.

What About the Risk of Suicide?

Parents should be concerned about the possibility of suicide when children are depressed. Among adolescents, the suicide rate has grown by over 300% in the past 30 years (Pfeffer, 1986). Suicide also has increased among preadolescent children. When adults are concerned about the possibility of suicide, it is important to ask children and adolescents *directly*. Parents and teachers are sometimes fearful that raising the issue of suicide will put the idea in children's heads, but there is very little evidence to support this fear. When teenagers are asked about suicide, they often are relieved to be able to speak openly about their frightening thoughts and feelings. It is important that questioning progress from probes such as, "Do you feel that sometimes your life isn't worth living?" or "Have you ever thought about hurting yourself?" to "Do you plan to hurt yourself?" "What has prevented you from harming yourself up to this point?" and "Do you think things will get better or worse?"

Children or adolescents who describe current suicidal thoughts should see a mental health professional as soon as possible. When a child shares suicidal thoughts with a school counselor, teacher, or coach, the adult should disclose this information immediately to the parent or caregiver. Although it is important for children and teenagers to have some degree of confidentiality, safety is paramount, and parents need to be notified so they can closely monitor their child.

What Are the Causes of Childhood Depression?

Depression in childhood and adolescence usually does not have a single cause. Part of the cause seems to be a hereditary predisposition for depression. Parents should be concerned about the possibility of depression developing in children when there is a family history of mood problems.

One of the most common external events associated with depression in children is exposure to marital conflict. Other events that tend to be associated with childhood depression are frequent geographic moves including changing schools, the death of a family member, and parental divorce. Children who lose a valued role (such as getting cut from the basketball team or losing a valued friendship) also can be at greater risk for depression.

What Can We Do to Help a Depressed Child?

Parents should get children who are depressed into counseling or therapy. The therapist also might work with parents directly but at minimum should communicate regularly about the child's progress and how to help him or her at home. In addition, therapy groups can be helpful for children, particularly those who have poor social skills and who have become increasingly isolated.

Treating depression in children and adolescents usually requires several therapies. Although antidepressant medication works fairly well with most adults, it is less consistently helpful in children. However, it might be worth considering, particularly in children who also have ADHD. Antidepressant medication treats the symptoms of both ADHD and depression. Teachers can help depressed children by giving them valued roles in the classroom and encouraging involvement in extracurricular and social activities. A teacher, coach, or scout leader who is concerned about the child and who can spend time with the child frequently, even for brief periods, often is helpful as a confidant and source of social support.

References and Resources

Hodgman, C., Kaplan, S., Kazdin, A., & Van Dalen, A. (1993). Managing depression in children. *Patient Care, 27*, 51-60.

Pfeffer, C. R. (1986). *The suicidal child.* New York: Guilford.

H. Russell Searight, Ph.D., is the director of behavioral sciences for the Residency Program of Family Medicine of St. Louis. He is the author of several textbooks and an adjunct associate professor in the department of psychology and Community and Family Medicine at St. Louis University.

Alcohol and Drug Abuse

H. Russell Searight, Ph.D.

Adolescents and adults with Attention Deficit/ Hyperactivity Disorder (ADHD) are at greater risk for abusing drugs and alcohol. Teenagers with ADHD who also have Conduct Disorder are at particularly high risk for substance abuse. One question many parents and teachers ask is, "When does 'normal' alcohol and drug experimentation become a serious problem?" This is a difficult question. Recent surveys found that over 80% of tenth graders and nearly two-thirds of eighth graders had tried alcohol. Slightly over half of high school seniors had used alcohol during the preceding month.

About two-thirds of U.S. teenagers have tried illegal drugs, with marijuana the most popular: 40% of U.S. high school students used marijuana, and about 25% of high school seniors reported marijuana use during the preceding month. Nearly 40% of teenagers also have used illicit drugs other than marijuana, amphetamines being the most common.

Occasional drug and alcohol use is very common among teenagers, and the consequences all too often are fatal. The leading causes of death among teenagers—accidents, homicide, and suicide—frequently are associated with substance abuse. About half of all teenagers who die violently had been drinking immediately before their death.

It is important to recognize that certain drugs are "gateway" drugs, leading to later, more serious substance problems. The most common gateway drugs are cigarettes, alcohol, and marijuana (Doweiko, 1990).

Because substance use is so common among teenagers, it is important for parents, teachers, counselors, and health care providers to know the difference between drug use, abuse, and dependence.

The majority of adolescents with drug problems *abuse* substances as opposed to being *dependent* on the substance. It is unusual for teenagers who drink to sustain liver damage or experience "DTs" (delirium tremens) when they stop drinking. However, for those teenagers who continue to use marijuana and alcohol, tolerance often does occur. Tolerance is a condition in which the teenager requires more of the drug to obtain the same effect.

Stages of Substance Abuse

Teenagers who develop serious drug problems seem to progress through five stages. In stage one, the adolescent usually makes a passive decision to try drugs or alcohol, almost always in a context of a peer group, party, or informal gathering. Most teenagers stop at this point and don't go on to more frequent drinking or drug use. However, "normal" experimentation can progress to more serious use for those teenagers who are more vulnerable—those with lower-self esteem or academic problems or who experience euphoric moods while under the influence.

In the second stage, teenagers begin to use alcohol and drugs more regularly, usually in the context of weekend parties. Because the adolescent's friends are also using drugs and alcohol, there can be more intense pressure to use larger quantities and a greater variety of drugs. During this stage, the teenager usually experiences reduced tension or anxiety and temporarily improved mood while under the influence.

In the third stage, the teenager has learned that there is a consistent relationship between using drugs and a short-lived sense of feeling better and more relaxed. The individual now actively seeks drugs and alcohol. In the past, the teenager used alcohol or marijuana provided by friends. Now, the teen begins to buy it for him- or herself and starts using it when alone. Substance abuse is no longer simply a weekend event; now the teenager uses drugs and alcohol to manage more stressful episodes during the week.

In the U.S., two-thirds to three-quarters of high school seniors hold down part-time jobs. Teenagers who are competitively employed are more likely to use cigarettes, alcohol, and marijuana, perhaps as a way of managing the stress of working in service-oriented jobs such as fast food and retail sales.

As substance abuse progresses to the next stage, teenagers become less concerned with their personal hygiene, their grades decline, and they find their friends among other substance abusers. As the pattern of use increases during this fourth stage, getting high or drunk becomes almost the singular focus of the day. Students skip classes and entire school days. The teenager sometimes gets high before going to school in the morning.

In the final stage, substance abuse affects the teenager's thought processes. Short-term memory and attention span become problematic. Reaction time is longer, and driving becomes dangerous. For those using marijuana, respiratory problems emerge with chronic coughs that won't go away.

What Causes Adolescents to Use Drugs and Alcohol?

Although experimentation is fairly common, teenagers who use drugs and alcohol are more likely to have parents who are substance abusers themselves. The child's peer group indeed plays a role in adolescent substance abuse, but peer influence is particularly strong when parental influence is low. Parents who do not model drinking or drug use themselves and who educate their children appropriately about the risks of substance abuse will be more likely to have children who are less influenced by substance-abusing peers.

Talking With Adolescents About a Substance-Abuse Problem

Many parents and teachers are afraid to raise the issue of substance abuse with teens because they fear alienating the adolescent or simply don't know how to talk about their concerns. One useful strategy is illustrated by the acronym WEEP. W is for *W*orry, E is for *E*vidence, E is for *E*ducation or *E*mpowerment, and P is for *P*lan (Ivy, Schneider, Burge, & Catala, 1994). Rather than accusing or criticizing the teenager, adults should begin the encounter by expressing their *own* feelings ("Susan, I am *W*orried about you"). Then, the parents specifically point out the *E*vidence for their concern ("Your grades have dropped from Bs to Ds, you are not keeping the midnight curfew we agreed on, and last night I smelled alcohol on your breath when you came home"). It is important that descriptions include concrete, observable behavior rather than focusing on feelings, beliefs, or attitudes (not "You don't care about anything, you're so disrespectful these days"). Parents should follow the evidence immediately with *E*ducation and *E*mpowerment ("You are a very intelligent young woman. You have done well in school and sports. Drinking has been getting in the way of your being able to use the gifts that you have"). It is extremely important that this confrontation include a specific and immediate *P*lan ("I think you need help to stop drinking. I have made an appointment for you with a counselor at 2:30 this afternoon. I will take you to his office"). Parents need to set up the plan in advance of the actual confrontation, and it must be a plan the family can follow realistically.

Because adolescents with ADHD are at particular risk for substance abuse, adults should be proactive about drug education while their children are younger. Aggressive drug abuse education might prevent later problems.

References and Resources

Doweiko, H. E. (1990) *Concepts of chemical dependency.* Pacific Grove, CA: Brooks-Cole.

Ivy, L., Schneider, D., Burge, S., & Catala, S. (1994). Sex, drugs, and rock 'n' roll: A student conference addressing sensitive issues. Society of Teachers of Family Medicine Violence Education Conference, Albuquerque, New Mexico.

Johnson, L. J., Bachman, J. G., & O'Malley, M. M. (1994). *National survey results in drug abuse from the Monitoring the Future study, 1975-1993.* Rockville, MD: U.S. Department of Health and Human Services/NIH Publication.

H. Russell Searight, Ph.D., is the director of behavioral sciences for the Residency Program of Family Medicine of St. Louis. He is the author of several textbooks and an adjunct associate professor in the department of psychology and Community and Family Medicine at St. Louis University.

Section 8

The Adult With Attention Deficit/Hyperactivity Disorder

What to Expect: Entering Adulthood With Attention Deficit/Hyperactivity Disorder

Christopher J. Nicholls, Ph.D.

How quickly they grow up! One minute it seems we are teaching our children how to tie their shoes; the next thing we know, they want the keys to the car. In the big picture, the time children spend at home with their parents is pretty short. Parents can have a lifetime of input into their children's lives, but all in all, children become adults very quickly.

How can parents best prepare their child with ADHD for the future? What should parents and their young adults expect? Are there any problems that seem to come up again and again? This article covers these and other subjects.

A Lifelong Disability

Although many of the early, core symptoms of ADHD seem to get better with age, this is a disorder that never really goes away. The troubles faced by the person with ADHD change with age and the different tasks of being an adult. For many, the support and guidance given by parents and teachers during the childhood years seem to disappear as the young adult leaves the nest. Parents can help to prepare for this transition if they expect certain trouble spots.

Independence

The transition out of the home is a difficult time for both the young adult and the parents. If college is part of the plan, then parents can hand off some of the responsibilities of watching over their young adult to a dormitory resident advisor or other supervisory person. The student can purchase meal tickets for the college cafeteria and rely on the college bus or the close-by shops and clubs common to most college campuses. In this way, parents can feel some comfort in knowing their child has a world specifically designed with the developmental needs of the young adult in mind.

It still might be a good idea, however, to explore (with your child) the resources available through the college's or university's disability resources or student services departments. Many colleges have an office designed to assist students with disabilities in various ways. Such services can add a layer of protection against the hard knocks of becoming independent.

Most people don't get to go away to live at a college campus, however. They face the issues of whether to continue to live at home (if they go to a local college or get a job) or get their own place to live. Often this becomes a "yo-yo" time of trial and error. Most 18-year-olds can't wait to get their own place to live, a job that will provide them with cash in their pocket, and the freedom of not having to be home by a certain time. However, many never really have had to pay for "everything" out of their paychecks before and suddenly find that there is "too much month at the end of their money!"

Some parents offer to have their young adult continue to live at home, rent and food (and laundry) free. This seems like a good way to ease entry into the adult world. If you wish to make this choice, then try to set it up so that the young adult has to take on more and more responsibility over time. Ask that your child make "rent" payments and contribute some money for food, utilities, supplies, etc. Help your young adult set up a budget and set aside money from each paycheck to pay the bills. Go over the household finances together—both income and expenses—and show your child how to set aside money for taxes, car insurance, retirement, etc. Most people learn these things as they are forced to deal with them. You can help by preparing your young adult ahead of time.

If your youngster will live at home, discuss and agree upon what the rules will be. Set guidelines based on your needs, and explain that if the youngster wants to live with you, he or she must go by your rules. Discuss what time at night the child must be home (or have called to say that he or she won't be home). Discuss your preferences on such issues as having friends/dates over, smoking/drinking/drugs, and use of the family car and other items. Don't be a pushover. It's your house! Don't be inflexible, however. Help your young adult learn to negotiate for change by identifying his or her own wants and needs, asking for them in a responsible way, and being willing to "pay" for them by his or her own responsible behavior.

Responsibility

We don't change overnight. It takes time to learn to be responsible, and you probably have been working on these issues since you first asked your child to pick up the toys. With increasing age, however, the responsibilities get tougher, and ADHD is a big risk factor for having lots of different kinds of problems.

It might be helpful to define responsibility as the ability to respond—in other words, we all make choices about what we do. Help your young adult think through various situations and make choices on the basis of good information, not impulse. Guide your young person by prompting him or her to make up a plan, think about the various outcomes of different choices, and live with these decisions.

What Are Some Common Areas of Trouble?

Credit Cards

Recommend using cards that require a deposited balance or must be paid off each month. If you cosign an account, require that you see the statements regularly.

Driving

Young adults with ADHD have a much higher rate of accidents. Actively teach defensive driving, insist that your child take extra driver education classes, make sure he or she takes the appropriate medications, and require your young adult to abstain from alcohol and drugs while operating a vehicle. Consider "safe" cars; avoid motorcycles. Require that your child buy his or her own auto insurance and pay for gas and auto repairs.

Alcohol and Drugs

People with ADHD are much more likely to have problems with drugs and alcohol. Actively discuss the ways alcohol interferes with judgment and coordination. Explain that nicotine is highly addictive and that although it treats ADHD symptoms (it does), tobacco smoke kills. Encourage your child to find the right type and dosage of medications to treat his or her symptoms and to take the medicine regularly.

Employment

Consider asking the young adult to visit with an employment or vocational counselor. Some jobs are just not a good fit for some people and are perfect for others. There is no perfect "ADHD job," so help your child identify the kinds of interests, skills, and talents he or she has and the style of work he or she can handle best. Match abilities and interests with the job. Help your young person avoid the frequent tendency of adults with ADHD to skip from one job to another because they get bored easily or can't follow the rules and duties of the job.

Relationships

"The grass is always greener on the other side" is particularly true for people with ADHD. Finding someone who will appreciate one's talents and accept one's troubles is hard enough when one is patient and self-assured. It is harder still if the person is impulsive and prone to thrill seeking. Explain that mature relationships involve prob-

lem solving, sharing, and mutual support. Help your young adult solve conflicts by talking and trying to find "win-win" solutions.

Deal With Emotional Baggage

Very few people have ADHD alone. Depression, anxiety, learning problems, substance abuse, anger control problems—all are common conditions that accompany ADHD. Be sure to treat each of these problems effectively. Encourage your young adult to seek professional help when needed. Most problems can be dealt with quickly, effectively, and at a reasonable cost. Ask for referrals from your doctor, if needed.

Self-Esteem

Many, if not most, adults with ADHD have taken some pretty big hits on their self-concept over the years. Help place the hurts in perspective. Point out the areas of strength and success. Actively praise and be proud of what your young adult does well, no matter how little the task. Explain that adults must pump themselves up when the going gets tough and that adults often don't receive from others the kind of feedback that parents and teachers gave them throughout their childhood. Young adults must learn to set their own goals and measure success by their own achievements. Consider hiring a "coach" to teach organization, time management, and other skills.

Allow Setbacks and Expect Ups and Downs

One of the hardest parts of being a parent is allowing our children to fail and to learn from their mistakes. Be there to support and help, but remember that your child is an individual and that you are not responsible for what he or she does. Be proud of your child's victories and comfort your child in failure, but don't fall into the trap of feeling that you have failed if all things don't go right. All parents try to the best of their abilities. Some do better than others. Your love and teaching prepares your child for adulthood. Your teachings will be there forever, in your child's heart.

Christopher J. Nicholls, Ph.D., is a health psychologist in private practice in Phoenix. A graduate of the University of Virginia, he specializes in children with traumatic brain injuries and attention disorders.

Medication for Adult Attention Deficit/Hyperactivity Disorder

Fred Rottnek, M.D.

What Is Adult ADHD?

ADHD is a medical condition that causes problems with concentration, impulse control, and sitting still. ADHD has not been studied as thoroughly in adults as in children, but researchers suspect that at least half the individuals who had ADHD as children will continue to have symptoms in adulthood. ADHD usually is diagnosed by health care providers when a person mentions having problems with confusion, unclear thinking, disorganization, or distraction. People often have trouble at work or at home with their family because of these problems.

If you are told you might have ADHD, a physician or psychologist (or both) will do some testing. They will ask you questions about your life and your activities. They also might have you perform tasks to assess your memory, concentration, and ability to manage distractions. If you do have ADHD, you will receive a treatment plan. Part of this treatment plan usually includes medication. Other parts include therapy with a psychologist or counselor and behavioral skills for you to practice on your own.

Medications for Adults With ADHD

As already mentioned, experts have studied ADHD in children much more than in adults. This is also true for the medications used to treat ADHD. With few exceptions, doctors prescribe the same medications for adults as for children. Often they must adjust the dosages more in adults because scientists haven't done enough studies yet to determine the right dose. Your physician will work with you to find the best medication and the best dose for you.

The paragraphs that follow describe the different types of medications used to treat adult ADHD, how they work, how they are prescribed, and their possible side effects. (Side effects are unintended actions of a drug that occur in some people as a result of how the drug works in the body. Some of the possible side effects of these drugs are fast heartbeat, edginess, and dry mouth. These effects are not wanted, and they don't help ADHD. They just happen. And they usually go away within a few weeks.)

Stimulants

These medications include methylphenidate (Ritalin) and pemoline (Cylert). They work by increasing your ability to concentrate. These are the best-studied ADHD medica-tions. Both come in a "regular" form in which the medication is absorbed in your body immediately and begins working right after you take the pill. Both also come in a "sustained-release" form, in which the medication releases slowly and evenly into your system over a longer period of time. People tend to respond better to one type or the other. Adults usually start on a low dose of stimulants. The doctor then might increase the dose until the ADHD symptoms decrease or are under much better control.

Many people have side effects for several weeks or months after they start stimulants. These can involve insomnia, edginess, loss of appetite, and headaches. You always should let your physician know of these problems.

Antidepressants

Medications commonly used to treat major depression also seem to be helpful in adults with ADHD. These medications probably work by changing the amount of chemicals found naturally in your brain. With these changes, you can get relief from your ADHD symptoms as well as the feelings of depression or nervousness that often occur with ADHD. Many studies have shown these medications to be safe, and most people take the medications once a day. The following are types of antidepressants.

Tricyclic antidepressants (TCAs)

These medications include imipramine (Tofranil), desi-pramine (Norpramin), and nortriptyline (Pamelor). These medications are the oldest antidepressants. Researchers have studied these medications extensively in childhood ADHD and many other adult medical conditions. Side effects involve dry mouth, constipation, and weight gain.

Selective serotonin reuptake inhibitors (SSRIs)

These medications include fluoxetine (Prozac), sertraline (Zoloft), and paroxetine (Paxil). These medications are often in the news because they have become popular for treating many psychiatric and medical problems. By changing the level of the brain's own chemicals (namely, serotonin), these medications can increase attention span and help ADHD. Side effects are mild and a little different for each of these medications. They sometimes cause nausea, diarrhea, edginess, or insomnia.

Other antidepressants

Doctors have prescribed many other classes of antidepressants to treat ADHD. Some are buproprion (Wellbutrin) and MAOIs (monamine oxidase inhibitors). These medications work like those already described; however, there are certain foods (such as cheese and chocolate) that you must not eat while taking some of these medications. Physicians typically prescribe these medications for people with ADHD who also have problems with depression and anxiety.

Antihypertensives

Doctors prescribe antihypertensives to treat high blood pressure, but they also have been helpful in treating children with ADHD, especially those who are hyperactive or tend to start fights. Now doctors are using these medicines for adults with ADHD, particularly those who show signs of hyperactivity. Some of these medications are atenolol (Tenoretic) and metoprolol (Lopressor). Side effects from these drugs include dizziness and headaches. These go away with dosage adjustment or as the person becomes used to the medication.

Combined Medication Therapies

Sometimes doctors will prescribe a combination of medications for people who aren't helped by just one. Some medications complement the work of the other medicine, or one medication increases the activity of the other. Combination therapy is especially helpful for people who have problems other than ADHD that these medications can help. Popular combinations are stimulants with TCAs or stimulants with beta-blockers. Side effects are similar to those described above.

Summary

If you are diagnosed with ADHD, medications might play an important part in your treatment plan. Doctors now are prescribing for adults many of the medications that they've used for years in children. All medications need adjustment in doses, and all can have temporary side effects. As with all medications, the keys to ADHD medications are listening to your physician's instructions and always taking your medications as prescribed.

References and Resources

Feifel, D. (1996). Attention-deficit hyperactivity disorder in adults. *Postgraduate Medicine, 100,* 207-218.

Wilens, T. E. Biederman, J., Spencer, T. J., & Prince, J. (1995). Pharmacotherapy of adult attention deficit/hyperactivity disorder: A review. *Journal of Clinical Psychopharmacology, 15,* 270-279.

Fred Rottnek, M.D., is a faculty family physician with Family Medicine of St. Louis. His interests include community medicine, health education, health care for the homeless, and behavioral science.

College Students With Learning Disabilities

Amy Ellis, Psy.D.

College students with learning disabilities have average to superior levels of intelligence and are talented and capable individuals. Most have developed a variety of strategies to compensate for some of the academic struggles they've experienced over the years. At most colleges, students with learning disabilities must go through the same competitive process of admission as students without learning disabilities. Further, most students disclose their learning disability only after they have been admitted.

A learning disability affects how a person takes in, retains, and expresses information. Learning disabilities are a result of nervous system dysfunction, usually genetic in nature, and are present throughout life. However, the problems associated with a learning disability can change, depending on the demands for learning and the setting. Further, a learning disability might manifest itself in only one academic area (such as math or foreign language) or affect an individual's performance across a variety of subjects and disciplines. The degree of severity varies from individual to individual (Duane & Leong, 1985).

There are over 100 different types of learning disabilities. Typically, a person displays a cluster of learning disabilities rather than just one. Most common learning disabilities occur in the areas of reading skills, reading comprehension, written expression, listening comprehension, mathematics, problem solving, oral expression, visual-motor processing, and speed of processing. In addition, many students with learning disabilities also struggle with attention/concentration and time management. Frequently, students with learning disabilities become frustrated because their disability is not visible. Faculty, parents, and peers often are unaware of the challenges faced by individuals with learning disabilities.

Most students with learning disabilities coming into the university setting are already cognizant of their learning disability from assessment in a previous academic setting. However, it is becoming more common for diagnosis of learning disabilities to take place at the college level. It is important that diagnosis be done either by an educational therapist or a psychologist. Assessment includes an IQ test as well as tests of academic achievement and information processing and a thorough history (developmental, academic, and familial). Some university campuses provide assessment for learning disabilities; others refer students to off-campus professionals.

Once a student receives the diagnosis of learning disability, it is important to determine the most appropriate measures for academic success. Many colleges offer study skills courses in addition to academic support services. The Individuals With Disabilities Education Act of 1990 requires universities to provide academic accommodations appropriate to the nature of a student's disability. The need for academic accommodations and services varies from student to student. Common accommodations and services can include note takers in the class to supplement a student's notes, exam accommodations, assistance with registration, priority registration, peer mentoring programs, study skills courses, and referrals to other campus and community resources.

Other suggestions for college students with learning disabilities include building on areas of academic strength, using a multisensory approach to learning (for example, using auditory, visual, and kinesthetic modalities in learning), becoming knowledgeable about describing the disability so they can advocate for themselves with faculty, sitting toward the front of the classroom, taking minimized course loads, reviewing notes as soon as possible after class to refresh memory and fill in any gaps, setting realistic goals, and linking up with campus support services.

College students with learning disabilities can be highly successful academically. Assessment is the first step toward self-knowledge and understanding of ability structure, which in turn is the prerequisite for accepting responsibility for one's own learning. Taking advantage of the necessary support services facilitates a successful college experience for students with learning disabilities.

References and Resources

Duane, D., & Leong, C. (1985). *Understanding learning disabilities: International and multidisciplinary views.* New York: Plenum Press.

Amy Ellis, Psy.D., is a certified psychologist with Learning Development Services in San Diego. She specializes in adults with attention and learning disorders.

Strategies for Success in College

Gretchen Gyving, M.Ed.

College students with ADHD face many new challenges. The structure and routines that allowed them to be successful at home do not transfer automatically to the college environment where they are living independently, often for the first time. Therefore, much of their success depends on their ability to find strategies that will help them cope effectively with their distractibility, hyperactivity, impulsivity, memory difficulties, time management difficulties, and poor organizational skills in their new environment.

The first step toward success in college for students with ADHD is becoming educated about their own unique patterns of cognitive strengths and weaknesses. As students understand their cognitive abilities, they are able to accommodate their areas of weakness and use their strengths to ensure success. Once college students with ADHD understand their cognitive abilities, they must learn how to advocate effectively for the accommodations that will allow them to maximize their academic potential.

There are many accommodations available to students at the college level. These include taking exams in an environment free of distractions, getting extra time on exams, either receiving an outline of the lecture notes or being assigned a note taker, and using a word processor during exams. A psychoeducational assessment will help determine which of these accommodations best match the student's learning profile.

Once students with ADHD have obtained the necessary accommodations, there are several strategies they can use in their day-to-day routines that will help them be more successful.

Distractibility

One area of vulnerability for college students with ADHD is the struggle to focus and sustain attention. Both internal and external distractions can serve to disrupt attention and concentration. Students can learn a variety of ways to manage these distractions more effectively. For example, students should study in a distraction-free environment. Turn off phones and pagers. Face desks away from windows. Use earplugs or soft, familiar music to screen out background noise. Request a roommate with good study habits.

In addition, students can learn to minimize the effects of internal sources of distraction such as daydreaming, forgotten tasks, and creative ideas (Nadeau, 1997). First,

students need to become active participants in the studying process. For example, students should take notes as they read and/or ask questions during lectures rather than passively reviewing the information. These individuals should get in the habit of using a day planner to minimize the number of forgotten appointments and assignments. Finally, students can write down and save creative ideas to ponder after they have finished their studying.

Hyperactivity

College students with ADHD also struggle with an excess of energy. This can be particularly disruptive in an environment that promotes such sedentary activities as sitting through lectures and hours of studying. However, students can learn to manage hyperactivity effectively and fidget respectfully. For example, taking notes during lecture, chewing gum, fidgeting with a variety of handheld toys, standing in the back of the lecture hall, and taking restroom breaks all involve body movement of some type. In addition, students can schedule classes with breaks in between, which will allow for movement and exercise. In addition, students might benefit from participating in athletic activities during free time.

Impulsivity

Impulsivity is a third area of vulnerability for college students with ADHD. These students are prone to making impulsive decisions. They tend to drop classes, skip lectures, and take on too many commitments at once without thinking of the long-term consequences. Impulsivity also can result in a loss of efficiency. Jumping into assignments without planning can lead to time-consuming mistakes and ineffective strategies.

It is important for students to determine whether a given class load will be manageable. Individuals with ADHD should not overload themselves. It is better to be successful in a few classes than to barely pass several classes. In addition, it is important not to make impulsive commitments. Rather than immediately agreeing to oversee a project, students with ADHD need to learn to say, "I'd like to, but I need to check my schedule." Also, developing a plan or strategy before beginning an assignment will minimize errors and the need to redo assignments. Finally, go back and "undo" mistakes quickly. Changing impulsive decisions at the outset is often much easier.

Low Frustration Threshold

Low frustration tolerance can be an area of difficulty for students with ADHD. Unfortunately, much of the educational experience requires repetitive, uninteresting material. Many students become bored with daily management and following through on tasks. Whenever possible, students with ADHD should team up with other students whose strengths complement their own areas of ADHD-linked weakness (look for students who are good at details and day-to-day management).

In addition, students with ADHD should look for assistance and training to improve their organizational skills. Student services departments frequently offer study skills classes. If possible, students should choose a variety of classes that will allow for a high degree of change and variety in subjects and assignments. Whenever possible, they also should choose professors who assign tasks matching their scholastic strengths. Finally, students can hire a tutor or coach to keep them motivated and on track with assignments.

Memory Difficulties

Students with ADHD often display poor short-term memory. They misplace items including class notes and textbooks, and they forget assignment due dates. Strategies for improving memory include carrying a day planner at all times and keeping all notes on scheduling and assignments in that planner. If note taking is difficult, students can use a tape recorder. Beepers and watch alarms as well as visual prompts such as self-stick notes are useful in reminding students of important tasks and deadlines. It is also helpful to develop routines because they place less demands on memory (Nadeau, 1997).

Poor Time Management

Time management is an area of weakness for many college students with ADHD. Students should plan to arrive early to classes, appointments, and meetings, to allow for unforeseen events. Arriving early gives students time to plan, focus, or reread the notes from the last class. However, getting to class early requires that students do two things. First, they must resist the temptation to do "just one more thing" before leaving for class. Second, they must build preparation time into their schedule, rather than letting "it's time to go" be the cue to start getting ready (Nadeau, 1997). To cope with procrastination, students might want to avoid classes that require long-term projects with huge reports at the end. Individuals with ADHD should commit themselves to a deadline and declare that deadline to the professor. Often, making a promise to others will help students with ADHD overcome their own resistance.

Students with ADHD should work with other students whenever possible. Teaming up with a conscientious student for study sessions will serve as a motivator. Another possibility is to hire a coach to help instill motivation. Finally, students should break assignments up into small parts and reward themselves for completing each section of the assignment.

Organizational Problems

Organization can be difficult for college students with ADHD. The most helpful strategy is to start at the end of a task and plan back through time. Students can mark in their day planners when an assignment is due and then work backwards, indicating the various dates by which earlier stages of the assignment must be completed. Students can reinforce these due dates by creating a large chart they hang on the wall and check frequently. This will reduce errors occurring as the result of "out of sight is out of mind." Finally, keep class schedules manageable. Full course loads often tax the organizational capacity of many students. Fewer classes might provide more opportunities for success.

Hyperfocusing

Another area of vulnerability for college students with ADHD is the tendency to hyperfocus at the expense of completing other activities. Students can become so involved in a task that they forget to attend class or complete other assignments. Individuals can manage this tendency to hyperfocus by scheduling time to become immersed in the activity when it will not conflict with other commitments, by providing a cue to interrupt the session (e.g., set an alarm or ask a roommate to interrupt the student), and by completing necessary tasks before engaging in such an activity (Nadeau, 1997).

If students with ADHD are able to gain a clear understanding of their learning strengths and vulnerabilities, advocate effectively for the accommodations that will allow them to maximize their potential for academic success, and implement coping strategies, college can be a rewarding, self-esteem-building experience. One of the primary elements in college that differentiates this level of education from previous educational experiences is that students are able to choose subjects they enjoy. Interest is an essential ingredient in success for students with ADHD.

References and Resources

Nadeau, K. G. (1997). *ADD in the workplace: Choices, changes, and challenges.* New York: Brunner/Mazel Publishers.

Gretchen Gyving, M.Ed., is an educator and therapist with Learning Development Services in San Diego.

The Impact of Attention Deficit/ Hyperactivity Disorder on Relationships

Marla Gil-McMahon, Psy.D.

The symptoms of Attention Deficit/Hyperactivity Disorder (ADHD) continue into adulthood for over 40% of the individuals diagnosed with the disorder (Murphy, 1996; Wilens, Spencer, & Prince, 1997). The three key symptoms of the disorder (inattention, impulsivity, and hyperactivity) affect relationships. This article describes some key strategies to help adults deal with these challenges.

Distractibility and Inattention

Problems with attention and distractibility can make it difficult for individuals to maintain attention in conversations with peers and family members. The adult with ADHD sometimes has difficulty listening to others and attending to subtle social cues and tends to tune out periodically in conversations (Nadeau, 1993; Ratey, Hallowell, & Miler, 1995). For many adults with ADHD, this has a detrimental effect on the ability to sustain a conversation or communicate effectively with a spouse who doesn't have ADHD. These challenges with attention can take the form of misunderstanding or not hearing what the partner said, which can lead to continued conflicts within the marriage and frustrations in a relationship.

Impulsivity

The adult with ADHD also can have difficulty with impulsiveness. Individuals with ADHD sometimes speak impulsively, talk out of turn, and say things before thinking about the effects of what they've said. They also tend to interrupt partners frequently, often putting more value on their own statements than their partners' contributions. Spouses without ADHD can feel misunderstood and might interpret these behaviors as purposeful and rude. Feeling misunderstood or not listened to interferes with effective communication, and both partners can begin to believe that they are not able to have a meaningful conversation with each other, leading to feelings of dissatisfaction and discouragement.

The symptoms of impulsivity impair the adult's ability to plan and organize. This in turn affects the couple's finances. The spouse with ADHD might spend money impulsively and fail to communicate the amount to the other spouse. Because of difficulties in planning ahead, the other person with ADHD might make purchases without considering how the other partner might feel about the cost and the effect of this purchase on other major household expenses (Nadeau, 1991).

These challenges can disrupt the best of relationships. Therefore, it is important to involve the spouse without ADHD in the process of understanding the diagnosis and managing the disorder. Without a clear understanding of the effects of ADHD and its treatment, the spouse without ADHD can become discouraged, angry, and resentful over the behavior of the individual with ADHD. The answer appears to lie in educating the partner about the disorder and identifying the common struggles encountered by other couples in this situation. This way the partners can begin to accept the disability together and begin to see other avenues to understanding one another. They can learn more effective ways to communicate with each other.

How to Work It Out

The following suggestions are offered to couples in which one or both partners have been diagnosed with ADHD.

Communication

1. Listen to your spouse.

   - Make time to sit down and hear about what your spouse has to say without external distractions (turn off the TV, stereo, and telephone).

   - Ask questions about what your partner is saying so that you can understand what he or she means (don't assume your partner is good at mind reading).

   - Show your partner that you respect and understand what he or she has to say (repeat what your partner just said to make sure you understood it).

   - Ask your partner what he or she wants out of this conversation.

   - Observe your spouse's body language as he or she speaks for clues of feelings or hidden emotions.

2. Use "I-statements" rather than blaming your partner.

   - "I feel hurt about what you did."

   - "I feel mad because you broke your promise."

3. Follow through on promises.

   - If you make a promise to your spouse, make sure you can follow through.

   - Don't take on something that is unrealistic or unreasonable!

- Promises you don't keep tend to pile up and can lead to resentments in the relationship.
- In order to follow through on your promises, do the following:
  — First, clarify what the promise is and be sure you agree about what it is.
  — Write down your promise on your calendar with a brightly colored pen.
  — Complete your promise as soon as possible. **(Do it today!)**
  — Talk to your spouse when you deliver your promise and see if it met his or her expectations. If you did not fulfill your promise, clean it up ASAP.

4. Express yourself in a responsible manner.
   - If you are angry with your spouse, **cool down** before talking.
   - Talk to a friend about your anger and get a second opinion.
   - Write down ideas about what you want to say to your partner. Write a letter or tape record your key points, then review your thoughts together.

Disorganization

Time management

1. Make a joint schedule and post it in a place where everyone can see it (e.g., on the refrigerator).
2. Communicate expectations. Talk about what you both expect, such as who will be doing housework, buying groceries, paying bills, etc.
3. Understand each other's schedule for the week. If your work schedule changes each week, let your spouse know about the changes.
4. Evaluate your week together. Check in with your spouse about the week and how he or she dealt with time management. See what worked and what didn't, and find ways to manage upsets as they happen.

Money/Budgeting

1. Sit down with your spouse and evaluate or create a budget.
2. Talk daily about the money you both spent so you and your spouse know how much is in the account.
3. One person should be responsible for paying bills, balancing the checkbook, etc.
4. Limit the number of credit cards you use.

Housework

1. Make a list of household chores and determine who is responsible for each task.
2. Create **structure** (an environment for order and routine) in your household. Understand that your household might need additional external structure so family members understand their responsibilities and remember to do them. Specify times for certain activities, such as dinner, and try to maintain a consistent time for each activity.
3. Create rewards for accomplishing goals.
4. Be careful not to expect too much. Reduce disappointment by keeping expectations realistic.
5. Modify the environment to fit the way you work. For example, if you work better with auditory stimuli, turn up the music or wear earphones to do your chores! If you do better without external stimuli, keep things quiet as you do the chores.
6. Designate one area that is off-limits to anyone but the partner with ADHD. This could be a designated room or desk over which the disorganized person has free rein. Let the person have this area all to him- or herself.

It *is* possible to have a great relationship with a person who has ADHD. Just remember that it takes time, management skills, acceptance, and lots of love.

References and Resources

Hallowell, E., & Ratey, J. (1994). *Driven to distraction.* New York: Simon & Schuster, Inc.

Nadeau, K. (1991, Fall). Till ADD do us part? Maybe not. *ADDendum, 6,* 15-17.

Nadeau, K. (1993). If your spouse has ADD: What's it like to be married to someone with ADD. *ADD Vantage, 3,* 40-41

Murphy, K. (1996). *Out of the fog: Treatment options and coping strategies for adult attention deficit disorder.* New York: Skylight Press.

Ratey, J., Hallowell, E., & Miler, A. (1995). Relationship dilemmas for adults with ADD: The biology of intimacy. In K. G. Nadeau (Ed.) *A comprehensive guide to attention deficit disorder in adults* (pp. 218-235). New York: Brunner/Mazel, Inc.

Whiteman, T., & Novotni, M. (1995). *Adult ADD.* Colorado Springs, CO: Pinon Press.

Wilens, T., Spencer, T, and Prince, J. (1997). Diagnosing ADD in adults. *Attention, 4,* 27-38.

Marla Gil-McMahon, Psy.D., has a degree in special education with a doctorate in psychology. She is an associate with Learning Development Services in San Diego.

Marriage and Intimacy

H. Russell Searight, Ph.D.

ADHD Symptoms in Adulthood

About 30% to 50% of children with Attention Deficit/ Hyperactivity Disorder (ADHD) continue to show some form of the disorder in adulthood. Adults with ADHD often do not have the pronounced level of hyperactivity seen in children. However, they are likely to be fidgety, which can show up as tapping the fingers, shaking the legs, and rocking in the chair (Wender, 1995). Adults with ADHD also will have difficulties with concentration. It might be very difficult for them to read more than a page or two without being distracted. The adult with ADHD chronically tends to lose things, including keys, wallet, or purses.

Emotionally, many adults with ADHD say that they have difficulty relaxing. They feel "wired" and appear to be on edge (Wender, 1995). Mood swings are very common and ADHD adults often seem "hot tempered." Usually their temper outbursts are short lived, and they quickly forget or get over their frustration.

In addition, ADHD adults tend to have problems with organization and task completion. They begin new projects but leave them unfinished for other new projects that they also leave unfinished. Difficulty managing stress is also common among adults with ADHD. Because of this difficulty, they sometimes become overwhelmed, particularly when there are multiple demands or deadlines looming. To friends and family, adults with ADHD seem to dart from activity to activity without putting significant effort into any one task.

Lastly, impulsivity is very common. Adults with ADHD take up hobbies and end them suddenly. They might make major purchases (such as a car) on the spur of the moment and interrupt conversations frequently. Adults with ADHD sometimes blurt out socially inappropriate comments because they often talk without thinking (Wender, 1995).

Impact on Close Relationships

Naturally, this behavioral pattern can create interpersonal conflicts in close relationships such as marriage. The impulsivity of adults with ADHD sometimes leads them to make decisions suddenly without thinking about the impact on their spouse or significant other. For example, booking a cruise for two weeks without consulting a spouse can lead to considerable anger and frustration. Similarly, making major purchases such as furniture, automobiles, or appliances on impulse often will leave the other spouse feeling left out and insulted. It has been suggested that adults with ADHD, because of their impulsivity, simply do not slow down enough to consider their spouse's perspective. The idea of planning or taking another person's schedule or needs into account might not occur to adults with ADHD, not because they are intentionally neglectful or uncaring, but because they respond without thinking first.

These difficulties also can carry over into communication. Because they often will speak before thinking, adults with ADHD can be overly blunt or even insulting in their comments to others. They usually are genuinely surprised when their partner is hurt or angry in response.

The emotional intensity and the sudden bursts of frustration can be frightening for the spouse of the adult with ADHD. Discussions about important issues can result in an angry outburst complete with door slamming and name calling. Fifteen minutes later the adult with ADHD might come back and apologize or return and simply carry on as if the argument never occurred. The spouse without ADHD usually values more sustained communication and resolution of differences.

The adult with ADHD, particularly after an emotional outburst, might be aware that his or her response was overly intense but might not appreciate the value of trying to understand or resolve conflicts. Similarly, trying to make a conjoint decision also can lead to resentment because of the lack of closure. The adult with ADHD might hop from topic to topic without reaching agreement on relatively minor issues such as where to go for dinner on a Friday night.

Maintaining an appropriate perspective on family priorities also can tax the attentional skills of the adult with ADHD. For example, it might be difficult for the person to realize that it's more important to show up on time for the son's or daughter's celebration, performance, or sporting event than to deal with a minor problem that has just surfaced and thus is foremost in the parent's mind.

Problem Solving and Communication Skills

In addition to medication, there are a number of specific strategies that can help increase relationship satisfaction among adults with ADHD and their partners. A structured format for problem solving often will keep the adult with ADHD on track. The following series of steps can help such couples: (a) state the problem, (b) brainstorm a range of possible options, (c) review the list of options generated, (d) discard those options that are unrealistic, (e) further narrow the range of available options in a systematic way, and (f) select one or two options to implement (Weinstein, 1994). It also might be helpful for the couple to set aside structured time every day (for example, between 6:30 and 7:00 every evening) to address family issues. Keeping a large calendar with all appointments and family activities, scheduled as many months in advance as possible, in a central place (such as on the refrigerator or over the kitchen table) provides frequent reminders.

It is also important that the partner with ADHD not use the disorder as an excuse for failing to follow through on important relationship commitments. The adult with ADHD does have an area of weakness, but it's an area of weakness that responds to environmental and pharmacological intervention.

When giving feedback to a partner with ADHD, it is important that the communication be behaviorally specific. Rather than saying, "You just don't seem to care about me," it is more helpful for the spouse to say, "I become very disappointed when we schedule lunch together and you arrive 30 minutes late." In addition, it is important to avoid trait-like labels such as, "You are so inconsiderate, you never show up on time," or "You have no sense of responsibility, you never get anything done." This type of feedback is not helpful at all. Instead, use very specific communication that includes suggestions to prevent the problem from occurring in the future ("If you see you're going to be late coming home for dinner, would you agree to call me an hour beforehand?").

Treatment of Adult ADHD and Relationship Dynamics

Identifying and treating the symptoms of ADHD and becoming more aware of the pervasive impact of the disorder can lead to an improvement in the person's ability to communicate and listen actively to his or her partner. However, many adults with ADHD might, at this point, feel guilty that they have wronged spouses, children, and employers (Wender, 1995). It is important that adults with ADHD take some responsibility for inappropriate behavior that has been harmful to others. But they also should recognize that they are now in a position to be more responsive and sensitive to important others in their lives. Rather than beating themselves up about what they were unable to do in the past, it is much more helpful for such adults to focus on what they would like their relationships to look like in the future.

In some long-standing relationships, the participants might have developed a pattern of interaction centering around the ADHD symptoms. For example, the adult with ADHD has been cast in the role as the "irresponsible husband" in contrast to the "responsible and stable wife." As these roles become equalized, there sometimes is some emotional threat or fear of losing control of the relationship, particularly for the spouse without ADHD.

More commonly, however, treatment leads to a much deeper intimacy. Because of improved attention and capacity for focusing, the adult with ADHD now is able to pay attention to and genuinely appreciate the spouse's feelings. Husbands and wives commonly report that they feel that the spouse with ADHD is finally "with them" and emotionally available for a sustained period of time (Bemporad & Zambeneddeti, 1996).

References and Resources

Bemporad, J. & Zambeneddeti, M. (1996). Psychotherapy of adults with attention deficit disorder. *The Journal of Psychotherapy Practice and Research, 5,* 228-237.

Weinstein, C. S. (1994). Cognitive remediation strategies: An adjunct to the psychotherapy of adults with attention deficit hyperactivity disorder. *The Journal of Psychotherapy Practice and Research, 3,* 44-57.

Wender, P. H. (1995). *Attention Deficit Hyperactivity Disorder in adults.* New York: Oxford University Press.

H. Russell Searight, Ph.D., is the director of behavioral sciences for the Residency Program of Family Medicine of St. Louis. He is the author of several textbooks and an adjunct associate professor in the department of psychology and Community and Family Medicine at St. Louis University.

New Insights Into Childhood Risks and Adversities and the Lives of Those Who Have Overcome Them

Mark Katz, Ph.D.

Robert Louis Stevenson once said, "Life is not so much a matter of holding good cards, but sometimes of playing a poor hand well." Many adults who currently enjoy meaningful and productive lives grew up under very difficult and emotionally stressful conditions that they couldn't change, no matter how hard they tried. Some were abused physically, sexually, or emotionally. Others witnessed a great deal of violence, often between people they cared deeply about. And others grew up in homes where those they depended on to take care of them weren't able to do so on any kind of consistent basis because of serious personal and psychiatric problems.

There are also many individuals currently enjoying successful and productive lives who did very poorly all through school. From the first day of first grade, they struggled. Some had learning disabilities. Others had attention-related difficulties. And some, we now know, experienced both in combination.

Researchers have been studying the life trajectories of these individuals, individuals who have overcome risks related to harmful outside influences and risks related to more internal influences. And these researchers are learning a great deal. They're identifying reasons why, for example, some individuals don't succumb to the harmful effects of multiple risk exposure. And for those who do succumb, who suffer emotionally for years only to stage a complete turnabout in their 20s and 30s, the researchers are learning how they're doing it, how they're making the best of turning-point experiences and second-chance opportunities. While there's still much to learn about the positive life trajectories of individuals such as these, much already has been learned. And this knowledge might prove very helpful to children, families, and young adults now confronting many of the same life circumstances.

The Effects of Multiple Risk Exposure

As the number of risks that we're exposed to increases, the chances of our suffering significant harm also increases. This is true for children and for adults. James Garbarino, Ph.D. (1995), has contributed greatly to our understanding of how exposure to multiple risks can affect the quality of our lives. Imagine placing four tennis balls in front of you, says Garbarino, with each tennis ball representing a single risk factor. Your job is to juggle the tennis balls. Most of us can juggle one ball. Some of us can juggle two balls. Now

imagine juggling three balls. A few of us might be able to do this, but not that many. Now imagine juggling four balls. You throw four balls into the air, and what happens? They all fall to the ground. Think of each ball as representing one risk factor. That's the effect that exposure to multiple risks can have on our lives. As the risks that we're exposed to mount, there can come a point where it's just no longer possible to function normally. Although we might not have been able to juggle three balls, we still caught one or two of them when we tried. Three balls didn't all fall to the ground. They all did, however, when we tried to juggle four balls. A 10-year-old child with attention deficits, growing up in a close knit, loving family, living in an affluent neighborhood, receiving individualized attention at a small structured school is having to juggle fewer tennis balls than a child with attention deficits who was removed from his birth parents' home because of neglect and who has lived in eight different foster placements.

Protective Influences

Protective influences can outweigh the effects of exposure to multiple childhood risks and adversities (Werner, 1995). And protection can come from many different sources. Sometimes, it originates from within. This is the case for children and adults. Our personal qualities and our ability to reach out to others can draw others to us in times of need. And our capacity to make sense out of traumatizing experiences that we have endured can allow us to restore shattered assumptions about the meaningfulness of the world and of our place in it (Janoff-Bulman, 1992).

Protective influences that are more internal in nature, that are related to certain qualities and skills that individuals possess, are frequently referred to as sources of resilience. Resilience is strength under adversity. It's the capacity to withstand the effects of exposure to known risk factors and adverse conditions, the capacity to "beat the odds," so to speak. "The world breaks everyone," Hemingway once wrote, "and afterward some are strong at the broken places." According to James Anthony, M.D. (1985), "The study of resilience may be among the most important research underway in child development and child psychiatry today" (p. 13). Norman Garmezy, Ph.D. (1992), refers to resilience as the nature of nature. He and other dedicated researchers feel that for too long we've focused our attention on studying what makes people sick, when our most important answers might lie in better understanding how and why some people stay well, despite all odds.

No doubt, researchers are learning a great deal from those who have fought hard to overcome the adversities and hardships they faced as children, those who have beat the odds, so to speak. Yet when Arnold Sameroff, Ph.D. (1992), examined the lives of families exposed to seven or eight risks, he said he didn't find any resilient children. That's because sometimes the odds we face will be insurmountable. All the strength, courage, and resilience we can muster still won't be enough to overcome them. The odds will have to change. And researchers are showing that they can change, given access to potential protective influences that exist within families, within special relationships, and within resources provided by our communities.

Important protective influences often can be found in families even when those families are experiencing great distress. In her work with families living in a homeless shelter, Ann Masten, Ph.D., cites examples of some mothers who saw it as their prime necessity to ensure that their child was outside waiting for the school bus each morning (Garmezy, 1992). Parents advocating for a child with special needs, trying to ensure that those needs are met, provide protection. So does an older brother or sister helping a younger family member understand a parent's illness, or an aunt or uncle or grandparent helping to raise a child because the child's parents are unable to do so.

And important sources of protection can be found within our communities. A school that offers smaller class sizes and can address each child's unique learning needs, highlighting each child's special strengths, talents, and interests, is protective. So too are high-quality recreation programs in disadvantaged neighborhoods that children and teenagers go to after school and stay at for hours. Special role models and mentors children get to know at school, during after-school activities, or through involvement in youth or church groups, are protective.

Protective influences exist within children, within families, and within communities (Werner, 1995). And together, these protective influences can outweigh the effects of exposure to a range of childhood risks. The evidence of this is now clear. And as we begin attending to protective influences that are capable of neutralizing the effects of multiple risk exposure in the lives of children and families, we begin to see child and family needs in a very different light. Our intervention plans now acknowledge that certain risks can persist for many years, meaning that children and families might need to be shielded and protected in special ways for many years. We adopt a lifespan perspective. Our notion of intervention now extends well beyond narrow professional disciplines. We're placing new importance on neighborhood resources that can shield children during after-school hours. We're beginning to evaluate schools for their protective value, knowing that some will buffer children better than others. Individuals who are admired by their family members and who are part of their circle of support take on very special significance. Society is giving added recognition to the role that mentoring relationships can play. A child's unique strengths and talents take on special importance, because their expression is key to developing a sense of mastery and confidence. We're always on the alert for new resources and materials that help children and families reframe adversities in a new way, that give them the words they'll need to validate and legitimize the pain they've endured. And we remain focused on the need to reinstill a sense of hope in the lives of children and families who feel futureless; who have given up trying to alter conditions and circumstances that researchers now recognize indeed might be unalterable for most, without access to new sources of protection, strength, and understanding.

References and Resources

Anthony, J. (1985). Resilience in children. *The Psychiatric Times,* 13-14.

Garbarino, J. (1995, April). *Raising children in a socially toxic environment.* Presentation to faculty and students, San Diego State University, San Diego, CA.

Garmezy, N. (1992, August). *Vulnerability and resilience.* Presentation at the American Psychological Association 100th Annual Convention, Washington, DC.

Janoff-Bulman, R. (1992). *Shattered assumptions: Towards a new psychology of trauma.* New York: Free Press.

Sameroff, A. (1992). *Abuse and neglect of children: Risk and resilience.* Time to grow: A television-based course in child development: Infancy through adolescence. Fountain Valley, CA: Coast Community College District.

Werner, E. (1995). Resilience in development. *Current Directions in Psychological Science, American Psychological Society,* 81-85.

Mark Katz, Ph.D., is the clinical director of Learning Development Services in San Diego. Information for this article was taken from the author's 1997 book, On Playing a Poor Hand Well: Insights From the Lives of Those Who Have Overcome Childhood Risks and Adversities, *published by W. W. Norton and Co. (New York).*

Resources

American Academy of Child and Adolescent Psychiatry
3615 Wisconsin Avenue NW
Washington, DC 20016
(202) 966-7300
Website: www.aacap.org

American Academy of Family Physicians
8880 Ward Parkway
Kansas City, MO 64114-2797
(816) 333-9700

American Academy of Pediatrics
141 North West Point Blvd.
Elk Grove Village, IL 60007-1098
(847) 228-5005
(847) 228-5097 (Fax)
Website: www.aap.org

American Association of Children's Residential Centers
440 First Street NW, Suite 310
Washington, DC 20001
(202) 638-1604

American Family Therapy Association
2550 M Street NW, Suite 275
Washington, DC 20037

American Psychological Association
1200 17th Street NW
Washington, DC 20037
(202) 955-7618

American School Counselors Association
5999 Stevenson Street
Alexandria, VA 22304
(703) 823-9800

American School Health Association
PO Box 708
Kent, OH 34240

American Speech Language Hearing Association
10801 Rockville Pike
Rockville, MD 20852
(301) 897-5700

Association for Children and Adults with Learning Disabilities
4156 Library Road
Pittsburgh, PA 15234
(412) 341-1515

Association of Educational Therapists
PO Box 946
Woodland Hills, CA 91365
(818) 788-3850

AT&T National Special Needs Center
2001 Route 46
Parsippany, NJ 07054

Children and Adults with Attention Deficit Disorder (CHADD)
8181 Professional Place, #201
Landover, MD 20785
(301) 306-7070
Website: www.chadd.org

Council for Exceptional Children
1920 Association Drive
Western, VA 22091
(703) 620-3660
Website: www.cec.sped.org

The Exceptional Parent
296 Doylston Street
Boston, MA 02116

Family Resource Center on Disabilities
20 E. Jackson Blvd., Room 900
Chicago, IL 60604
(312) 939-3513

Foundation for Children with Learning Disabilities
99 Park Avenue
New York, NY 10016
(212) 687-7211

National Association for the Education of Young Children
1834 Connecticut Avenue NW
Washington, DC 20009-5786
(800) 424-2460

National Information Center for Handicapped Children and Youth
PO Box 1492
Washington, DC 20013
(703) 893-6061

Glossary

Academic therapist—an educational specialist who teaches remedial skills but does not necessarily help with homework.

Accommodations—modifications in a curriculum based on child's individual needs.

Advocate—to speak up and support oneself or a particular cause.

Attention Deficit/Hyperactivity Disorder (ADHD)—a disorder of the nervous system (neurobiological) characterized by abnormally high activity, impulsivity, and a short attention span.

Attention-Deficit/Hyperactivity Disorder, combined type—the diagnosis given when the individual meets both sets of inattention and hyperactive/impulsive criteria.

Attention-Deficit/Hyperactivity Disorder, not otherwise specified—the diagnosis given when the individual demonstrates some characteristics but an insufficient number of symptoms to reach a full diagnosis. These symptoms, however, disrupt everyday life.

Attention Deficit Disorder without hyperactivity—a subtype of the disorder that demonstrates primarily inattention, not hyperactivity.

Auditory discrimination—the ability to detect differences in sounds and to sort and compare them with each other.

Autism—a severe disorder of behavior and communication characterized by extreme self-absorption.

Behavior modification—a way to change or modify present behaviors; techniques to help correct behaviors.

Bilateral—on two sides.

Chunking—grouping related directions to aid recall by saying them in one breath; breaking activities into short segments.

Coaching—an instructional activity that helps individuals achieve their goals by building organizational and time-management skills.

Cognitive development—the growth of thinking skills.

Cognitive skills—thinking skills.

Concept—a general idea or characteristic applicable to several objects or events that helps to organize the knowledge about the world.

Conduct Disorder—a pattern of socially disruptive behavior that sometimes develops along with ADHD.

Consistency—maintaining routine and structure; similar patterns.

Cue—an aid to improve understanding. Cues can be facial expressions, hand gestures, and tone of voice. Other useful cues include colors and markers to help the child tune in and respond appropriately.

Cursive handwriting—a handwriting technique that employs a fluid, script-like stroke.

Depression—a pattern of withdrawal in behaviors, listlessness, and general loss of pleasure in usual activities, sometimes accompanied by weight loss or gain, loss of sleep, and suicidal thinking.

Developmentally delayed—a child who acquires specific skills after the expected age.

Dexedrine—a stimulant medication. It comes in both short-term and longer-acting form.

Diagnostic and Statistical Manual for Mental Disorders—this book is a reference tool for psychologists and psychiatrists. It lists all mental health challenges and discusses their cause and effect.

Diagnostic specialist—a professional skilled in both testing and curriculum. The diagnostician helps identify the child's strengths and weaknesses and suggests appropriate tools and interventions for success.

Dietary supplements—nutritional supplements (pills), added to normal diet, such as vitamins.

Emotional arousal—being tired, stressed, or overwhelmed.

Empathy—a sensitive understanding of personal interactions and emotions.

Expressive language—includes the skills involved in communicating one's thoughts and feelings to others.

Family system dynamics—the way family members interact with one another.

Family therapy—a type of counseling in which the whole family is involved in resolving a particular problem.

Genes—the parts of the chromosome that carry information about specific traits passed from parent to child.

Genetic inheritance—a trait passed on from parent to child.

Homework coach—a person who helps the child with daily assignments from school.

Hyperactivity—abnormal excessive physical action accompanied by restlessness, low tolerance for frustration, and short attention span.

Hypoactivity—abnormally low level of physical activity.

IDEA—Individuals with Disabilities Education Act, a law that protects disabled children within the school environment.

Impairment—physical weakness or damage or a functional problem.

Intelligible—clear, understandable speech.

Language disorder—any difficulty in understanding and using language.

Language delay—the development of language at a slower rate than most children of the same age.

Language impairment—any difficulty in understanding and using language.

Learning disabilities—learning problems related to thinking or language skills, reading, mathematics, and writing.

Mainstreaming—educating children with special needs in the regular school environment with the help of special teachers.

Math facts—addition, subtraction, and the multiplication tables.

Methylphenidate—a stimulant medication. Ritalin is one trade name.

Model—to provide an example of a technique or another behavior to demonstrate a desired response.

Motor—involving muscle movements

Multidisciplinary team—a group of professionals and parents working to provide a supportive environment for a child within the school setting.

Muscle tone—the amount of tension present in muscles at rest.

Nonverbal communication—communicating without words by using gestures, facial expressions, body language or tone of voice.

Oppositional Defiant Disorder—a disorder that describes a child who resists social demands and argues frequently with adult authority.

Oral—pertaining to the mouth.

Pediatrician—a doctor who specializes in the health, development, and diseases of children.

Psychoeducational therapy—an integrated approach to managing ADHD. It uses a variety of techniques and coping skills to help the person with ADHD succeed.

Psychologist—a specialist in the way children think, act, and behave.

Psychostimulants—prescription medications that typically burn glucose rapidly. They are fast-acting and leave the body rapidly.

Receptive language—includes the skills involved in understanding language.

Reinforcement—to reward desired behavior.

Resilience—the ability to succeed and survive despite limitations.

Section 504—a specific part of the Rehabilitation Act of 1973 that protects children with attention disorders if they are failing to learn within the school environment because of their disability.

Self-discipline—the ability to begin to be responsible for one's actions and decisions.

Semantics—the aspect of language concerned with meaning or content.

Siblings—brothers and sisters.

Social skills—a cluster of skills to help a person comfortably interact on a successful personal basis with friends, parents, and peers.

Speech-language pathologist (SLP)—a person who is qualified to diagnose and treat speech, language, and voice disorders.

Strategies—ideas and techniques to encourage change.

Syndrome—a group of related symptoms that characterize a disease or disorder.

Time out—a technique to remove children from a situation. Child sits to side of the room or activity until he or she can demonstrate self-control.

Tourette's Syndrome—a syndrome involving gestures, grunts, tics, and repeated action.

Tremor—the trembling or shaking of a muscle group.

Tutor—a person who helps the child understand and complete homework, sometimes providing specific help with required subjects.

Vigilance—the ability to stay focused within a conversation.

Visual attention—the ability to focus on specific items within the field of vision.

Visual discrimination—the ability to detect differences in objects, forms, letters, or words.

Visual-motor memory integration—the ability to look at, remember, and copy or reproduce designs, patterns, or handwriting from the board to paper or from a book to paper.

Vowels—the sounds associated with the letters *a, e, i, o, u,* and *y* made by allowing air to pass through the nose or mouth without friction or stoppage.

Written language—the ability to transmit knowledge and ideas effectively on paper.